"I know that a calm and connected teacher is a calm and [illegible] educators should have the opportunity to read this book and have the support to implement its practices. In a world consumed by a global pandemic, Joanna Schwartz's insistence on the importance of mental health in schools has never been more timely and important."

—Annelise Cohon, Senior Policy/Program Specialist, National Education Association

"This book is crammed with an extraordinary array of simple and practical ways to connect with young people, to understand what their behavior might mean, to understand our own assumptions and biases, and to help them (and ourselves) to cope when it is all too much."

—Marg Thorsborne, restorative practitioner, trainer, and author

"This is an eye-opening, practical, and engaging book that is written to be revisited over and over. It provides tools to help our students thrive, with a focus on the importance of teachers caring for both their students and their own overall wellbeing. This is a must read for EVERY teacher, at every grade level."

—Stacey R. Siegel, elementary school teacher, Philadelphia, PA

"This is the book I wish I had when I first embarked on my journey in education. Joanna writes from the perspective of a fellow teacher who knows, who understands, and who has developed actionable opportunities for readers to foster their own vulnerability, empathy, and self-compassion in this work. Thank you, Joanna, for highlighting not only the importance of self-care but also the necessity of community-care."

—Danna Thomas, Founder of Happy Teacher Revolution

"I was blown away by the resources, the organization, and the ideas for connection found in this book. This book offers the right tools, strategies, and, more importantly, the emphasis on relationship that a classroom needs to be trauma-informed and restorative in nature. It is a great resource that I imagine most teachers will return to over and over."

—Joe Brummer, author of Building a Trauma-Informed Restorative School

"I love this book. It is inspirational, practical, wise, and vitally important. It covers much that I recognize from my own work in relational and restorative practice, yet in a way that is fresh, informative, and utterly compelling."

—Dr Belinda Hopkins, Director of Transforming Conflict Ltd

of related interest

The Trauma and Attachment-Aware Classroom
A Practical Guide to Supporting Children Who Have Encountered Trauma and Adverse Childhood Experience
Rebecca Brooks
ISBN 978 1 78592 558 0
eISBN 978 1 78592 877 2

The Simple Guide to Complex Trauma and Dissociation
What It Is and How to Help
Betsy de Thierry
Foreword by Graham Music
Illustrated by Emma Reeves
ISBN 978 1 78775 314 3
eISBN 978 1 78775 315 0
Simple Guide series

The Simple Guide to Child Trauma
What It Is and How to Help
Betsy de Thierry
Foreword by David Shemmings
Illustrated by Emma Reeves
ISBN 978 1 78592 136 0
eISBN 978 1 78450 401 4
Simple Guide series

The Teacher's Introduction to Attachment
Practical Essentials for Teachers, Carers and School Support Staff
Nicola Marshall
Foreword by Phil Thomas
ISBN 978 1 84905 550 5
eISBN 978 0 85700 973 9

Building a Trauma-Informed Restorative School
Skills and Approaches for Improving Culture and Behavior
Joe Brummer with Margaret Thorsborne
Foreword by Judy Atkinson
ISBN 978 1 78775 267 2
eISBN 978 1 78775 268 9

The Teacher Toolbox for a Calm and Connected Classroom

Teacher-Friendly Mental Health Strategies to Help You and Your Students Thrive

Joanna Schwartz

Foreword by Michael McKnight

Jessica Kingsley Publishers
London and Philadelphia

First published in Great Britain in 2021 by Jessica Kingsley Publishers
An Hachette Company

1

Figure 17.1 is reproduced with kind permission of National Child Traumatic Stress Network.
Figure 19.1 is reproduced with kind permission of CASEL.

Front cover image source: www.ianrossdesigner.com

A CIP catalogue record for this title is available from the British Library and the Library of Congress

ISBN 978 1 78775 404 1
eISBN 978 1 78775 405 8

Printed and bound in the United States by Integrated Books International

Jessica Kingsley Publishers' policy is to use papers that are natural, renewable and recyclable products and made from wood grown in sustainable forests. The logging and manufacturing processes are expected to conform to the environmental regulations of the country of origin.

Jessica Kingsley Publishers
Carmelite House
50 Victoria Embankment
London EC4Y 0DZ

www.jkp.com

Contents

Part 4: Resources Section

Foreword

As I sit to write the forward to the first book by Joanna Schwartz, it is the Martin Luther King holiday as well as our 11th month of being held within a global pandemic. We have recently witnessed the storming of the United States Capitol as well as the many summer protests for racial justice in America that continue to bubble underneath the surface of American culture. As of this writing, America is closing in on over 400,000 deaths due to the Covid-19 virus. Families and their children are experiencing more and more stress as all of these waves of difficulties wash over us. At this time, many of our schools remain closed and teachers are working to provide the best education possible remotely or in a hybrid model. Some of our educators are required to provide both at the same time—an almost impossible task! Educator stress is at an all-time high as well.

Prior to the pandemic, children remained the poorest age group in America. One in six children—more than 11.9 million—were poor in 2019. Nearly 73 percent of poor children were children of color. I would suggest that these statistics are now even worse due to the recent stress put on our economy by the pandemic. Stressed families have stressed kids, and these young people carry that stress with them daily as they enter our classrooms and schools, remotely or face to face.

I first met Joanna back in 2016. We met online, through a network for trauma-informed school professionals. I was immediately drawn to the name of the workshops she was providing, Toolbox for Teachers. I have had a personal passion for creating "reclaiming environments" for at-risk students for decades and I am always on the lookout for tools that can help teachers. I was a classroom teacher for 14 years, teaching adolescents removed from regular schools, and was an administrator for over a decade in a school for troubled students, aged 5–21. I now work for the New Jersey Department of Education. I still get to teach, now at Stockton University as an adjunct, teaching future teachers. Not long after our connection, Joanna invited me to come see a workshop she was holding at Temple University in Philadelphia. I left that workshop with a large smile on my face; here was a teacher, currently working in the large urban school district of Philadelphia, that gets it.

In learning more about Joanna, I began to understand where her vision of what can be done in classrooms and schools comes from. Joanna not only has a master's degree in Education but she also has a master's degree in Counseling, spending some time as a child and family therapist. Knowing this immediately took me back to the work of a mentor I have read for years, Dr. Nicholas Hobbs. One of the perks of getting old is the opportunity to connect the dots of a long legacy of working and teaching our most challenging children and youth. Hobbs held many teaching jobs over his career and is worth a Google. He is best known for his idea concerning Re-ED, a vison of working with troubled children and youth that is still used today. Hobbs wrote about the role of the "Teacher-Counselor" in his book, *The Troubled and Troubling Child*, in 1982. Joanna's combination of teacher and counselor takes that concept and expands it to teachers teaching in any school and any classroom. This integration is critical in today's classrooms and schools.

The Teacher Toolbox for a Calm and Connected Classroom: Teacher-Friendly Mental Health Strategies to Help You and Your Students Thrive is filled with tools that any teacher can pick up and use immediately. The work is broken into three sections: The Case for Relationships; How to Deal with Adverse Childhood Experiences, Trauma, and Chronic Stress in the Classroom; and Weathering the Storm: How to Prevent and Process Meltdowns, Burnout, and Other Natural Disasters. The book allows for the development of the Teacher-Counselor skills so necessary for educators today and still so lacking in most of our formal training.

Joanna recognizes the critical nature of connections in the classroom. She provides not only the rationale for the importance of connection and relationship in classrooms but many things teachers can pick up and use immediately with their class to make and deepen those connections. We know that the brain learns best in a state of "relaxed alertness," and this book is filled with activities teacher can use to create that state for all the students in their room. In Part 1, she asks teachers to pause and consider their legacy. She provides the research behind why relationships are critical to learning and then provides tools and many activities for working on creating those connections. In Part 2, Joanna takes us on a journey into the world of adverse childhood experiences and the brain as it reacts to stress. She highlights the need to intentionally build teacher resiliency and the importance of taking care of ourselves so we can continue to meet student needs. Her use of reflective questions in each section also helps teachers stop and check in with themselves. She writes about Social Emotional Learning practices for both students and teachers that again will assist in creating environments of care and learning. Lastly, in Part 3, Joanna writes about dealing with meltdowns and emotional flooding in classrooms. She provides practical strategies teachers can use to calm these storms rather than escalate conflict. Joanna also provides many ways of working with students who carry in high levels of anxiety and how to recognize and work effectively with these young people.

As a classroom teacher, I truly believe you will love the strategies that Joanna has put together in this friendly and easy-to-read book. These include using check-in wheels, learning about the cognitive triangle, creating feeling word walls, creating your own personalized Mission Statements, using emotional timelines, mood notes, teaching steps to a good apology, writing "what I wish you knew" notes, and so many tools and activities to integrate into your practice.

You will be able to instantly tell that Joanna is a practicing teacher. These tools and activities, both for the students as well as for the teachers supporting them, will also begin to change your approach to discipline in the classroom. That shift occurs when discipline issues are recognized as emotional regulation issues. These tools will assist you in creating a class and school environment focused on regulating the brains and bodies of not only our students but also the adults who guide them. It takes a calm brain to calm another brain.

This book won't make teaching easy. Teaching is a complex and demanding vocation. What it will do is help you make your classroom a safer, calmer, and more connected place. It is in environments of belonging that learning can flourish and grow. The research is clear: teachers have the opportunity to change lives, and this book will provide you with a pathway and the tools needed to become a turnaround teacher.

Michael McKnight
January 18, 2021

Acknowledgments

From the bottom of my heart, I'd like to thank: my dear old Dad, Arthur Schwartz, for spending time proofreading and for his many hyphens. Editing skills aside, I feel blessed to have so much love and support from my father and my mother, Anna Mae Schwartz, as well as my extended family. Catherine Allard, even though you're not a teacher, you've taught me what unconditional positive regard, deep listening, and friendship truly mean. Odilia Kirshenbaum, I hope you realize how much of this book you inspired. Thank you for giving me a glimpse into what kids really think and feel. You and Aminda Kirshenbaum both mean so much to me! I'd also like to thank Wendy Sousa from Adoption Rhode Island and Cordelia Wheelock for going out of their way to provide me with clear and helpful feedback about the manuscript. Diane Cady, thank you for many hours of reassurance, encouragement, and excellent editing, and Elisabeth Bodnaruk for your fine proofreading eye! Thank you, Mandy Howe, for your beautiful illustrations! Patricia Jennings, thank you for your shining example and so much of your life-changing research. Dr. Erin Rooney, thank you for showing up both as a fantastic friend and a wise voice in the editing of this book. Dr. Beth Berman, I want you to know how much I have appreciated your exuberant encouragement along the way, your valuable feedback, and, of course, your precious friendship! Speaking of precious friendships, Christina Almeida, thank you for keeping me afloat during the most challenging part of writing this book. I feel blessed to have you. I'd also like to thank all my teacher friends who encouraged me and shared feedback. Special thanks to Susan Fields for stepping in to coach me through the rough early stages, and to my friend Maria Ottinger. Maria, I think our many years of obsessing together about teaching have finally led to something! A huge thanks to my students at Kirkbride Elementary for reminding me every day how blessed I am to be a teacher.

Ike, for changing the entire course of my life. And lastly, of course, to all of my **teachers**!

A Missing Wing and Where This Book Comes From

Over the last 20 years of my life, I have been obsessed with a missing wing. In fact, it was this obsession that brought this book into being. Let me explain.

Historically speaking, teacher preparation programs have only outfitted new teachers with knowledge about academics. Then, once teachers are in the classroom, they receive hours and hours of professional development about the teaching of science, social studies, math, literature, and so on. But since education is a human pursuit, it must deal not only with *what* we're teaching but *who* we're teaching. To do this, we need insight from psychology—the scientific study of the human mind and its functions. Without it, education is like a bird with only one wing. This explains why, for so long, education has struggled to get off the ground.

My own encounter with this particular aerodynamic snafu began in 2001 when I started my career as a teacher in Philadelphia. As I honed my own teaching skills and worked with other teachers, I became fascinated with what it was that made some classrooms marvelous and others miserable. Ten years later, I started a career as a mental health professional working with trauma-impacted families and youth. In my new role, I received excellent supervision and learned a lot about humans and the reasons for their behaviors. My career in mental health was going great, except for one thing: everywhere I went, I was still plagued by a series of questions about *schools*! "What's the role of mental health in schools?" I wondered. "How practical are these kinds of psychological strategies in the classroom?" I thought. And always, "Why aren't people telling teachers this stuff?" Finally, unable to quash the voices in my head, I sat down to attempt to write this information in an honest, engaging, and practical way. I wanted to create the kind of tools I myself had needed as a teacher.

Since 2014, I have shared these professional development workshops—

Toolbox for Teachers—with thousands of educators. I've also been in the unique position of using the tools firsthand in my own classroom (you guessed it—I couldn't stay away!). It has been so gratifying to share these tools with so many other teachers, and now getting to use them with my own students makes me feel I've come full circle!

I hope that these tools will finally give teachers and students what they deserve—the chance to soar!

A Personal Note to the Reader

An important clarification about the purpose of this book.

You may be reading this book because you're looking for tools to help your students thrive. You'll find them here. So that they will make the most sense to you, I've also done my best to corral these tools into a coherent order. But, as much as it would help if they would just line up quietly in their correct places, truthfully, these concepts are not linear. They're more like a rowdy bunch of kids lining up for lunch, always elbowing up against each other, arguing about who goes first and who is in whose spot. So, whether you choose to read the book gradually (maybe taking one chapter per week?) or not, I feel confident that you should be able to find lots of tools to help your students.

But serving our students is only part of this book. The other part is *you*. As I wrote every page of this book, I tried to keep *you* and *your* happiness forefront in my mind. That's not only because—as research bears out[1, 2, 3]—a happy, healthy classroom begins with a happy, healthy teacher.

It's also because I'm guessing that you, like me, spend a vast amount of your "one wild and precious life"[4] caring for and paying attention to your students (aka "your kids"). I bet you've also searched out and received enormous amounts of professional development intended to help you improve your instruction. In my opinion, improving ourselves as teachers is an important part of providing our students with the best possible education.

However, you also need to know that this is *not* another book intended to give you more ways to improve and more things *you* need to do for *your* students. This is not another trend in education that you need to stay on top of. God knows you're probably not in need of any more professional development, and my guess is that you're already plenty good enough just as you are!

I wrote this book, and especially Part 3, because I wanted to remind you that even though teachers are expected to effortlessly and heroically face down each and every challenge that society places at our door, we are humans after all – beautifully complex and imperfect human beings: bewildered but also brilliant, weak but strong, pessimistic but full of hope, and utterly deserving of our own care and attention That means that although you're caring for the needs of so many young people, *you* and *your needs matter too*. Just like your students, you're a full spectrum human being, and that's a wonderful thing to be.

Now, shall we begin?

All pages marked with ★ can be photocopied and downloaded at www.jkp.com/catalogue/book/ 9781787754041

Preface: Standard Sizes and the Need for a Full Spectrum View of Schools

Everything we will talk about in this book is based on the revolutionary idea that students and teachers are humans too, something that educational institutions all over the world seem to have forgotten.

To illustrate my point, consider for a moment that our educational system is a lot like a big, automated shipping warehouse. In the warehouse, machines run to and fro on tracks to pick up merchandise and prepare them for shipping. The machines are programmed with mathematical formulas that tell the robots how to grip and carry merchandise so they know what pieces to pick up and what tracks to run along. The robots' ability to grasp and carry those containers depends heavily on the containers coming in predictable, standard sizes.

But what happens when this efficient system has to move things along that are not standard-sized? For example, imagine that one day these robots have to move something that deviates from their programming, something quite alive and dynamic.

A puppy, for example.

What might happen when the machine rolls down the tracks to pick up its unsuspecting cargo? The puppy, being a puppy, may have wandered off on his little paws in search of something to eat, or maybe he curled up to sleep, or perhaps he is whimpering in bewilderment at the strange sights and sounds. Then, when the robot arrives, its enormous metal phalanges don't fit correctly around the puppy's wiggling body, and the puppy may start to lose it. Perhaps, in his panic, the puppy tries to bite back at the offending metal "mouth" and pees in alarm, causing the machine's circuitry to short out. The machine freezes, holding its squirming, panicked cargo in mid-air.

The shipment never arrives because a puppy simply cannot be manipulated in the same way as a standard-sized box! A puppy is a unique living being, just like the teachers and students who populate our schools.

Maslow before Bloom

Like a machine with faulty programming, our schools have historically made the crucial miscalculation of placing academic progress before overall wellbeing. But until schools start to prioritize Maslow's Hierarchy of Needs over Bloom's Taxonomy of Learning—that is to say, wellbeing before academics—they will continue to spew out disastrous results: one out of five students report being bullied, loads of school violence, and hordes of teachers quitting due to overwhelming challenges.[1, 2, 3, 4, 5, 6]

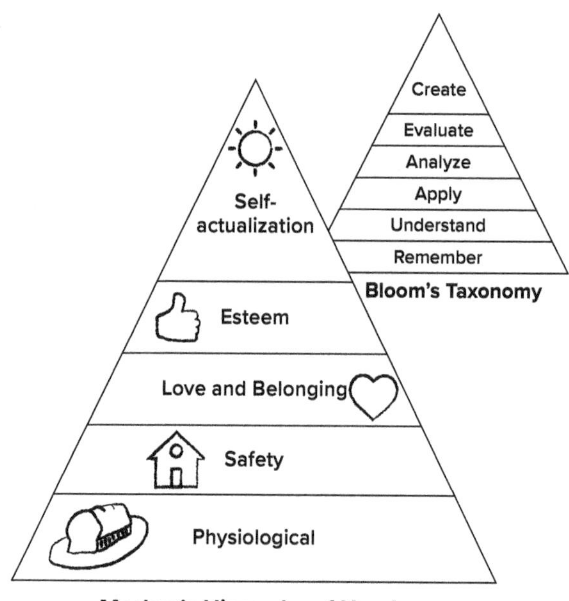

Figure P.1: Maslow's Hierarchy of Needs before Bloom's Taxonomy of Learning

Over the last several decades, teaching has been named in study after study as one of the most stressful jobs in the world. In one recent eye-popping study,[7] nearly 93 percent of teachers report "high degrees of stress." It has been reported that half a million teachers move or leave the profession each year, costing the United States about 2.2 billion dollars annually, not to mention the enormous loss of human potential.[8] Since we also know that students struggle in schools with stressed-out teachers, and vice versa, something in this burned-out equation needs changing![9]

Schools need to replace the one-size-fits-all robotic model of education with one that instead values our shared humanity. "Shared" because being a good teacher is not just about supporting students, but also recognizing that, like students, teachers are humans with their own backgrounds and experiences. Put simply, *we are people first, and students and teachers second.* When educational institutions recognize and honor this fundamental fact, it enriches and adds nuance and art to our work in the classroom. It also gives us a full spectrum view of what's happening.

A full spectrum view

What do I mean by a **full spectrum view**? Maybe an analogy will help.

As far back as 1054 AD, Japanese and Chinese astronomers began writing about a unique star that seemed to be exploding in the sky above them. Later astronomers became fascinated by this mysterious pattern of lights when it reappeared in the seventeenth and eighteenth centuries. These lights became known as the "Crab Nebula," one of the most studied astronomical objects outside the solar system. Over the years, whenever astronomers looked at the Crab Nebula, they felt relatively confident that what they saw was an accurate depiction of what was out there. But for most of its history, astronomers also lacked a crucial piece of information about the Crab Nebula. That vital piece of information is that, like much of life, things are more complicated than they initially appear.

As you may remember from high school physics, light is a tricky thing. Our eyes use something called visual or optical light to perceive the world around us. But unbeknownst to early astronomers, visual light is only a small part of all the light out there, as measured on the electromagnetic spectrum. Other forms of light are invisible to our eyes, such as infrared, ultraviolet, radio, and X-ray. To see something like the Crab Nebula accurately, then, you need **a full spectrum view — a perspective that captures the entirety of what's happening.** When NASA combined images from different telescopes that included all types of light, the resulting image showed that the familiar supernova wasn't familiar at all. Seen through the full spectrum, the Nebula wasn't just a simple crab-shaped outline of white lights. Instead, it transformed into a dazzling array of colorful wavelengths of light spanning nearly the entire electromagnetic spectrum. Its unexpected beauty and complexity stunned astronomers all over the world.

In this book, we'll take a similar full spectrum view—not of the stars, but of what goes on in our classrooms—to get the most accurate picture of what's truly happening. We will bring to light the hidden dynamics of our classrooms in order to build relationships and manage instruction with more ease and enjoyment. We'll look at interactions from the inside out and consider how individuals are "wired" psychologically and biologically. From another vantage point (drawing on Cognitive Behavioral Therapy[10] and research on the neurobiological effects of chronic stress and trauma), we'll take a look at individuals to see what happens when things get hard; how chronic stress, trauma, and adverse childhood experiences show up in our classrooms. Finally, we'll get into the tools that will help you work creatively and compassionately with tough dynamics like meltdowns and burnout.

While the educational machinery that is in place may be largely out of our control for the time being, there is still so much that we *can* do to create a calm and connected classrooms and school communities for ourselves, our students and the world at large.

Growth mindset versus fixed mindset

A growth mindset, rather than a fixed mindset, is key to the work we will be setting out to do in this book. These terms refer to the work of Stanford psychologist Carol Dweck, who described two underlying habits of mind (mindsets) that individuals adopt towards different areas of their life.[11] Simply put, having a **fixed mindset** means that we believe we have a static and limited ability in certain areas of life. We may think that we are "not a math person" per se, or that we'll "never be an artist," or that, essentially, we don't have what it takes to do x, y, or z. On the other hand, if we have a **growth mindset**, we believe our intelligence and abilities are malleable and can develop and improve over time. Individuals with a growth mindset embrace mistakes and challenges as part of the learning process. Instead of thinking that one is simply not good at x, y, or z, those with a growth mindset might instead consider that they're simply not good at it *yet*.

One remarkable study compared the achievement of 7th graders (12–13-year-olds) with fixed and growth mindsets throughout 7th grade.[12] Even though students in the study began the year on a similar academic footing, those with growth mindsets outperformed those with fixed mindsets simply because they believed that intelligence is not fixed and that the brain grows with repeated practice. As a result, when things got hard (as they tend to do in 7th-grade math and science!), these students simply put in more effort and tried new strategies, correctly believing that it was this effort and repeated practice that would make the difference! In short, having a growth mindset gives us the power to transform outcomes, and we'll harness that power to fuel our growth throughout this book.

Figure P.2: One of my student's interpretations of growth mindset!
Source: Kimberley Theo

Where are we headed?

Positive student–teacher relationships are the keystone to everything discussed in this book, and we will lay the groundwork for them in Part 1, paying particular attention to their hidden dynamics. In Part 2, we'll look at how trauma, adverse childhood experiences, and chronic stress impact everyone in the classroom, including us. And in Part 3, we will discuss what to do when things do not go according to plan, when meltdowns occur, and how to sidestep burnout. In all three sections of this book, we will explore how to:

- re-frame discipline as helping your students regulate their emotions (co-regulation)
- practice using communication tools that demonstrate how to empower students, not have "power over" students
- take a broader, more human, more compassionate lens on behavior (ours and our students).

One last note: to be clear, I'm not proposing that the tools in this book are the secret to unraveling the stress-laden profession of teaching, especially in underfunded and under-resourced schools with poverty-impacted students and staff shortages. Until systemic, racial, and societal influences on schools change, teachers and students will almost inevitably feel burned out and overburdened. For this reason, we must continue to fight tirelessly to force legislators and administrators to respect, humanize, and prioritize the sacred spaces that our schools are. Meanwhile, it's my deepest hope that these practices will be of service to you as you change the world through your teaching, one lesson at a time, one student at a time.

Questions for reflection

- Think about growth and fixed mindset. What kind of mindset do you think you have about people's abilities in general? To what extent do you believe people can grow and change with practice?
- How might a teacher's fixed or growth mindset impact the kind of mindset their students have about what they can and cannot do?
- What three adjectives might you use to describe your leadership style? Can you explain why you think these adjectives fit?
- On a scale of 1–10, to what extent do you believe your workplace takes into account the full spectrum of an individual's needs? Why did you rate it this way? What ideas do you have about how things could be improved?

PART 1

The Case for Relationships

1

A Legacy of Relationships

Imagine with me the following situation, if you will. One morning, a long time from today, one of your current students wakes up and walks downstairs to make themselves a cup of coffee. They sit down at a kitchen table by a window and, in the dim morning light, run their eyes over the day's news. Suddenly, their eyes catch on something that makes them pause. Under a section titled "Obituaries," a familiar name leaps out at them. That name is yours! Surprised, your former student calls out to their spouse, "Honey, look! My teacher passed away. I remember them! They were so ________!"

They were so *what*?

What would they say?

Dear reader, **how do you want your students to remember you?**

If you are reading this book, I will venture to guess that you, like me, wish to be remembered as the kind of teacher who made a difference in a young person's life. Maybe you wish to be remembered as what psychologist Julius Segal called a *charismatic adult*—"a person with whom they [the child] can identify and from whom they gather strength."[1] Maybe you want to be remembered as an adult who, as Fred Rogers said, "loved others into being."[2] Have you yourself had such an adult in your life? All those descriptions touch something in my soul because I certainly did.

When I was about 30 years old, a football-loving, elderly, Black, urban cowboy named Isaac Johnstone decided to take me "under his wing." A few years earlier, Ike founded a non-profit youth empowerment equestrian program in Philadelphia. One day, when I randomly stopped by to see the horses, we struck up a friendship. Seeing that I was having difficulty transitioning into the next stage of my life, Ike became my teacher and mentor by filling in all the emotional cracks that I'd developed over my traumatic teenage years and tumultuous early adulthood. Because I didn't feel I mattered much to anyone, he made it his mission to make me feel heard, seen, felt, and known. "Young lady," he'd say, as I led enormous horses around the stable to practice my self-confidence (his idea!), "one day, you're going to be so confident you won't even recognize yourself!" "Listen to your gut," he'd bellow whenever I approached him with a problem I couldn't figure out. "I believe in you!" he'd insist, day after day. And always, "Love yourself!" He repeated these mantras day after day until I finally understood that I did mean something to someone and that I had value and a place in this world. To this day, several years after his death, I can still hear his voice reverberating around inside me and making its way into my classroom, where I sometimes fail—but always try—to offer the same liberating love and acceptance that Ike gave me.

That's all well and fine, you may be thinking, but what about school? Are relationships really *that* important for learning?

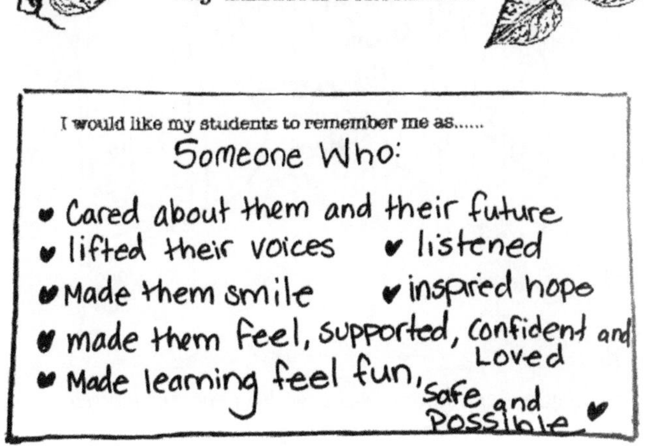

Figure 1.1: Teacher Mission Statement

Researchers who have investigated positive student–teacher relationships (warm, affirming, empathetic, consistent relationships with clear boundaries and high expectations) find that they do much more than just make classrooms feel good—they are crucial to a classroom's success. In fact, positive student–teacher relationships are correlated with an overwhelming amount of favorable outcomes. A 2019 *Education Week* article cites an educational research analysis that looked at 46 different studies. The conclusion states that "**strong teacher–student relationships** were associated in both the short- and long-term with **improvements on practically every measure schools care about**: higher student academic engagement, attendance, grades, fewer disruptive behaviors and suspensions, and lower school dropout rates" (my emphasis).[3]

Figure 1.2: How one teacher wishes to be remembered
Source: Melissa Donner

As if that wasn't enough, positive student–teacher relationships have also been correlated with increased teacher job satisfaction. Teachers who have positive student–teacher relationships consistently report feeling more joy and overall satisfaction with their work.[4]

As it turns out, positive student–teacher relationships can get students where they need to go behaviorally and academically and can even make us happier. Plus, as you know, they can touch and transform lives and leave behind a legacy for you as a teacher that lasts long after you're gone. Strong relationships are powerful tools, perhaps the most powerful in this entire book. That's why, as you will soon see, building positive student–teacher relationships will be the beating heart of this book.

CREATE A MISSION STATEMENT

Use the Mission Statement template provided in the Resource Section (or make one of your own) to create a Mission Statement showing how you wish to be remembered by your students. Hang it up by your desk or at the front of the room to remind yourself of your goal. Maybe consider sharing it with the students in your classroom and invite them to make one of their own.

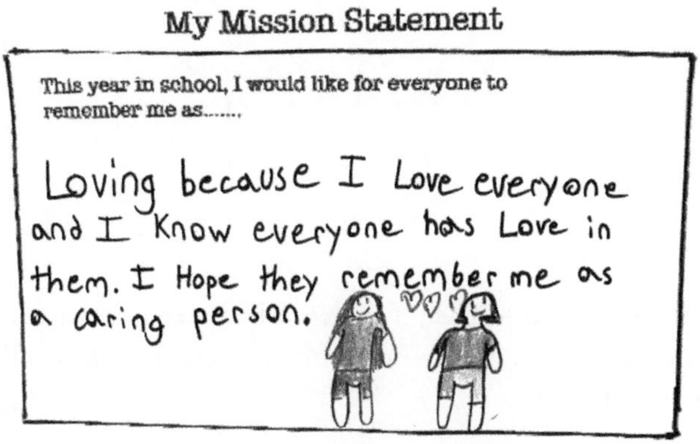

My Mission Statement

This year in school, I would like for everyone to remember me as.......

Loving because I Love everyone and I Know everyone has Love in them. I Hope they remember me as a caring person.

Figure 1.3: A 5th grader's Mission Statement

Questions for reflection

- Thinking back to your own childhood, did you have a teacher who was able to build positive student–teacher relationships? What were the most significant life lessons you learned from them?
- Whether they were a teacher in a school or just a special person in your life, who has been your greatest teacher? How did they influence who you are today and the life you live?
- Think about the example of your future student reading your obituary one day. How do you imagine they might fill in the blank: "I remember that teacher! They were so________"?
  - How would your best student respond? How about your most challenging student?

2

The Invisible Backpack

What Counselors Know about Mental Health That Teachers Need to Know Too

Back when I was a new teacher, if someone had asked me what was on my students' minds when they were at school, I might have drawn them a pie chart that looked like this:

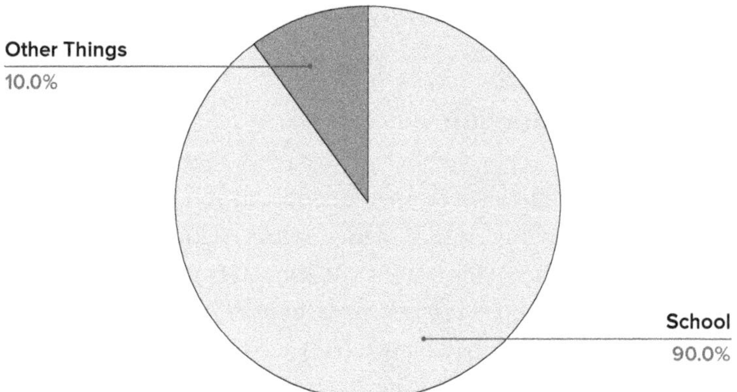

Figure 2.1: What my students think about

Given my young age and lack of life experience, I could only imagine that my students' attention would be focused on what was happening in school, as mine had been as a child. Likewise, I'd have carved out a small piece of the pie to "other things"—so named because I just wasn't sure what those other things could be. But when we use a full spectrum lens to understand our students, we may be surprised to find that there's a whole lot more happening than meets the eye.

Like the heavy backpacks they lug into school each day, so many of our students also carry a heavy, invisible backpack filled with difficult and sometimes traumatic childhood experiences. Not surprisingly, recent child development research shows that these stressful experiences can profoundly shape and limit the extent to which students participate in learning. That means that it is *vital* to know something about the contents of the "Other Things" portion of the pie chart. With this knowledge in hand, we can build relationships and powerfully influence how available our students will be for learning!

Nyla, and why what you don't know can hurt you

Nyla was a bouncy 4th-grade girl with round cheeks and hopeful brown eyes. Despite her surface exuberance, she qualified for therapeutic services because a close family member had been murdered less than two years before. As part of my work as a clinician treating co-victims of homicide, I worked with Nyla and other students at her school, where she was offered school-based mental health services to help process her grief and loss.

In the therapy room where I met with Nyla, just down the hall from the classrooms, I was frequently touched by Nyla's sweetness and desire to connect with me. I also heard all kinds of details about Nyla's home life. One of the most important pieces of information that she shared with me was that she often stayed up late watching horror movies in a (woefully misdirected) attempt to stay awake and avoid having nightmares about her father's death (nothing keeps you alert like a scary movie!). The result was that during the school day, she would be cranky and defiant until fatigue would overtake her and she'd slump over her desk and fall asleep. She also confided that she routinely became jumpy because she imagined that the scenes from the horror movies might come to life in her classroom (no doubt made worse by the loud and sudden sounds so common in urban schools!). Although her behavior in school was understandable to me because I knew what was happening behind the scenes, it was understandably frustrating and exasperating for her teachers.

Even though teachers spend the most time with students, it's often guidance counselors and therapists who are privy to the most critical information about our students' lives behind the scenes. This discrepancy between what teachers and counselors know about students' lives is especially unfair to teachers, who need at least some information to decode student behavior. That's why it can be such a game-changer to get some sort of quick read on how our students are doing each day at school.

The medical profession has an entire protocol for this. Just think of a typical visit to the doctor. To make sure you're stable when you come in the door, your doctor will check your vital signs. They'll listen to your heart and respiration rate, take your temperature, and check your blood pressure too. Assuming everything is in order, your doctor can then move on to talking about your achy joints or whatever brought you in that day. Even if you came in for other issues, your doctor first needed to make sure that you didn't have more pressing problems that needed to be addressed. The same goes for our students.

Think, for example, about Nyla's story. If her teachers had some kind of vital signs check on her, they might have found out why she was always so cranky. Her sleepiness and hair-trigger responses would have become much easier to understand and empathize with. Even if they didn't know the entire story, just a little bit of information could have made an enormous difference in how they interpreted her behavior. The lens would have shifted from "What's wrong with this child?" to the well-known trauma-informed refrain of "What has *happened* to this child?" In the pages that follow, we will discuss some of the tools you can use to make this shift and check in with your students' vital signs.

Why don't counselors and mental health professionals share important information with teachers?

From the counselor's point of view, in most cases, privacy concerns prevent them from telling teachers the nitty-gritty of what's happening with their clients. To share this information, they need to first ask their clients for permission to share confidential information, and often clinicians may be hesitant to do so because this request may make their client reluctant to share more details in the future. It may set up a feeling that the therapist is betraying their confidence ("I trusted you with my story, and now you want to tell that person my business?!!"). Some also fear that knowing everything about students can be too much for teachers and cause "empathy fatigue" and vicarious trauma, which are real considerations for those close to trauma. Last, some counselors hesitate to share their clients' personal information with teachers because they imagine teachers will sensationalize these personal details and that they won't have the same consideration for their clients or the same depth of empathy and clinical understanding. This perception that teachers can't have the same depth of clinical understanding is evident in the clinical world's preference for referring to trauma-informed education as trauma-sensitive education, implying that teachers lack enough awareness to be trauma-informed, they can only be trauma-sensitive. In my experience, that is not true.

Questions for reflection

- If you were a parent, how would you feel about a counselor sharing your child's information with their teacher? Are there times when this would or would not be okay?
- To what extent do counselors at your school share vital student information with teachers? Why do you think this is the case?
- Do you have a student whose behaviors are puzzling? Make a list to show all the explanations you can think of that might throw light on their behavior.

Why Did You Do That?

The Cognitive Triangle

Christina and the *Check-In Wheel*

"Christina" is a bright, artistic, and insightful teenager. A few years ago, when Christina was 14, her mother was scheduled for surgery at the hospital. At the same time, her beloved cat, Blossom, also happened to get a bladder infection (when it rains, it pours!). While her mom stayed overnight for the surgery, Christina went to stay at her friend's house. The next morning, not surprisingly, Christina found it hard to focus on what was happening in school. Curious about what she was experiencing, I asked her to draw me a pie chart of what had been on her mind in school that day. This is what she drew.

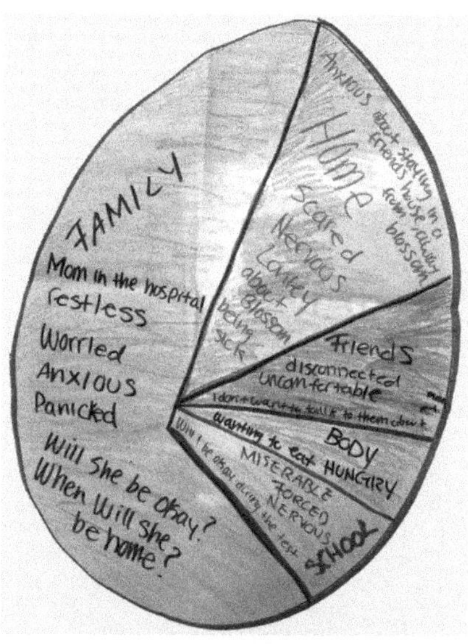

Figure 3.1: Christina's Check-In Wheel

When you look at this pie chart, what do you notice, and how does it compare to my imaginary pie chart from my early days of teaching, depicted above? For one, I'm sure you noticed that Christina's pie chart is a fair bit more realistic because it gives us a bird's eye view into what those "other things" could be. But if you look closely, I'll bet you'll also notice that it's pretty much the inverse of the pie chart in Figure 2.1! As it turns out, school is pretty insignificant, and those "other things" take up the lion's share of attention.

We can also immediately see that she's dedicated a huge section of the wheel to thoughts about her mom. Since she's staying overnight at a friend's house during her mom's operation, she's also worried about her sick cat being home alone. She says she feels "disconnected" from her friends and uncomfortable talking to them about her mom. She also writes that she is hungry (too nervous to eat breakfast?), and feels "miserable, forced, and nervous" about an upcoming test at school.

How might these below-the-surface thoughts and feelings translate into the observable behaviors we would see in school?

To connect how Christina's thoughts and feelings might translate into behaviors, we need to take a closer look at how an interaction that starts on the inside can explain why individuals act the way they do on the outside. Knowing how this interaction works can help you get to the root of puzzling student behavior. Let's look at the *cognitive triangle*, an essential psychological tool created by psychiatrist and founder of Cognitive Behavioral Analysis, Dr. Aaron Beck.[1]

The cognitive triangle—thoughts, feelings, behaviors—oh my!

The creators of Disney's popular 2015 movie, *Inside Out*, must have had the *cognitive triangle* as part of their inspiration. In it, we watch while a young girl named Riley struggles to adapt to a new school and house when her family relocates. As we watch events unfold in Riley's exterior world, we also observe the same events from the "inside out," from the point of view of Riley's five basic emotions: fear, anger, sadness, joy, and disgust. These entertaining Pixar characters are located in a sort of headquarters in Riley's brain from where (unbeknownst to Riley) they monitor each new situation and jostle over who gets to make decisions for Riley.

Let the body speak its mind

Have you ever felt butterflies in your stomach when a crush looked your way, or felt your heart seem to sink when you found out disappointing news? That's because, contrary to what many people have traditionally believed, feelings or emotions are not airy-fairy, mushy-gushy, unreal things. Instead, emotions are a very real physiological response of neurotransmitters and electrical signals experienced in our bodies. In fact, in 2013, a group of scientists in Finland was able to map out the exact locations where emotions are experienced in the body.[2] They found that the locations were the same, even across different cultures. For example, participants reported that happiness and love were reliably experienced as increased activity across almost the whole body, while depression diminished feelings in the arms, legs, and head. Volunteers said they felt danger and fear in their chest, and interestingly experienced the feeling of anger as an activation in their arms. This is good news for those of us who struggle to identify our feelings, because being able to identify patterns of sensations in our body (a heavy feeling in our heart area signifying sadness, for example) can help us to more consciously identify our emotions. You can begin by teaching your students to use physical sensations to decode feelings by increasing their familiarity with sensory words (fuzzy, tingly, pulsing, burning, bubbly, etc.). Then, help them make the connection to sensations in their body and explain how these sensations give us clues about what emotions we're experiencing—something many adults are still learning to do! You might find *Connecting Feelings and Sensations* and the *Feelings List* in the Resource Section at the back of the book to be helpful.

Just as the crew in Riley's head influenced her decisions, the cognitive triangle posits a direct relationship between what individuals think, feel, and do. Because it is so central to how humans operate, an immense amount of observable behaviors show up in the classroom simply because of the cognitive triangle.

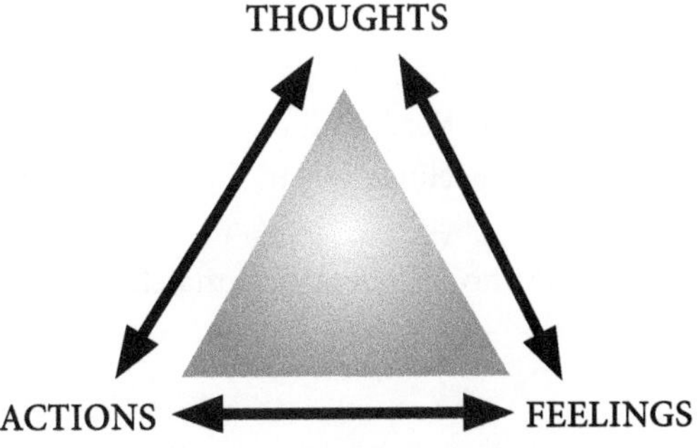

Figure 3.2: The cognitive triangle

Here's an example of how the cognitive triangle works in real life. Imagine that, one morning, you are walking down the hallway at work when you see a colleague walking towards you. "Good morning," you call out cheerfully, but they hurry past you and don't respond. You might have the **thought**, "Wow, that was rude! What did I ever do to them? What a jerk!" This thought may lead rapidly to a **feeling** of irritation or hurt, fear, or even self-righteous anger. "Who do they think they are? What did I ever do to them?" The next time you see that colleague, these thoughts and feelings may re-emerge and propel you into action (a **behavior**). Maybe you choose to double down on your efforts to be friendly, or you ignore them, or perhaps you send them an email letting them know *exactly* what you think of their snooty behavior. Once you do act, you'll probably also have a whole new round of thoughts and feelings about what your behavior was and what happened (and so will the other person undoubtedly!). Then, you act based on this new batch of thoughts and feelings. So will they. And around and around we go on the cognitive triangle merry-go-round. Even though we like to think that we are rational beings fully in charge of what we do, the cognitive triangle reminds us that our conscious and unconscious thoughts and feelings direct our actions from behind the scenes.

Some tools inspired by the cognitive triangle

In many cases, students may lack emotional literacy—awareness and a lexicon to describe their feelings. This makes it harder for them to understand why they do what they do, and harder to decode the reasoning behind others' behaviors. We can help boost their emotional literacy by increasing their ability to name feelings.

Some strategies

- Create a Feelings Word Wall (can have words and images). You can use the Feelings List in the Resource Section to get you started.
- Have students draw a character to match their feelings.

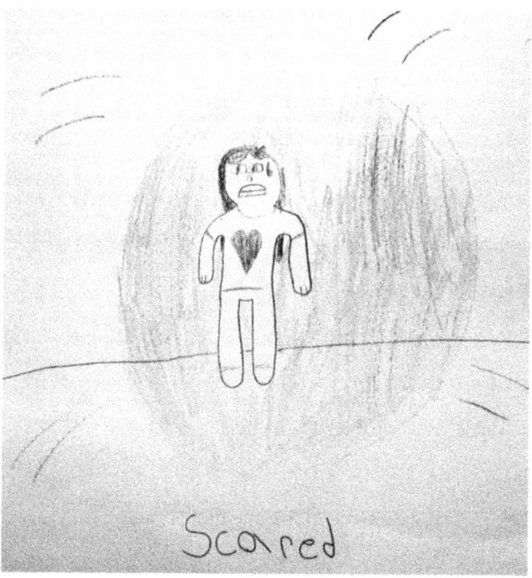

Figure 3.3: A student's description of what "scared" would look like as a character

Figure 3.4: A student's drawing of "nervousness"

- Assign groups an emotion to write a poem about. They should include synonyms in the poem (happy = joyous, thrilled, exultant, content, etc.) and say when we feel that emotion.

When the poem is finished, snap a photo of students acting out that emotion and showing off their poetry!

- Teach students the sign language gesture for each emotion. Post pictures of volunteer students showing the sign language gesture for each emotion with a corresponding label.
- Get them to write and talk about their feelings by asking: "What color would your feeling be?" "How big is it?" "What would it look like?" "What kind of voice do you imagine it has?" "How would you act it out?"

Figure 3.5: Thoughts, feelings, and behaviours are like a tree and its roots

You can also imagine the interaction of thought, feelings, and behaviors as a tree growing in the soil. We can see the plant's observable parts: the trunk, the branches, the green leaves, all above ground level. This visible part is like the behaviors we see outwardly. But hidden below the soil's surface are roots that receive and send information to the parts of the tree above the ground and are responsible for the way the tree grows. Similarly, while we can only see people's behaviors, they are connected to the hidden root causes of those behaviors—thoughts and feelings. (To take it a step further, those thoughts and feelings can be influenced by the surrounding soil, much as our thoughts and feelings can be powerfully influenced by largely unconscious influences such as our age, gender, race, class, nationality, history of trauma, attachment styles, sensory needs, etc.)

Christina's behaviors

Let's get back to Christina. Thanks to the *Check-In Wheel* she drew, we already understand Christina's thoughts and feelings. We don't need to dig around under the soil, or guess at her thoughts and feelings, as we would normally need to do. So let's go the other way around. How might her thoughts and feelings translate into observable behaviors?

Let's put ourselves into Christina's shoes. Can you imagine or remember a day when you had to go to a meeting at work, but something else worrying or stressful was on your mind? Maybe you had just received a phone call with alarming information from the doctor, had a terrible fight with your partner, or were worried about paying the rent. Or many other things. That day, as you sat in a meeting plagued by your worries, what thoughts ran through your head? If a camera recorded your every action as you struggled with these thoughts and feelings, what might it have seen you *do*?

Depending on how well you keep your composure, I'd imagine that you would have sought out ways to prevent yourself from losing it during the meeting. You may have tapped your pencil, looked out the window, sighed, texted a friend, jiggled your leg, chewed on your fingernails. You may have rolled your eyes once or twice at a colleague, annoyed at the information that was being conveyed and worried about more pressing matters. You might have opened your laptop and checked your email, distracted yourself with social media, excused yourself to go to the restroom, stepped outside to get some fresh air, or maybe you made a plan to call your best friend after work. In your defense, you found normal and natural ways of **coping**.

Questions for reflection

- How do you make decisions? Do you feel you listen mostly to your feelings and your gut? Or do you prefer to make decisions by rationally thinking things through?
- Imagine you're cast in the role of Christina in a movie about her day. You are only given the image of her *Check-In Wheel* to guide your

performance. As the camera rolls, what would you decide to do in class, around school, at lunch, before and after school?

- If you are working with a group, choose one participant to play the role of Christina. The other group members can "direct" Christina's actions when she is in class, around school, and at lunch. What kinds of situations might occur as a result of her actions? How might other characters react to Christina and interpret how she is behaving?
- What new insights about Christina and her situation came to mind as you acted this out?
- How might you share the information in this chapter with your students in a developmentally appropriate and engaging way?

4

Coping Skills

Dealing with What We're Feeling

Coping skills, or coping strategies, are what we do consciously or unconsciously to make ourselves feel better when under stress and to bring our nervous system back to homeostasis—a relaxed but alert state where we function best. Chewing your nails, listening to music, praying, gardening, stretching, calling a friend, and many more things (both healthy and unhealthy) are examples of coping skills. They distract us, relax us, focus us, or center us until things calm down enough for us to get back to a baseline level of functioning. They help us move past difficult times with more ease.

But being confined to a classroom means that options for coping strategies are much more limited. If we feel stressed, we can't suddenly decide to go take a bath, curl up in a corner, pop by the salon for a manicure, go for a run, and all those other real-world activities that normally center us and calm us down. Instead, we employ subtler strategies like those described in the imaginary meeting mentioned in the previous chapter.

Sometimes when we're very stressed, we also find ourselves in a state of **hyper-arousal**, and we'll use coping skills to help us return to our baseline level of functioning. For example, when our nervous system is hyper-aroused, we become hyper-vigilant about what's happening around us, and we experience anxiety, jitteriness, and an intense need to release this extra nervous energy. We might burn off this excess steam at home by playing a game of basketball, going for a run, or doing an intense workout, for example. But in the classroom, students may have to release some of this tension by jiggling their leg, tapping their foot, drumming their fingers, spinning in their chair, pacing, calling things out impulsively, and so on. Even though their behaviors may be an attempt to calm down an overly anxious nervous system, from the outside a student in this state may just look like a student who can't sit still.

Using exercise to calm down

Back in 2015, I experienced in a very public way how powerful exercise can be to calm down an over-reactive nervous system. Thanks to my mother, I applied for a place in a nationally televised competition for women in the workplace (MSNBC's *Grow Your Value*). I was selected, and the culmination of the contest required that I deliver a 60-second speech to a crowd of 500 people and a team of celebrity judges. I was beyond terrified! Backstage, doing interviews and photo-ops, I was way outside my bandwidth for handling stress—so sweaty and tense, it felt like my heart was going to jump right out of my throat! I knew I needed a chance to *move* so that I could relax. So, shortly before my big moment on stage, I slipped out a back door to go for a run! As I ran around my hometown of Philadelphia, I could feel the tension draining away. When I came back 45 minutes later, it was almost my turn to step on stage. Thankfully, the exercise had brought me out of my hyper-aroused state, and I was feeling calm and cool. Freed from my nervous system's stranglehold on my emotions, I delivered a speech I was proud of—and ended up winning the competition!!

Other sensory strategies to deal with feeling hyper-aroused (too "hyped up") include deep, slow, belly breathing with slightly longer exhales than inhales, squeezing a stress ball, listening to calming music, throwing a ball against a wall, lying under weighted blankets, deep breathing, and drinking warm water.

On the other extreme, we may also find ourselves in a state of hypo-arousal in which our nervous system is decompressing from repeated or intense stress. In this state, we may feel fatigued, numb, empty, and want to avoid talking to anyone, doing anything, or taking in any more stimuli. A friend of mine found themselves in this state after their father had an emergency heart operation during the same week as the 2020 presidential election in the United States, two very high-intensity events! After both situations resolved, he told me that the repeated stress left him feeling "numb and hollow." He'd likely shifted from a state of hyper-arousal to a state of hypo-arousal. When we're in this state, if we have the luxury of being at home, we might curl up on the couch, stay in bed, and turn off our phone and social media in order to avoid more stimulation. Being in a state of hypo-arousal in the classroom, however, can lead to students covering their heads with a hoodie, asking to go to the nurse, putting headphones on, staring into space, doodling, avoiding being called on, and so on.

Hypo-arousal—When It's All Too Much

Some strategies for getting out of a hypo-aroused (too low energy) state include smelling essential oils, doing jumping jacks or exercise, splashing cold water on the face, singing, briefly holding ice packs, finger painting, rocking in a chair, and more.

When we see students in hypo- and hyper-aroused states, we can make the mistake of thinking they are difficult and disengaged. It can help us to know, though, that in many cases they may just be using instinctive coping strategies to regulate a stressed-out nervous system. Remember how you acted in the aforementioned meeting when you felt stressed? If we didn't know better, you could also be seen as acting up or being difficult! But because we know better, we know that none of your actions meant that you were trying to get attention or that you had a bad attitude. None of these explanations work because you were just trying to cope!

Name it to tame it

It's also important to know that you can help students who seem to be over- or under-activated, or just having a hard day, by doing what psychiatrist Dr. Dan Siegel calls "name it to tame it." When you "name it to tame it," you state what you're observing about the other's emotional experience. You might say something like, "It looks like you're feeling frustrated; why don't we take a break?" Or, "Seems like you're feeling nervous about your game tonight—what can I do to help?" You can also do this with your whole group. It's a great way to help regulate the entire class at once ("Seems like you guys are feeling anxious about the results of your SATs/math tests, etc. Would it be helpful to talk about it a little bit more?") Stating what you observe non-judgmentally can provide them with a sense of being understood, of feeling "felt," and for many students who have struggled to experience being seen by their caretakers, this can be transformative.

If, during that meeting, you were disciplined, shamed, or threatened because of your behavior, you would feel irritated, resentful, and misunderstood. After all, as they say, you weren't trying to give anyone a hard time; you were simply *having* a hard time. Unfortunately, when we don't realize that children may misbehave and seek our attention in the wrong way because they are living in stressful situations and acting out their pain, we can unwittingly punish them for their misbehavior. It's as though the behavior were a symptom, and we're making a misdiagnosis. Then, by punishing harshly, we provide the wrong medicine, and the patient ends up in more pain.

To be clear, I'm not recommending permissiveness just because a student has other things on their mind on a particular day. For example, whatever behavior is totally unacceptable in your classroom—hitting, running, throwing things, etc—still remains unacceptable. On many occasions, you may need to try different strategies: provide consequences or clear feedback on behavior, kindly but firmly redirect, use the Connection before Correction strategy that we will talk about in Chapter 11. But as Mark Katz says in his book *On Playing a Poor Hand Well*, "If only we knew what happened last night, or this morning before he/she got to school, we would be shielding the same child we're now reprimanding."[1] Next time you find yourself frustrated with a student's puzzling and frustrating behavior, dig a little deeper. You might be surprised at what you uncover.

Using the *Check-In Wheel* as a tool

Below are some ways that you can use the *Check-In Wheel*, just like Christina. It can help you to navigate strong emotions (yours or your students') and get at the real reasons behind behavior.

(You can find a copy in the Resource section.)

- Staple many copies together to make a "check-in journal" that students can keep in their desks. They may choose to pull out this journal during trips to a Cool Down Corner/Peace Center. They may also choose to share it with you as part of a morning routine.
- Make smaller-sized versions of the *Check-In Wheel* that children can drop off in a confidential jar or box on your desk.
- Use as a grab-and-go template for a Writer's Workshop literacy center. Make copies and place in a clear plastic pocket on the wall or anywhere students can easily access.
- Share it as a resource for counselors.

- Try it out as a self-care strategy for *you.*
  - A note about using the *Check-In Wheel* as a self-care strategy for you: if you think you don't have the time to fill out a *Check-In Wheel,* take advantage of the fact that just naming feelings *accurately* has a therapeutic effect on your nervous system. Try closing your eyes for just 30 seconds and name three feelings you are experiencing. Try to be as specific as possible. Instead of "I am feeling sad," say, "I am feeling heartsick/miserable/in despair." Instead of saying, "I feel angry," try saying, "I feel enraged/furious/resentful." You may start to feel better just by finding precisely the right word to name how you're feeling.

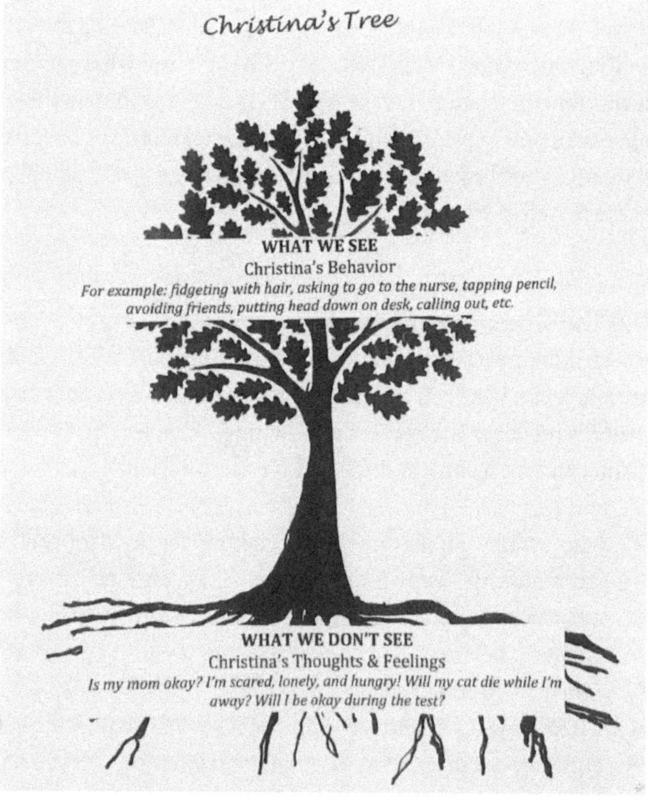

Figure 4.1: We can observe Christina's behaviors because they are above ground but her thoughts and feelings are invisible to us

Where Do You Feel Feelings?

Did you know that emotions are experienced in our bodies as physical sensations? These sensations—tight, warm, heavy, tingly, fluttery, prickly, bubbly, to name a few—provide essential clues about what emotions we might be experiencing. For example, a heavy, sinking feeling in your heart could indicate that you are feeling sad or disappointed. In contrast, a burning, fiery sensation in your gut and tension in your hands and arms could mean you are angry, etc. Children and adults often lack this crucial awareness. Here are some strategies to help:

- Explicitly teach that body sensations are clues to what we are feeling.
- Use the *Connecting Feelings and Sensations* chart in the Resource Section to prompt students to identify their emotions.
- Describe hypothetical situations to students and ask them to imagine themselves in those situations and name what sensations come up. (For example: You get soaked in a rainstorm walking to school. Your backpack and clothes are sopping wet. On the way into the classroom, the principal yells at you for being late.) Then, ask them to name the accompanying internal sensations in their bodies and what emotion goes along with those sensations.
- Create a Sensation Word Wall with words and images or incorporate it into your Feelings Word Wall.
- Ask children to chart their emotions on a timeline of the day and indicate with an emoji how they were feeling, along with a short description of why.
- Have students draw and create a character to match their body sensations.
- Write about sensations. For example: What color would your sensation be? What would it look like? How big would it be? If it could talk, what would it say? How would you act it out?

Figure 4.2: Student sample of an "Emotion Timeline."

Source: Christopher Oteri

Questions for reflection

- When you were a child, or now as an adult, has anyone ever come to a hurtful conclusion about what you were doing and why? How did it make you feel? If you could go back in time and talk to that person who misunderstood you, what would you say? What do you wish they had known?
- Think about a student with whom you have a challenging relationship. If they were asked what you think and feel about them, how do you think they would answer? Is it true or false?
- Did you ever react to something in the heat of the moment only to regret saying it later? What happened?
- Fill out a *Check-In Wheel* of your own (see the Resources Section). How did it feel to do that activity? Did any of your thoughts and emotions surprise or upset you? Why? How might you use this tool in the classroom?
- If you found out that a child is having a hard day because of something happening at home, what might you do? Make a list (see Figure 4.2).
- How might you share the information in this chapter with your students in a developmentally appropriate and engaging way?

Vital Signs

Easy Ways to Check in with Students

This chapter is chock-full of practical strategies to check in with your students. Just a few words of caution about privacy and boundaries before you dive in…

When you do these activities, it is a good idea to decide and communicate ahead of time whether students volunteered personal information and stories will be shared with the classroom or just seen by you. Some of these activities can be private (*Check-In Mailbox*, for example), but other activities (like *What I Wish You Knew* or *Name a Number*) can be made either public or private. If they are made public, be sure to be very clear with all your students that the information shared needs to stay within the classroom community for the good of all concerned.

It's also essential to give students a heads-up that there are times when you won't be able to keep their information confidential. While most information shared in your classroom can be dealt with in the classroom, other situations that children may disclose—about problematic home situations, for example—will require you to contact the guidance counselor, administrator, or even a child protective service agency. Children may feel you've broken their trust if you don't give them a heads-up before this happens. There is a sample script in the Resources Section (*Sample Script: Sharing Confidential Information*) that will help you have this conversation before these situations occur.

Also, sharing some information about your own life outside of school can be transformative. It not only helps you build relationships with students, but also lets them know that you are a real person, just like them. Sharing stories from our lives, something older generations have done for millennia, can also provide context and guidance for students as they grow into their own identities and turn to us to "digest" the world around them.

Not sure what to share and what not to? As a general rule of thumb, don't share so much that your students feel they need to be taking care of you instead of the other way around. And consider steering away from topics that may be too personal (financial worries, romantic life, arguments with loved ones, etc.). Try to focus on more G-rated topics and surface-level concerns that are still important to you (your dog got a check-up, you went to a basketball game last night, you have a sore throat today, a story from your childhood, etc.). It can be hard to thread the needle between oversharing and being authentic. But given how important it is to build these relationships in the first place, it's worth a shot!

WHAT I WISH YOU KNEW

The strategy comes from a Denver-based primary school teacher named Kyle Schwartz. When Schwartz posted about this activity in 2015, it went viral, and she subsequently wrote a book about it. In this activity, you give students a chance to tell you something they wish you knew about them. Schwartz suggests putting them on sticky notes and either posting them or sharing them privately with the teacher.

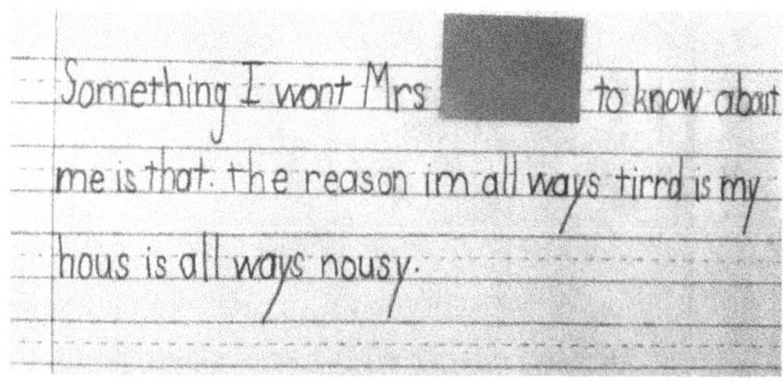

Figure 5.1: A 1st grader shares the reason she is always tired is because her house is always noisy

Before you give out these notes, it could be helpful to give suggestions of the type of things that they might write (e.g., I wish you knew that I sometimes come to school late because I'm taking care of my little sister, or I'm very excited about the quinceanera party I have next month, etc). Tell your students that the goal of sharing these notes with you is to help you understand and support them because you know that they have lives outside of school. If you are planning on sharing their notes publicly, make sure they know that and give them the option to indicate whether they'd like to keep it private.

This could also be done as a *dual journal* in which students write to you and you write back. You may want to choose one child per week to be your dual journal "pen pal."

NAME A NUMBER!

Ask students to think of the numbers from 0 to 5, with 0 meaning they are having the worst day ever and 5 meaning they are having the best day ever. Ask them to share with you a number that indicates how they're doing that day. Students could show their number by holding up their fingers, sharing during a classroom meeting, or sharing on a Google spreadsheet with an optional box provided if they wish to elaborate on why they chose the number they chose.

Name a number can be particularly helpful when checking in with students when they anticipate having a stressful event later in the day (a spelling test, standing up to a bully at recess, having a conversation with an authority figure, doing an oral presentation in front of the class, etc.). Before the stressful event, ask them to imagine how stressful that event will be and ask them to assign a number to it. Then, after the event happens, ask them to give a number indicating how stressful the event actually turned out to be. Reflect on how their estimate might have differed from reality. These activities can help individuals prepare for future stressful events because they can see that they might be over-imagining their difficulty and underestimating their own ability to deal with it.

It can also be helpful to ask the kids what it would take to move their number up a few notches, or give them a real or imaginary balloon and ask them to blow it up to the size that the problem is, and then ask what it would take to let the hot air out! You might ask, "What can we do to make this better?" and "How can I help?"

Along those lines, if a child is having a difficult day because of something worrying them at home, it can sometimes help to ask if they would like you to "hold" it for them during the day. Tell them that you will be in charge of worrying about it, and that if they like, you can "give it back" to them before they go home. This profound gesture of caring can be very touching and freeing for both children and adults!

CHECK-IN MAILBOX

Make yourself available to students by using a check-in mailbox. Much like the *What I Wish My Teacher Knew* activity, a check-in mailbox allows students to share personal information with you. It is simply a box where students can put notes that are meant exclusively for you. After sharing with the students what it is for, you might want to keep it in a quiet, private classroom area where curious students won't be tempted to check out other students' mail. I suggest finding either a box that is lockable or a piggy bank with a combination lock. You may want to designate colored index cards or special colored notes next to the box that students can easily grab. This way, shy students can access them independently.

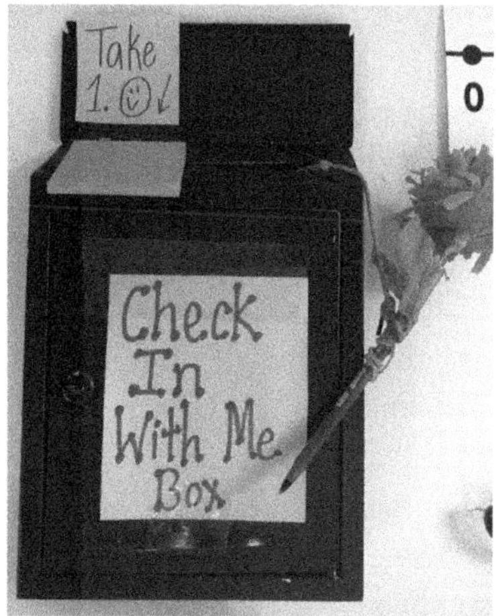

Figure 5.2: A check-in mailbox

MOOD NOTES

The strategy comes from Erin Castillo, a teacher in Northern California. In this activity, kids write their names or initials on the back of sticky notes and stick them to a section of a bulletin board/poster/chalkboard that describes how they're feeling. You can use this on a rolling, voluntary basis for students, or you might want to invite students to do it as they walk in the door in the morning. You may want to keep in mind that some students will not want to make their mood public every day (just as sometimes when you're feeling very private, you just don't feel like sharing). Note that you can differentiate two sections for students who are having a hard day—one to indicate that they don't want anyone to personally check in with them, and one for students who wouldn't mind checking in with you or another teacher/counselor about how they're feeling.

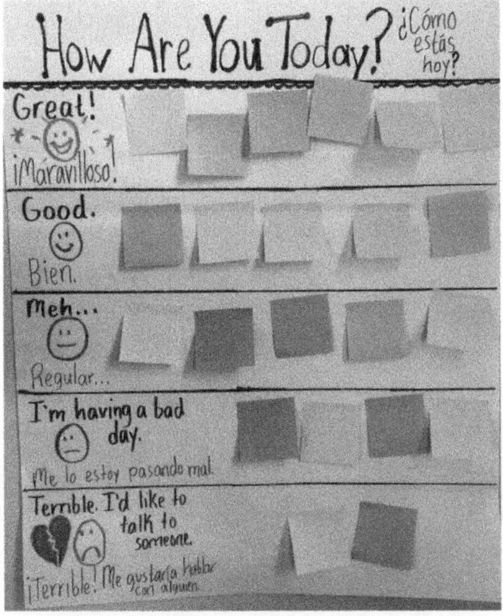

Figure 5.3: My (bilingual) interpretation of Erin Castillo's Mood Notes

HANDLE WITH CARE

This model, which is being embraced in many cities across the United States, allows school professionals to stay connected with law enforcement officers in the community. In this model, if a law enforcement officer encounters a child during a call, that child's information is forwarded to the school before the school bell rings the next day. No specific details about the circumstances of the police visit are provided to teachers; instead, school teachers are simply told to "Handle with Care" such-and-such a student. This knowledge gives teachers and other school professionals a heads-up that this child likely had a difficult time the night before and that they may need a little extra TLC that day at school.

CHECK-IN PARTNERS

Often in classroom meeting models, students are asked to share an emotion/feeling word that matches their feelings that day. However, many individuals feel resentful and panicky about sharing their thoughts and feelings with a large group, especially when they are having a hard day.

Instead, we can give students a chance to check in by allowing them to partner with a single person as a "check-in partner." These partners can work together for two to three weeks to enable students to get to know one another before switching, or they can change daily. This more intimate grouping makes it more likely that students will feel comfortable opening up, especially if they can choose their partners or are chosen by another student.

Partner check-ins can be more productive when we can empathize with other people, something that can be hard to do when we're only given a single word to go by (good, sad, worried etc.). For example, if I am your partner and I just say, "I'm worried," you may only have a vague sense of how I'm feeling and it will be harder for you to put yourself in my shoes. But if I say, "I'm feeling worried because my old dog had a seizure last night," you have some needed information that can help you more vividly understand the situation and more easily empathize. That's why in the following sample check-in script, students have the opportunity to share not only how they're feeling but also, briefly, why they're feeling that way.

Sample script or partner check-in

Partner A: "How are you feeling today?"

Partner B: "I am feeling ________ because ________. How are you feeling today?"

Partner A: "Thank you for sharing that. I am feeling _________ because ___________."

Partners can also respond to more traditional community meeting questions about favorite hobbies, music, foods, and many other topics.

TWO BY TEN

Also referred to as the "two-minute intervention" by researcher Raymond Wlodkowski, the Two by Ten strategy is a way to get a conversation started with students and build trust and rapport.[1] The idea is to chat with a single student for two minutes a day for ten consecutive days (ideal for hard-to-reach, stand offish, or disruptive students). Conversation can revolve around anything outside of academic concerns: their new sneakers or soccer jersey; their favorite basketball player, music, YouTuber, food, hobby, etc. It's a time for the teacher to provide unconditional positive regard for the student and speak honestly and open-heartedly about their own life, interests, and hobbies. These brief, consistent bursts of getting to know challenging students can help students finally feel they can let down their walls and trust. It also may help you to see difficult students in a whole new light.

CLASSROOM NEWSPAPER

One of the most appealing elements of social media is the possibility of checking in with friends and family and learning what's new with them. You can give your students the same opportunity by creating a classroom newspaper. You can do this in an elementary school classroom by laminating a few pieces of paper and allowing students to write their news on that paper using dry-erase boards or sticky notes. You can also designate a particular section of your classroom to be the "newspaper bulletin board" where students post their news on index cards or sticky notes (if you do so, you may want to designate one student as the "newspaper editor" who is in charge of handing out and keeping track of the material). The daily newspaper can be stored in an area where students can access it in their free time or when work is finished. As part of your morning routine, you can have a student volunteer (in my classroom, we call them the "town crier") to read the students' news stories aloud.

Students who are listening are encouraged to respond with non-verbal signals of support: the ASL sign to agree with what someone has said, a thumbs up, an air drawing of a smiley face for happy news, invisible tears or a frown face to empathize with upsetting news, etc. You might also choose just to have the classroom receive the news in silence to allow space around what the children have shared. Sometimes children share upsetting information, and when they do, you may want to ask them if they would like the rest of the class to respond ("What can we do to take care of you today?" "Would you prefer to not talk about today, or is it okay if some of your peers check in with you about how you're doing at recess?").

Checking in with students in remote learning spaces is more difficult, but also more crucial. Here are some possible ways to conduct remote check-ins.

Options for remote learning "check-ins":

- Create a shared Google document where children can share recent news, or their "highs and lows," or "yays and yucks."

- Have students visually check in by showing how they're doing with a thumbs up, thumbs sideways, or thumbs down. Consider taking a screenshot of that moment so you can review it later.
- If students show thumbs down, offer them the option to send you a message privately in the chat explaining what's up.
- Ask students to put an emoji in the chat to show how they're feeling.
- When possible, scroll through the chat after having a live meeting with your group. Often kids will slip in little messages about how they're doing into the chat, which can easily be overlooked.
- Use a platform that allows students to upload videos and share them with you or the classroom. Consider asking them to use a video sharing platform to explain their number of the day or just their news. One particular platform I find useful is called "Flipgrid." I am sure there will be many more by the time this book is printed!

STUDENT-LED PROFESSIONAL DEVELOPMENT

Although the strategy is not technically a one-on-one check-in, a student-led professional development session offers groups of students an opportunity to share their feedback with teachers. In this very student-centered model of professional development sessions, students offer teachers opinions and ideas about how to make lessonws more interesting, current, or relatable. School leaders can use students' feedback to make lessons more engaging.

TEACHER–STUDENT CONNECTION ACTIVITY

In this activity, as described by a 2017 article in *Edutopia*, the staff members scan which students have meaningful relationships with teachers and which don't.[2] To do this, share a virtual document online or post rosters of the entire school in one place where teachers can walk around and examine them (a gymnasium or library would be perfect). As teachers rotate around the room, they put check marks and their initials next to students' names under columns labeled "Name/Face," "Something Personal," "Personal/Family Story," and "Academic Standing" to note to what extent teachers are familiar with each student. When teachers have finished reviewing the whole school, it becomes apparent which students are tightly connected with teachers and, just as importantly, which are mostly out of the loop and maybe need someone at school who knows a little more than just their name and face. This awareness can be a game-changer in itself, but a follow-up step is to invite teachers or other staff (cafeteria and custodial staff included!) to reach out to the out-of-the-loop kids to make sure they become more connected and known within their school community.

PERSONALIZED DOORWAY GREETINGS

Made popular by various viral videos, teachers greet students at the door with personalized greetings to get the day started on a warm and fuzzy note and take stock of how students are doing. For younger grades, this is done by hanging a sign outside the door with images to show which kind of greeting a student prefers: a hug, high five, fist bump, etc. Students indicate which greeting they prefer, engage in that greeting, and then head into the classroom to start the day.

There are also contact-free options to say hello—saluting, curtsying, bowing, or bowing with folded hands (Namaste). Another option for those athletically inclined is a dance greeting. As each student approaches you in the line, you need to remember what their favorite dance move is and "dance hello" together!

VIRTUAL OR ACTUAL CLASSROOM DIRECTORY

Almost like Facebook, but each student has one page where they can share photos, details, news, etc. In a virtual learning environment, students may also choose to post links to their favorite videos, YouTube channels, songs, and favorite online resources. Be clear about your expectations for what kinds of materials are appropriate to share. Spend time each week spotlighting one student's page.

Checking in with our LGBTQ+ students

For gender-nonconforming students, it's even more critical that we have a vital signs check with them. A LGBTQ+ friendly classroom empowers all students to be who they are, and that includes being aware of the language we use and respecting students' preferred gender expression. This requires having conversations that may initially feel awkward or uncomfortable, but it's preferable to making hurtful assumptions. Some simple ways we can make our classrooms into more LGBTQ+ friendly spaces are:

- Avoid using language that reinforces only binary gender identity. For example, address the class as "class," "students," "kiddos," "game changers," "future leaders," etc., instead of "boys and girls" or "ladies and gentlemen."
- When you introduce yourself, identify what your preferred gender pronouns are (she/her, he/his, they/their). "My name is Mr. Quan. The pronouns I'd like you to use for me are he and his."
- Address bullying against the LGBTQ+ community in a respectful, direct way.
- Work with your counselor to find LGBTQ+ resources in your community.
- Show support for LGBTQ+ students with a sticker on your name badge, computer, and other visible places.
- Ask sensitively for students to let you know privately or publicly what gender pronouns they prefer you use. ("How would you like me to refer to you in class?")
- Ask for permission to tell other teachers if a student's gender identity differs from what other teachers may believe. ("Is it okay for me to inform other teachers about your pronouns?")

Questions for reflection

- Have you ever asked your students if they think you care about them outside of school? What might they say?
- How do you usually check in on your students?
- After reading this chapter, are there any particular strategies that you might want to use to check in with your students?

6

Curiosity

It May Have Killed the Cat, But It Can Save Your Classroom

It's important to not only understand the invisible backpacks that students are carrying, but also why it's so easy for us to misread behaviors and over-react, particularly when we're stressed. This can make our students feel like we are being unfair and too hard on them, and drive a wedge between us that's hard to remove. So what's really happening when we over-react to behaviours? How can we break free of that pesky habit?

As it turns out, there's a neurobiological reason for this. Because our brain is wired to act quickly to prioritize our survival, we are prone to misread situations under stress. Unfortunately, a classroom's intrinsic qualities—the time urgency, constant demands, and the need to quash difficult behaviors quickly—are the very things that naturally throw our brain into a stressed, survival state. This survival state doesn't look for the nuanced reasons behind behaviors, a crucial component of good class management. Instead, in its panic and pressure to act, our brain quickly reads others' behaviors as *safe* or *unsafe*. This can be a dangerous oversimplification because in our rush to respond to "unsafe" behaviors quickly, we're likely to misread what's actually happening and miss out on important information.

There's a touching Pfizer commercial that shows how surprising and hurtful our snap-second misperceptions can be. In it, we see a teenager furtively spray-painting a brick wall in a dark alley. When he finishes, he walks down the alley and up the stairs into an apartment building where his mother is feeding breakfast to a little girl in the kitchen. As though to convey how long she's been waiting for him, she looks at her watch with frustration and throws the boy an exasperated, withering look. Dodging her glare, he walks out of the room and steps into a bedroom where we are surprised to see a young girl in a hospital bed attached to what looks to be a breathing machine. The teenage boy and the little girl greet each other lovingly, and then he reaches over to open the curtains. As she turns to look, the little girl's face suddenly lights up. There, just outside her window, is an astonishingly beautiful mural of vivid graffitied flowers encircling the words, "BE BRAVE." Appearing in the doorway, his mother sees what he's done and suddenly realizes where her son has been. Through happy tears, she mouths the words 'Thank you."

This commercial is so powerful not only because the boy's gesture is so touching, but because it defies our expectations! From the beginning, it's easy to misread the boy as a delinquent and vandal, so his kind gesture turns our perceptions on their head. As the viewer, we can understand why the teenager's mother jumped to a conclusion about what happened. After apparently being out all night, her teenage son walks in the door, looking secretive and saying nothing. All the ordinary signs point to him being up to no good. The problem is that he has actually been up to something very good (or at least well-intentioned!). It's so easy to jump to what a "simple story" of what's going on and miss the actual, more nuanced story.

Simple story

Let me be clearer about the meaning of a **simple story**. The idea of a simple story draws inspiration from Chimamanda Adichie Ngozi's description of a "single story," as described in her 2009 TED Talk.[1] Ngozi's concept of a single story refers to confining our understanding of other cultures and other people to a single interpretation, which can cause critical misunderstandings. When I say "simple story," though, here I'm talking about the split-second assumptions we create all the time about the world around us. When you're truly in danger—a threatening man is coming after you with a knife, a car is careening your way, for example—a rapid-fire, simple story ("This is dangerous—get out of here now!") is essential to keeping you alive. Because our brain is designed to assimilate information quickly, we come to rapid conclusions about what's happening in the world around us all the time. Then we run these narratives in our heads to help make life more understandable and reliable. But what happens when our simple story isn't correct? For example, what happens when we assume that a potential employer hasn't called us back because we're no good but really they have just been out of town? Or when we assume our co-worker is showing up late because they are irresponsible and lack discipline but really they're late because they're taking care of an elderly parent? Clearly, there is danger to having a simple story, especially an incorrect one!

Mind trap ahead! Watch out!

The *Fundamental Attribution Error* (*aka the Attribution Error or Correspondence Bias*) is our brain's inclination to under-emphasize situational reasons for one's own behaviors while over-emphasizing personality-based reasons for others' behavior. That means that when we witness someone else's behavior, our brains are wired to view that person's behavior as an intrinsic part of who they are and not related to the situation's context. On the other hand, we believe that our behavior has nothing to do with who we are, because, for us, it's situational. For example, if your partner shows up late to the restaurant for your romantic dinner, it's because they are fundamentally uncaring and selfish, but if it's you who shows up late for dinner, it's clear that it's situational. You didn't get a good night's sleep, you were under the pressure of a deadline, you had to wait for the cable man to come, etc. It was certainly not because you are fundamentally uncaring and selfish (like your partner!). When it comes to other people, we judge their behavior to mean something permanent about their basic character, but for us, well, it's all relative. Perhaps a bit unfair and definitely something to be on the lookout for!

In those cases, by misreading others, we can miss out on precious opportunities for connection. For example, in the commercial described above, although the boy is probably avoiding his mother because he's afraid of getting in trouble for coming in late, it's a shame because he has such an exciting secret to share. Instead, he hurries out of the room, alone with his secret. More poignantly, as he walks out of the room, he's also alone with the story of *who* he is. He's a profoundly loving brother and talented artist, not a vandal or rebellious teenager who stays out late all night up to no good.

What would have happened if, instead of glaring at him, the boy's mother had paused and said, "You're coming in late. I've been so worried about you and wondering where you were. What can you tell me?" The door might have opened up enough for the boy to let his mother in, and from there, real communication could have started.

How often do we miss out on the truth of who we are? Have you had the experience of people believing an inaccurate story about you? It is devastating. It makes you wonder, what must be happening in our own hectic classrooms where we often have hair-trigger responses to behavior? Where we are forced to quickly compose simple stories about our students? How often do we miss out on the truth about what's actually happening and who our students truly are?

From my classroom to yours: Hit the pause button with "Take 4 Before"

According to a study investigating teachers' ability to manage stress,[2] one of the most helpful ways to regulate your emotions, reduce your stress levels, and see more clearly what's happening around you is to practice mindfulness. There is much more information about this in Chapter 32, but one way you can incorporate it is by practicing what I call "Take 4 Before." Start by placing one hand on your belly and one on your breastbone. Then take four slow, calm breaths through your nose and feel your belly expanding on the exhale (belly breaths and longer exhales are known to be more calming). In my classroom, we regularly do this together at trying times (such as when the classroom phone rings once again, when a student is escalated, or before I try to mediate a difficult conversation for my students), by telling them I need to "Take 4 Before" and then taking this breathing break. It's also helpful to do when someone is too escalated or emotional to speak clearly and rationally. At these times, I'll sometimes ask the students to match my breathing as we take four breaths together. Other times, I will tell them they are free to look away as we breathe because looking away from others is also a natural mechanism for calming down.

We don't know what we don't know

But "when we know better, we do better," as poet Maya Angelou said to Oprah Winfrey.[3] So how do we do better? How do we sidestep the brain's tendency to panic and misperceive situations?

Remember our friend the cognitive triangle? Let's use it to help disrupt this problematic cycle.

As you remember, before we act, we usually have a thought or feeling that propels us into action. Remember the example of your colleague who didn't return your hello? Before you decided to give them a piece of your mind, or ignore them, or something else, remember that you had the thought "Who do they think they are? What did I ever do to them? What a jerk!" What if, instead, you suddenly noticed that you might have jumped to the assumption that your colleague was *purposely* ignoring you? At that moment, could you also consider that maybe a cranky toddler kept them up all night? Or their pet died? Maybe they had a terrible headache? Maybe their mind was on an argument they had with their partner and not how much they hated you?

But what if they *were* purposely ignoring you, you might be thinking? What if the teenage boy who was staying out all night really was up to no good? To be clear, I agree that sometimes people are ill-intentioned, acting out of malice, and sometimes don't have our best interests at heart. But it's also true that sometimes our first take on a situation is the wrong one and we may be missing information. In the lingo of Landmark, the personal development program, **we don't know what we don't know.**[4]

So how do we know for sure if the narrative we're telling ourselves is what actually happened? Or how do we know if this is one of our blind spots?

As we've mentioned, if we allow ourselves a chance to be curious instead of reactive when responding to behavior, we can open the door for conversation, and this means we might be able to find out what *actually* happened. Then we can respond accordingly.

For example, one morning, just as I began to ring the chime to start class, I noticed that Nick, one of my 2nd graders, was still out of his seat, talking loudly to Andrea. My first thought was, "Ugghhh! Why is he still out of his seat?" I felt myself getting irritated and was tempted to play the role of disciplinarian. "What do you think you're doing out of your seat, young man!" But instead, I stopped. I remembered how much I hated it when I was falsely accused of something I didn't do. I reasoned that there was possibly a legitimate thought, feeling, or situation behind Nick's actions. So, in a neutral tone of voice, I asked what was happening. I said, "The chime's ringing. What's up?" Nick paused for a second. He seemed relieved that he didn't appear to be in trouble, and he raised his hand to show me a copy of one of his beloved Dog Man books. He explained that he and Andrea were still talking because they had decided they could take turns reading it. When I rang the chime, they were still making plans for switching ownership of the beloved book at lunch. Even if it meant they were a few seconds late getting started, I was surprised and pleased that they were trying to take turns with a book! It was also refreshing to see my 2nd grade students take the initiative to solve a problem independently—something I'm always trying to get them to do!

A punitive response might have frustrated and confused them (and maybe even made them think twice before trying to solve a problem independently in the future). Instead, pausing and becoming curious about what was happening allowed the lines of communication to open so that Nick and Andrea could get the actual story out.

Does pausing and pondering mean letting students off the hook? No, but it does mean that the consequences for behaviors are more fitting to what's actually going on, instead of what we imagine to be happening. For example, in this case, instead of giving Nick a time out or dealing with his behavior punitively, pausing and pondering let me see what was really happening. It also brought to light that Nick was missing a skill I could help him with: learning how to stop one activity when it's time for another. As Viktor Frankl, an Austrian neurologist, psychologist, and Holocaust survivor, said, "Between stimulus and response there is a space. In that space is our power to choose our response. In our response lies our growth and our freedom."[5] So, for simple situations that require re-direction—especially in cases where we are likely to over-react or misinterpret what's going on—try just pausing in that space and pondering. Allow a second for curiosity to emerge. Then check to see whether your narrative matches what's actually going on. You might find that stopping to pause and ponder can lead to more peaceful outcomes for everyone involved.

Try the following process: Pause Plus Ponder Equals Peace to help you pause and ponder to consider what's happening (there is also a template in the Resources Section).

Pause Plus Ponder Equals Peace

1. Become aware of your response to what's happening.
2. Pause for a few moments to breathe calmly.
3. Ponder the possibility that you might be making up a story about what's happening and that you may be missing information.
4. Decide if you want to act.
5. If you decide to act and inquire about what's happening, use a neutral tone of voice. Say something like "I've noticed ________. I'm wondering what's actually going on." Or "I noticed that _____. I am wondering what you can tell me about that."

Questions for reflection

- Think about Viktor Frankl's famous quote: "Between stimulus and response there is a space. In that space is our power to choose our response. In our response lies our growth and our freedom." What meaning does this quote hold for you?
- Can you think of a situation in which a teacher might be influenced by the fundamental attribution error when evaluating a student's behavior? What about when meeting with a parent or co-worker?
- Think about your most challenging student, one you struggle with a lot. Now write out a flowchart that shows what a typical problematic interaction between the two of you looks like. What happens first? What typically happens next? And then what? Can you identify a pattern to these interactions? Can you identify a point where you might be able to stop this cycle from repeating, maybe by using "Pause and Ponder"?
- Are there any insights from this chapter you'd like to share with students? How might you do that in a developmentally appropriate and engaging way?

7

The Story I'm Telling Myself

How to Repair Ruptured Relationships and Sidestep Hurtful Narratives

We can use the "Pause and Ponder" process to quickly find out what is happening in our classrooms. But what happens when we notice that the narratives we are telling ourselves about students are ongoing, emotion heavy, and driving us nuts? By choosing to strategically share these private narratives openly with our students, we can repair trust and free ourselves from painful misunderstandings.

Brené Brown, a researcher who writes and speaks about vulnerability and courage, shared the following personal story about the power of sharing "the stories that we tell ourselves." In a popular Netflix special,[1] she shares that she and her husband went for a swim in a lake one summer day while on a family vacation. As they started to paddle around, Brown noticed that her husband seemed to be keeping his distance. Every time she tried to talk to him about how special it felt to be swimming in the lake together on their vacation, he would reply curtly and swim away. She started to wonder if her aging body was driving him away, and the more he stayed away, the more she constructed a painful story about how her partner was no longer interested in her. By the time he finally swam back her way, she was overwhelmed with dismay. But instead of descending further into grief and frustration, she decided to lay her cards out on the table and be vulnerable. There's a *story I'm telling myself* about what's happening, she told him. As she shared her fear that he was not responding to her bids for attention because he wasn't attracted to her anymore, her husband also felt it was safe to be vulnerable. As it turned out, instead of being repulsed by her aging body as she'd imagined, he'd actually been fighting off a panic attack about a terrible nightmare he'd had the night before. As he swam around, the nightmare came to mind, and he felt so panicked that he couldn't talk about it, so he was swimming away to calm himself down. Brown never would have found out the true story without first being vulnerable enough to share *the story she was telling herself.*

Much of the way we see our relationships, including those in our classrooms, is driven by these stories and narratives we tell ourselves. As we've said, as humans, we are wired for stories because they help us make sense out of what's happening. But these stories can get twisted in some pretty problematic and predictable ways. Some of these familiar, maladaptive stories are:

- I'll never be able to get them to understand me.
- He/she is just trying to control me.
- I'm not worthy of love.
- The best way to deal with them is to avoid the whole issue.
- They always act this way.

For example, several years ago, I had a student who frequently called answers out and seemed to want to monopolize classroom conversations. For a while, I told myself the story that he was spoiled and unwilling to share airtime with others. But as I got to know him better, I started to see that he was actually quite gifted and his calling out and monopolizing the conversation was really because he wanted to show me how quickly he was mastering the material. This realization helped me to change the way I saw him. I ended up giving him a private notebook to write in during class so that he could record his answers to my questions and write down his new and exciting ideas. It didn't completely reverse his disruptive behavior, but it did make a big difference.

If we don't get to the root of behavior, over time the simple, negative stories can become toxic, requiring us to find ways to mend the ruptures in our relationships. It's helpful to know that this pattern of having challenges in relationships and then mending them is normal and natural. In fact, in psychological terms, it's known as the *rupture/repair cycle*. This is a normal and natural pattern that happens between individuals in relationships with one another (teachers and students, parents and children, siblings, co-workers, couples, etc.). It's normal for difficulties to come up whenever we are around someone for a long time; misunderstandings arise, hurtful things are said and done, and there is a rupture or challenge in the relationship. We may feel angry, hurt, betrayed, or disappointed. When this rupture happens in healthy relationships, it also gets repaired with open and honest communication between the two parties. Children in families with healthy rupture and repair cycles learn to trust that ruptures will be safely repaired and that problems in relationships with others, including authority figures, are normal and workable ("problem mentionable, problem manageable," as Mr. Rogers said).[2] For these children, this safety makes them feel more secure and comfortable expressing their feelings the next time a challenge comes up. They know that even if there are ruptures in relationships with their caregivers, things can be talked about, ironed out, and will go back to normal. Even though they have made a mistake, they are still safe in their care-taker's affection. They sense that they have what Carl Rogers called "unconditional positive regard."[3]

But many children don't experience a healthy rupture and repair cycle. Their parents and care-takers may have had ongoing explosive battles at home, lower-level disagreements that never really resolved, or conflicts that were regularly "solved" with the silent treatment. When these children made mistakes, or a problem came up at home, the "guilty party" was chastised, judged, isolated, and criticized. It was unclear to the children if, once things went wrong, they could ever be made right again. They didn't receive unconditional positive regard and worried they wouldn't be loved because they upset the grown-ups around them with their perceived imperfections. As they grew, they learned to fear causing any kind of problem, hurting anyone, or making any kind of mistake. In their experience, problems spelled certain disaster and the loss of love and affection.

Now imagine these children in the classroom where the nature of our job requires that we provide lots of – possibly triggering – corrective feedback. Because students may read this frequent feedback as a rupture in their relationship with you, they may over-react, fearing you don't care for them anymore because they've "made a mistake." That's why even the littlest corrections and redirections ("Please put your feet on the ground," "Please remember to tuck in your chair") can throw them into a state of panic and defensiveness. For them, making mistakes is a big deal and so they may act as if they've been treated with outrageous unfairness when you provide any kind of corrective feedback, no matter how small. There is a place for both negative and positive feedback, but you may recognize that the usual 5:1 positive to negative ratio may not be quite enough for these students. To keep them on an even keel, they may need a good amount of reassurance and repair!

Thought about in this way, it makes sense that so many of our students with broken rupture and repair cycles would also be hesitant to get close to adults. Getting close to people means risking being open to people who may hurt us and trusting others to accept us for who we are. It also means trusting that we'll be forgiven when we make mistakes without lots and lots of drama. For many children, this is a longed-for but hard-to-imagine reality.

Fortunately, the classroom is a great place to heal. By modeling consistent warmth and dependability in your communication with children, you can help them learn that even when things go wrong in the classroom, it's okay; in fact, it's a safe place for them to be exactly who they are.

I'm sorry: Why apologies are so important

Relationships can bring meaning and joy to our lives, but ruptures in our relationships can be extremely painful and stressful. Knowing how to patch things up with a good old-fashioned apology can go a long way towards repairing the damage done. But for most of us, sincerely apologizing is a hard thing to do. In many cases, we fear that we'll lose the other's respect for our authority by apologizing. We fear that if they see we're human too, it will make us vulnerable to attack. In truth, if we apologize sincerely, instead of attacking us, the other person may soften their own defenses because they feel touched by our bravery in opening up (it takes a boat-load of courage to be vulnerable!). The good thing about receiving a sincere apology is that the rupture in the relationship can finally heal. We can once again relax and trust the other person because they've shown openness to our needs, to our point of view. We count; our needs matter.

In an interview with Brené Brown, clinical psychologist and relationship expert Dr. Harriet Lerner asserts that a good apology tells us that our feelings make sense, which is especially transformative for those who grew up in homes where adults didn't validate their reality.[4] So how do we make a good apology? Dr. Lerner shares that there are several key ways to apologize well; here are some of them:

1. First, be careful with using the word "but" because it can cancel out the sincerity of your apology ("I'm sorry I spoke to you in a nasty way, but I was feeling stressed"). Instead, wait to explain your side until another time when the other person is not as upset and might be more open to receiving what you have to say (think connection before correction).
2. Second, take responsibility for *your* actions, and don't accidentally enrage the other more by apologizing for their feelings ("I'm sorry if you felt x, y, z"). Instead, apologize for

what *you've* said or done ("I'm sorry that I spoke to you in a nasty way; that must have hurt your feelings").

3. Third, don't apologize as a bargaining tool, or just to get the other person to move on, or to get an apology back from them.
4. Lastly, offer to make amends for what you've done. For example, if you've broken something, replace it; if you've hurt feelings, make a commitment not to repeat the hurtful behavior again in the future.

Questions for reflection

- As a child, how did your parents and care-takers handle conflict? Was there a healthy or unhealthy rupture and repair cycle? How do you imagine that this style of handling conflict influenced you and the way you handle conflicts today?
- Is there a situation in your life where it may be helpful to share with someone else "the story you are telling yourself"?
- Can you think of a time when you apologized to a student or colleague? What happened?
- Think of a time when you received a very good apology. What made it so effective?
- Think of a time when you received an inadequate apology. What made it so unhelpful?
- How do you show your students you are safe enough for them to trust? After reading this chapter, what new strategies might you use to model that you are a person your students can trust?

8

Cards on the Table Conversations

How to Find Out What's Really Going On

I'm not much of a gambler, but I do know that in poker, there comes a moment when players have to stop and come clean about what cards they've been holding. They have to lay their cards on the table, literally. This is a good metaphor for ruptures in relationships because sometimes there comes a moment when things just need to be addressed for what they are before anyone can move forward. For example, maybe you have had a problem simmering for a while with one of your students: they start showing up late; they used to participate all the time, but now they don't; they've started calling out answers, etc. You have a sense that, clearly, *something* is going on, but you're not sure what. The only thing you know for sure is that it's time to get things out in the open before the situation gets any worse. It's time to repair a ruptured relationship with what I call a *Cards on the Table Conversation.*

This type of conversation helps to create a classroom in which students feel emotionally safe. By offering ourselves as authentic and even vulnerable human beings, we make students feel safe and address and correct dangerous power imbalances that can show up in the classroom.

To show you what I mean, consider four types of leadership as they relate to power.[1] They are known as *Power Over, Power With, Power Within,* and *Power To* styles of leadership. As you may be thinking, these leadership styles aren't just limited to classrooms: they can be seen in politics, faith communities, sports teams, workplaces, and families.

Individuals who have a *Power Over* style of leadership believe that power is a limited resource, and, as such, it must be carefully guarded and protected. To maintain power over people, this kind of leader will use fear and intimidation to make sure they can stay in charge. They will dehumanize, humiliate, and find ways to punish those who resist or oppose their authority. For students who have experienced trauma, a *Power Over* style of leadership can remind them of the pain and struggle they experienced during traumatic situations in which others wielded power over them.

With *Power With, Power To,* and *Power Within* leadership styles, on the other hand, the leader sees their role as sharing power, collaborating, empowering, and giving others a voice.[2] Instead of believing they need to hoard power for themselves, they believe that when they share power, it doesn't shrink but expands! Their leadership style has much in common with the values of *servant leadership*, in which the leader seeks to empower and uplift individuals. These leadership styles are preferable to the *Power Over* leadership style because they are based on equity, compassion, empathy, and the belief that we are stronger together. This is the kind of leadership we want in our classrooms and schools. *Cards on the Table Conversations* and other open-hearted types of conversations like these are in line with these deeply empathetic and human-centered leadership styles.

Sharing power with the "Little Teacher"

In my classroom for the last several years, I have done something my students and I call "Little Teacher" or "Junior Teacher." Usually, I spend the first two months of school practicing our routines and transitions. Then, around the end of October, I let the students take charge of these activities while I watch from the sideline (and coach when needed). Each day, a different student is placed in charge of leading the class during activities like lining up, unpacking and packing up, moving students into literacy centers, walking to and from lunch and recess together, going to and from the rug, etc.—all the things that I would typically be in charge of leading. The Little Teacher also leads a morning routine, which includes saying good morning to the class (in the language of the day), saying the date, and leading a quick tai-chi stretch. They even lead the line to lunch, recess, or wherever—a job they particularly relish! To make sure the Little Teacher doesn't become a Little Tyrant, we also have repeated and ongoing discussions about what an important responsibility it is to be in charge of the class and why it's important to be fair (not picking their friends to line up first, for example). Of course, I am always there to monitor.

Over the years, I have seen firsthand how this activity builds self-confidence and gives students the sense they are an important part of our classroom community!

A *Cards on the Table Conversation* is longer and more thoughtful than the usual, daily quick redirections we provide in the moment ("I need your work to be neat when you hand it in," "Please walk carefully on the stairs so we can all stay safe," "Remember to speak kindly to your partner," etc.). It doesn't have to be isolated from consequences or be a replacement for accountability. In fact, it's not something that you will do every day. But on those occasions when you need to get to the root of a problematic pattern, clear the air, or patch up a ruptured relationship, having a *Cards on the Table Conversation* can help immensely.

As with all the scripts in this book, think of this script as a general guideline. Your desire and intent to connect and your body language and tone of voice convey immense amounts of information to your listener, much more than any specific words. Still, as a guidepost, it's important to remember that it's helpful to connect before we correct, regardless of exactly what we say. Doing so will help ensure that the other person will be open to hearing what we have to say. It also helps to be vulnerable before asking the other person to be brave enough to share what's really in their heart. Whether you use these words or not, following these general guidelines can make it easier for shy or reluctant students to open up.

Cards on the Table Conversations

1. Hi ______________. How are you? Can we talk?
2. Don't worry—everything is okay. But I want to make sure we can talk when things come up.
3. You're important to me and I'm noticing that ___________ (your work is not getting done, our last conversation made me feel tense, you're coming in late every day, you look frustrated when it's time to work on math, etc.).
4. The story I'm telling myself about this is ___________. (Apologize if it's appropriate to do so)
5. I wonder what's actually happening, though. I'm not sure I have the whole picture.

6. Would you help me to understand?

Tips for *Cards on the Table Conversations*

- You may want to use this conversation along with the *Lifesaver* discussed in the next chapter to sort out reasons for behavior. Before you decide what course of action you want to take to help your student change their behavior, you can take a shortcut by using this script to check with the student about the *reason* behind their behavior. If you want, you might even venture to tell them about the *Lifesavers* activity you filled out. It may touch them to know how much work you've put into trying to understand them!
- Not every *Cards on the Table Conversation* has to include you sharing a vulnerable emotional response, but some will. For example, suppose you are trying to determine why your student has suddenly stopped doing their homework. In that case, the "story I'm telling myself about this" might simply be "The story I'm telling myself about this is that it's been hard to manage schoolwork plus the soccer team." Even though you are not sharing an emotional confession, your student will still value that you are sharing what you've been thinking. This transparency can go a long way!
- In cases where you are using this conversation to repair a relationship following a challenging emotional situation, you will need to reveal how you perceive the situation on an emotional level, as we've been discussing. For example, you might say, "The story I'm telling myself about this is that you haven't participated lately because I hurt your feelings the other day when I said your essay didn't meet my expectations of you." This statement reveals to your student that you know there is an emotional component to what's happening and that you might be partly responsible for what's gone wrong. Saying it out loud gives students the message that you are tuned in to how they may be feeling (a *vital* part of making people feel "felt"). It also communicates that you believe problems can be managed by talking about them, even the sticky emotional ones. It can be freeing and reassuring to students that teachers care enough to talk about even the "invisible" emotional parts of what's happening.

- Your *Cards on the Table Conversation* may need to include a sincere and effective apology. For tips on offering a good apology, check out the section "I'm sorry: Why apologies are so important" in Chapter 7.
- Lastly, before you have this conversation, you may want to think about whether this is a good time for them to talk. If they are hungry, thirsty, distracted, or in a bad mood, you may want to ask, "Is this a good time for us to talk together about something that's been on my mind?" If it's not, make a plan to reschedule.

To wrap it up, we can use the *Pause and Ponder* process to quickly investigate the root of behaviors in challenging situations. For more persistent, chronic, and emotional problems, we can also have a *Cards on the Table Conversation* to find out what's really going on and repair ruptured relationships.

Questions for reflection

- When was the last time you repaired a ruptured relationship? What did you do?
- Blaise Pascal said, "Justice and power must be brought together, so that whatever is just may be powerful, and whatever is powerful may be just."[3] Thinking about the four styles of leadership we discussed earlier (*Power Over, Power With, Power Within*, and *Power To*), what does this quote mean to you?
- Do you know anyone who has a *Power Over* style of leadership? What do the people they lead seem to think and feel about being treated this way?
- Can you think of a student who might benefit from a *Cards on the Table Conversation*? Take a moment and sketch out what you might say using the scripts (you can find another copy in the Resources Section).

9

I Need a *Lifesaver!*

Make a Plan *Now* for Difficult Behaviors

Even if we manage to pause and ponder when we see problematic behavior and are conscientious about repairing ruptured relationships, it can sometimes still be hard to decode persistent misbehavior. It can lead you to take others' behavior personally, but focusing entirely on yourself can lead you to overlook the many other reasons for student behavior (and make you feel pretty terrible about yourself as well!).

So what should you do? Clear, consistent, and fair consequences can help with many, but not all, children. As we've discussed, it can be game-changing to have an open conversation with students (like the *Cards on the Table Conversations* discussed in Chapter 8) about what's really going on. But sometimes, students have no answers to provide, at least not in the moment. It doesn't help that students often lack words to describe emotions and come up short or say, "I don't know," when asked why they did what they did. This lack of answers might make you want a more systematic way to decode puzzling or difficult student behavior.

As you may know, in applied behavioral analysis, you probe for an antecedent, behavior, or consequence to explain problematic behavior. But suppose you don't have time to track the antecedent, behavior, and consequence over time and want a direction to go in *now*. In that case, you can think about a specific problematic pattern and ask yourself, "What are all the reasons this person might be doing this thing?" and, "If this reason is the correct one, then what might be some possible next steps to help them to modify this behavior?" To help you stay organized, you can use the *Lifesaver* activity to deduce what might be causing a behavior. I recommend doing it with your colleagues to get more ideas, but you can also do it alone. Here's how it goes:

LIFESAVER ACTIVITY

1. Think about one challenging behavior that one of your students has. Tell your colleagues about it or think about it yourself. For example, you might choose to focus on a student sleeping in class, calling out answers, never participating, etc. If you are working with colleagues, write it in the middle of the *Lifesaver* (there is a template in the Resources Section) where it says "Challenging Behavior." Resist the urge to explain the reasons behind the behavior too much at this point. Just say what you see and what you've noticed, when it occurs, when it started, while being as objective as possible.

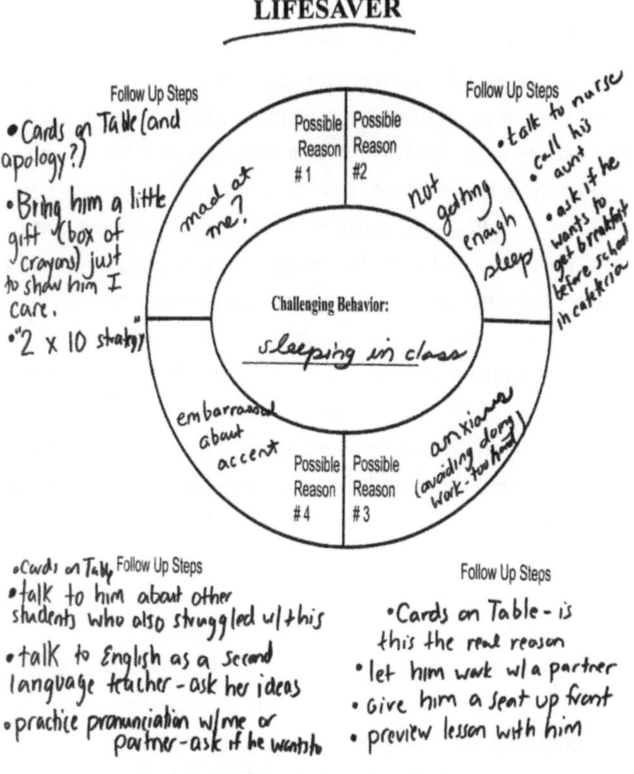

Figure 9.1: A sample completed Lifesaver

2. Now, brainstorm as many possible reasons as you can think of for this behavior. For example, for "sleeping in class," you might brainstorm that: (1) They are sleeping because something is preventing them from getting enough rest, (2) they are feigning sleep because

they are bored with the content being taught, (3) they're forcing themselves to sleep because they're anxious about the material being too hard, (4) they're worried about participating because they're new to the school, (5) they're embarrassed that they are learning English and have an accent, or many other reasons. When you do this, it's imperative to consider physical and sensory needs as well as social and emotional needs (like problems in relationships with teachers and peers). You should also consider academic needs that might prompt the behavior (is the work too hard or too easy?) and whether the behavior is trauma- or anxiety-related. You can find more information about sensory needs, trauma, and anxiety-related behaviors later in this book.

3. Select four of the most likely explanations for the behavior. Using the *Lifesaver* template (or draw your own version), write down one possible reason in each of the four sections of the lifesaver image. There is a copy of the *Lifesaver* template in the Resources Section.
4. Brainstorm what follow-up steps might be helpful for each possible explanation. In the white space outside of the *Lifesaver*, write down what your follow-up steps might be. For example, imagine that you have decided that the student is sleeping because they are not getting enough rest. You might write down that follow-up steps are calling home to talk to parents/care-givers, checking in with the school nurse, checking with colleagues to see whether his/her siblings are also falling asleep in school, etc. You might decide to track what time they fall asleep to see if there is a pattern. You might decide to give them a chance to move around more frequently or set up a cozy area in the room to allow them to take a quick catnap if needed.
5. Now, consider each of these possible reasons. Which one seems most likely?
6. Try out your interventions. Do they work? If yes, great! Continue on this path. If not, take another look at your *Lifesaver* and re-examine the other three reasons, given what you've observed. Choose which one makes the most sense now and repeat the process.

Question for reflection

- Freddy, a student in your class, is frequently distracted by other things (technology, books, doodling, etc.). When you call on him, he needs a lot of coaching to respond correctly. Use the *Lifesaver* template in the Resources Section to plot out possible reasons for his distracted behavior and plan possible follow-up steps.

10

Like Porcupines on a Cold Night

How Attachment Theory Affects Your Classroom

Do you hear me? Do you see me? Does what I say matter? Every human being you meet wants to know the answer to these fundamental questions. That's because they get at the heart of attachment theory, a working model of how we see the world and the safety of our relationships with others. Let me share a story to show you what I mean and why these concepts are crucial to creating a calm and connected classroom.

A few years ago, I went to see a doctor about getting a biopsy for a lump in my breast. This visit was my third appointment about this lump because, at every previous appointment, I flatly refused the possibility of the surgeon leaving an aluminium tag as a marker in my breast. I was so resistant to the idea that I had walked out of an earlier appointment and made repeated phone calls to my primary care doctor to discuss my options. In my opinion, I didn't see the need for a piece of metal to be placed in my otherwise healthy body; it seemed unnatural, and I wasn't sure how it would help. Even though I heard all the doctors' reasons for the tag and read studies about how innocuous it was, I remained passionately opposed and very anxious about the whole situation. My personal doctor suggested that I see one more specialist to talk the possibilities over.

When I got to the specialist's office, the new doctor and I went through the same motions as before, again discussing the need for the biopsy and again reviewing the benefits of the aluminium tag. Even though she was friendly and gentle, I still wanted no part of the tag, and the visit was shaping up to be another impasse.

I remember that she took out a sample metal tag and gave it to me to hold. Previous doctors had also done this. But then she did something extraordinary. Instead of continuing to insist on her opinion, she sat down next to me so we could look at the tag *together*. For a few minutes, we just sat in silence and looked at the tag, the two of us. The whole time we sat, she didn't say a word. No "What do you think?" or "See how small it is?" Nothing. She just sat next to me and peered gently into my palm with me. As I looked down at the despised object, I felt the sense this doctor was finally trying to see it the way I saw it. No pressure, no judgment, no agenda, just sitting together considering this little piece of aluminium. Suddenly, I didn't feel so alone in my struggle. I felt that this doctor really saw me, understood how I felt, and valued what I thought. She was replying in the affirmative to my unspoken questions: Do you hear me? Do you see me? Does what I say matter? Trying to hold back the tears that had built up over weeks about the pending operation, I turned to her and said, "Okay, I'll do it, but only if you'll be my surgeon." She smiled warmly and nodded.

That day, when my doctor sat next to me and waited for me with sensitivity and patience, she illustrated a key principle of building relationships: that of **attunement**, or making others feel that their needs are being sensitively considered and attended to. According to attachment theory, a theory that explains a sort of internal working model of relationships that we all have, our sense that others are attuned to us—even on a non-verbal level—originates in our very earliest interactions with care-givers. We depended entirely on our care-givers to correctly read our smiles, cries, whimpers, and pleas for affection. If our care-givers were attuned to us, they responded to our moods and emotions appropriately so that we felt heard, seen, witnessed, and *felt*. This attunement provided enormous relief to our young selves because it assured us that we had a way of communicating our needs in this new world in which we found ourselves, especially because we couldn't yet do so in words. If we felt lonely, confused, angry, sad, hungry, hot, cold, or in need of reassurance, we knew we could count on our care-givers to care for our needs. Because we were regularly taken care of, we formed what is known as a "secure attachment" with our care-givers, a sense of safety in relationships resulting from consistent, attuned parenting. Later in life, we could use this working model of safe relationships as a base from which to confidently explore the world and form and maintain healthy relationships.

Attachment theory and the porcupine problem

German philosopher Arthur Schopenhauer has said that humans are like hedgehogs or porcupines on a cold night.[1] To protect ourselves from the cold, we want to draw close to others to keep warm. But when we do, we end up continually pricking each other with our sharp quills and hurting one another so that we have to retreat. This unconscious dynamic of seeking intimacy and then needing space emerges every time we find ourselves in close relationships with others.

So what separates the securely attached from the insecurely attached? It comes down to how regularly care-givers consistently and sensitively respond to their distressed child. Unlike safely attached children, insecurely attached children have learned that reaching out to care-givers for help when there is a problem doesn't make things better; instead, it can make things even worse! When challenges arise, instead of receiving comfort from care-givers, insecurely attached children are often dealt with harshly. They are often shamed, ignored, or criticized for not being strong enough, smart enough, whatever enough.

Why would a parent do this? What makes it so hard to provide children with a sense of safety? While care-givers may deeply love their children, their own life challenges may sometimes make it hard or impossible to do the labor-intensive work of attuning to young children day in and day out. It can be hard to consistently respond to the constant demands of infants and young children if you're worried about paying bills, for example, or embroiled in an unhappy marriage, fighting an addiction, or any number of other ordinary and extraordinary life challenges. Many parents may even have lacked this kind of secure nurturing experience as children and don't yet know how to provide it or even why it's important. (Word to those of you who are parents: if, after reading this section, you're feeling worried that you're not forming a safe enough attachment with your kids, don't worry too much. For the most part, if parents fail to provide attunement from time to time, it is not disastrous for children. In fact, there is research that denotes that parenting doesn't need to be perfect to avoid damaging children; it just needs to be "good enough."[2])

However, when their interactions with their parents are negative day in and day out, children can receive the message that turning to others is more a source of pain than comfort. In the vacuum that develops, they develop "insecure attachment styles"—worldviews that help the child navigate the world without a secure attachment figure. They may believe that others will abandon them, and so they must cling on fiercely (anxious attachment), or that they can only rely on themselves (avoidant/dismissive attachment). Less commonly, individuals who have experienced significant neglect or trauma may have a fearful avoidant (disorganized) attachment style and exhibit traits of both insecure styles. You can see these four basic attachment styles described in Figure 10.1.

<table>
<tr>
<td>Secure Attachment
• Confident
• Can have emotional closeness with others
• Trusts readily
• Not afraid of communicating their concerns
• Solves problems collaboratively
• Positive attitude towards themselves and others
CORE BELIEF: I am safe with others. I can confidently explore the world, make mistakes, and give and receive love.</td>
<td>Anxious Attachment
• Dependent
• Struggles with emotional highs and lows
• Fearful of losing relationships
• Clingy before separations
• Thirsty for nurturance
• Negative attitude towards themselves, positive attitude towards others
• Prefers to have others' help to process strong emotions/conflicts
CORE BELIEF: I need others to be safe, but they will let me down and leave me.</td>
</tr>
<tr>
<td>Avoidant/Dismissive Attachment
• Keeps themselves at a distance from others
• Can be highly competent, seeks out independence
• Positive view of self/critical view of others
• May consciously or unconsciously push others away
• Prefers to be alone to process strong emotions and conflicts
CORE BELIEF: I don't need anyone. I can take care of myself. I'm safest on my own.</td>
<td>Fearful/Avoidant Attachment (also called disorganized attachment)
• High anxiety in relationships
• Both actively seeks and actively avoids closeness
• Unpredictable
• Has extreme fear of rejection
• Can be self-harming
• Negative view of self and others
• Usually develops as a result of childhood trauma and/or significant neglect
CORE BELIEF: I don't deserve love. There must be something wrong with me.</td>
</tr>
</table>

Figure 10.1: Four types of attachment style

Okay, I get attachment theory—now what do I do?

You may be wondering what to do with all this information? To start with, let's talk about how these different attachment styles show up in *your* classroom. Because insecurely attached children haven't learned that they can trust the adults in charge, they enter school already very uncertain that grown-ups will be reliably attuned to their needs. They may even be convinced that this will not be the case. This can make them resistant to trusting you and the other teachers around them. That's why it can be so *hard*, but not impossible, for insecurely attached students to trust adults enough to form safe attachments. These kids can be more prickly and more difficult to love, and you may feel like they are pushing you away or over-reacting to every perceived slight. In the words of Dr. Russell Barkley, "the kids who need the most love will ask for it in the most unloving of ways."[3]

But as we've said before, the good news is that classrooms are excellent spaces to heal and try out new ways of experiencing the world. This is even true on a neurobiological level! Because our brain can change and grow based on experiences (this is called neuroplasticity), we can develop new and healthier neural circuitry based on the quality of our day-to-day interactions with others. Later positive experiences can counteract early negative experiences, and the brain can recalibrate to take in this new way of seeing the world. This means that at any point in time, we have the potential to unlearn unhealthy patterns of thinking, acting, and perceiving the world and instead to learn healthier ones!

In our classroom, we can create conditions where children are more sensitively attended to, seen, heard, and witnessed, even if they never experienced this before. By doing this, we let students know that they can be real with others about their needs and that it's safe for them to be vulnerable. We are building secure attachments.

Although it is anything but easy, once we have established a safe attachment bond with insecurely attached students, they become more respectful, more focused and engaged, and can even build more trusting relationships with others around them. This ability to trust in others can carry over to other areas of their lives and have lasting, positive effects for the rest of their lives.

Tips to build secure attachment with your students

- Give specific praise (e.g., "The stripes you drew on the tiger make him look so real!" *not* something general like "Awesome drawing! You're a great artist").
- Give praise related to effort versus final results ("I can tell you put so much time into this story!" *or* "Wow, I can see you put a lot of effort into finding juicy rhyming words for your poem").
- Use phrases that focus on hearing and seeing what the child is expressing ("**I hear you saying that** you want more time to finish your work"/"**It sounds like you're** confused about which course meets your long term goals"/"**When I listen to you talk**, it makes me wonder if...").
- Help name what emotions children are expressing non-verbally ("I see a big smile on your face! It looks like you are feeling proud of your performance!").
- Remind them of things you remember about them or things they've told you ("I remember you said your little sister is learning to talk! What has she been saying to you lately?"/"I remember you said that you like to listen to music. What have you been listening to lately?").
- Share that you think about them even when you don't see them ("Last night, when I was out walking my dog, I remembered what you said about air pollution in class yesterday. You really got me thinking!").
- Be mindful about mentioning not only the places students need to grow, but also where they "glow." The usual ratio is five positive interactions to one negative interaction,[4] but you may find that trauma-impacted children need more of these "glows" to balance out the "grows" than typically developing children. To achieve this balance, try putting a bunch of coins or counters on your desk one day. Every time you say something negative, put a coin in your left pocket, and every time you say something positive, put a coin in your right pocket. What's your balance at the end of the day?
- Consider allowing students to record video responses as homework assignments. Shy and reluctant students may feel more empowered to show their true colors over video. You can have them share their opinion of the news, recite their multiplication facts, detail the causes of the American Revolution, etc. The added preparation time and creativity that recording videos allows may help them to let their guard down enough to really shine!

I feel invisible!

The theme of stopping to see and notice our students, despite all that is going on around us, and the mad rush towards the finish line, was brought home to me one day thanks to a little girl named Mara. One morning as we were unpacking at our desks, I noticed that instead of putting her things away, she was just standing at her desk looking miserable. I asked her what was on her mind. "I just feel...invisible," she said quietly. Looking carefully at Mara, my heart sank. I knew that her parents were in a bitter custody battle and that she was often shuffled between homes. She looked like she was tired of all the emotional ups and downs. "What must it be like for her to be caught up in a war between adults?" I thought. Realizing I was not always fully present enough to *really* see her, I stopped what I was doing to give her my full attention.

"You're not invisible, Mara! I see you," I said. "I see that you put on your sparkly earrings today and that you put your hair into two braids with two purple hair bands. I see that you are wearing your sparkly green socks today. I see that you are tapping your foot a little bit. I also notice that you are starting to smile around the corners of your mouth. I see *you*, Mara!" I told her, widening my eyes to emphasize the point. Her lips spread into a big grin as she flung her skinny little arms around me. "Thank you, Ms. Schwartz!" she said. And then she walked into the classroom closet to hang up her things and get ready for the day ahead.

Teacher's invisible backpack: Why your attachment style matters too

Just as our students carry an invisible backpack of their own experiences, so do we. Whether we like it or not, our childhoods and unique ways of seeing the world can impact the way we teach. In the case of attachment, as we've discussed, an individual's attachment "style"—or internal working model of relationships—comes from early relationships with care-givers. We use this lens throughout our lives to understand how others will treat us and what we can expect from them. As research bears out, these internal working models make their way into the classroom because, in addition to students behaving in ways consistent with their attachment styles, teachers show up with attachment styles of their own. In an eye-opening study, a majority of teachers entering the profession were found to have insecure attachment styles.[5] The study even hypothesized that these early negative experiences consciously or unconsciously motivated teachers to want to work with young children so they could provide corrective emotional experiences for them.

One situation in which our own attachment styles frequently come into play is when we discipline or provide consequences for students. For example, teachers with secure attachment styles have been found to set age-appropriate boundaries for behavior and have high expectations for students.[6] On the other hand, teachers with insecure attachment styles may interact with students in ways that echo maladaptive beliefs about how relationships work. For example, individuals with avoidant dismissive styles have had to learn to lean on themselves and their own perspectives from a young age and are less comfortable with closeness. That resulting rigidity and independence means that they tend to be less likely to try on the other's viewpoint or compromise. Having their own viewpoint and managing things on their own is one of the avoidant attachment's superpowers after all (and their Achilles' heel!). This can also mean they come across as more controlling, less nurturing, and as having lower expectations of students.

On the other hand, teachers with an anxious attachment style have learned through early experiences to be fearful of losing connections with those close to them. In the classroom, this fearfulness can translate in to being afraid of losing relationships with students and being hyper-vigilant to conflict to avoid major upsets. As a result, when conflicts come up, anxiously attached teachers tend to placate challenging students and try to sidestep situations that might make their students upset with them. Anxiously attached teachers also tend to acquiesce to students' needs when it might be more helpful to consider their own needs and preferences instead.[7]

What do you need to know now?

The next time you find yourself in conflict with a student, consider that our habitual ways of reacting likely have roots in what we learned from a very young age about how safe or dangerous relationships are. But these ways of responding are by no means fixed. At any point, if we're willing to look at our patterns, we can seek out healthier ways to grow and develop.

Questions for reflection

- Look at the different attachment styles in Figure 10.1. Think of the students in your class. Who might fit in each category? What about their life outside of school and their behavior makes you think that?
- Which attachment style do you think you might have?
- Think about a recent conflict you were a part of. How might your style of handling that conflict be consistent or inconsistent with your attachment style?
- What is your reaction to the statement "Classrooms are excellent spaces to heal and try out new ways of experiencing the world"?

11

A Feedback Sandwich

Connection before Correction

The classic concept of "connection before correction"—validating the other's point of view before trying to change their point of view—can be life-changing when we need to get others to change their behavior. So what exactly is connection before correction, and how do you use it? Let me give you an example.

Imagine that you and your best friend have been going to the same sandwich shop for years. We'll call it Smithy's Sandwiches. Your friend really loves this place because they're clean, their prices are reasonable, and they have a decent menu. But then one day, you discover a new sandwich shop a few blocks away. We'll call it Joe's Old Time Sandwiches. Joe's has all the same winning qualities as Smithy's Sandwiches, but they also have a special for teachers (your friend is a teacher), and they offer avocado at no extra cost (both you and your friend love avocado). The owner is super friendly, and you can't wait to tell your friend about it. You feel certain that if your friend only knew how much better the new place is, she'd definitely switch. But when you talk on the phone that night, she's totally resistant. Even though you know she would be better off trying out the new place, she is set on Smithy's Sandwiches. It works for her, and it's what she's used to, she says. To get her to switch, at the very least, it will help for you to acknowledge how she feels and her current reasons for not wanting to change ("I hear you. It seems so hard to try somewhere new when Smithy's has been our go-to place for so long! It's true—they do have a decent menu and reasonable prices."). Only then can you bring up Joe's Old Time Sandwiches, and maybe get her to consider going there for lunch with you next Tuesday ("I do really think you'll like this new place. They have a great menu and reasonable prices like

Smithy's but they also have a special for teachers and free avocado on the side. What do you say we try it out on Friday?"). What you need to do is **connect before you correct**.

Speaking of sandwiches, this well-known connection before correction strategy is also at the heart of the feedback sandwich, a time-trusted managerial tool with which you are probably already familiar. First, the relationship is reinforced with a positive comment, after which there is an opportunity for growth. Lastly, the conversation closes on a positive note. Think of the connection statements as putting money into the emotional bank before you take money out.

To use this *Connection before Correction Sandwich* in your classroom, you will want to preface the talk by naming the problematic behavior in a neutral tone of voice ("I'm noticing that ____________."/"It's been hard for you to get started on your work."/"It's been challenging for you to get along with your rug partner."/"You've been late to class every day this week," and so on). Then you can put together a *Connection before Correction Sandwich.*

Connect correct connect

Step 1: Connect

Connect with how the other person is feeling. Authentically try to acknowledge and validate how they feel. Put yourself in their shoes.

I can appreciate that you feel ___________.
I imagine that it's hard to _________________.
It makes sense to me that you think/feel _________________.
I bet you'd prefer it if ____________________.

Step 2: Correct

Next, supportively guide the other person to a new, desired behavior.

I also need you to _________________ so that ___________________.
It's also important that you ___________ so that ___________________.
I would appreciate it a lot, though, if you could also _________________.
I think you could be even more _________________ (productive, confident, efficient, etc.) if you _________________.

Step 3: Connect

Last, warmly reconnect with the other person.

Does that make sense to you?
What do you think?
I'm here for you/I've got your back. Just let me know if you need help with this.
I'll check back on you later to make sure you're alright. Is that okay?
I really appreciate you trying so hard/doing this/making this effort, etc.

One example is a student who is talking too much in line. You want the behavior to stop, and if you decide to use the *Connection before Correction Sandwich,* your conversation could go like this:

Teacher (in a matter of fact, neutral tone of voice): Marquis, I noticed that you are talking to Angela in line a lot lately. **I know that you are super social; you are so good at being a friend to everyone in our classroom (Connection).**

Marquis: Yeah, I guess I am a good friend!

Teacher: **Yep. You are. I really like that about you, buddy (Connection)! I also need you to be quiet in line, though (Correction).** You know how we talked about what happens when people talk in line? How things get chaotic, and people can get distracted and fall or bump into others?

Marquis: Yeah?

Teacher: So, even though you are a super social guy, I need to be able to count on you to stay quiet in line so we can get to where we are going safely. **Make sense, buddy (Connection)?**

Marquis. Yeah, okay.

Teacher: I knew you'd understand. I know how important it is for you to make sure others are safe and taken care of. Now, let's get back to the others. Ready (Connection)?

Here's another possible *Connection before Correction Sandwich* as it might play out with an angry parent who shows up unannounced just as you are closing up the classroom for the night. Notice that there are several connections included here because of how angry the parent is and because the teacher knows that a calm listener will be more receptive to what is being said.

Parent (storming into the classroom): Hey Ms.! I'm sorry to disturb you, but I heard Carlos took my son's hat today. I just wanna know, if you're supposed to be in charge, how come this happened? Aren't you supposed to be the teacher? What's going on here?

Teacher: **I can appreciate that you must feel very upset. I'm glad you came in to talk with me today. I'm sorry to hear this happened (Connection).**

Parent: Damn straight, I'm upset! What kind of school is this anyway?

Teacher: **I know this must be very frustrating. It makes sense to me that you are concerned. (Connection). Can you tell me a little more?**

Parent: Well, my father gave it to my son. We want it back; it's really important to our family.

Teacher: **Oh, I see! The hat has lots of sentimental value too! Oh, wow. I'm glad you came to me (Connection).** I'm going to investigate this. Can you wait a moment while I put a note in my plans for tomorrow to talk to both boys? I want to make sure I get the story straight so I can figure out exactly what happened here... Okay, I have it written down. Is there anything else I can help you with?

Parent: No, I guess that sounds good...

Teacher: Oh, I'm glad! It's good you came in—your concerns are always important to me.

Parent: I appreciate that.

Teacher (smiles): Of course! Ms ________, I know this was a very upsetting circumstance. You were so right to come to me about it. I'm glad you let me know. **I would also appreciate it in the future, though, if you could email me before coming in? That way we can set up a time to talk and I can be more prepared (Correction)?**

Parent: Sure, I can do that. I didn't realize…

Teacher: Don't give it another thought. **Please know that I'm here for you. I'll check back in with you tomorrow. Sound good (Connection)?**

Parent: That should be fine. Thanks for hearing me out, Ms. Have a nice night.

Questions for reflection

- What do you think of the feedback sandwich?
- Think of a situation where you might use the feedback sandwich. On a separate piece of paper, plan out how your part of this conversation would sound.

- What did you think of the above sample conversations? How might you tweak them to match the types of students and families you serve?
- How might you incorporate this strategy into your interactions with students?
- How might you share this information with students to help them guide their own interactions?

12

Do You Hear Me?

Active Listening and Reflective Listening Statements

In the previous example of the angry parent who comes in to find out what happened to their child's hat, the teacher was able to turn the temperature down in the situation by using the *Connection before Correction Sandwich*. But I would venture to guess that another reason for their success was that the parent felt they were actually being listened to—a rare occurrence for most people!

In my life, my Aunt Marilyn Kaltynski is one of the best listeners I know. I am so glad to have such an excellent listener to turn to in times of trouble. What about you? Do you have a good listener in your life? How does their ability to listen help you to cope with life's ups and downs? The ability to listen deeply to others and get at the heart of what they are saying is a relationship-building skill that every single human should have in their toolbox.

So what is it about deep and reflective listening that can calm others, undo damage, and help us bridge relationships? Here's an example to illustrate.

Imagine that a family in the community wants to thank you for your hard work and has kindly given you a $100 gift card! Maybe it is to Target or another store that has a lot of fun teacher goodies. So one day, you set out for the store, and you stock up on lots of things you've needed and wanted for your classroom. Maybe you toss some much-needed construction paper into the cart, markers, stickers, colored pencils, ink and cardstock, and other odds and ends that would make your classroom a better place. You are as pleased as punch with your purchases. The next day you bring the bag full of goodies to your classroom, and you put it on the floor by your desk. You're running late, so you head over to the teacher's lounge in a hurry, say hi to a colleague, and excitedly tell them about the family's generosity and your shopping trip. You make some copies, then set up for a busy day of teaching.

When the day is over, you walk over to where you left your bag, happy to be able to unpack. But there is nothing there! The bag is totally gone. You search everywhere, but the bag, full of your precious goodies, is nowhere to be found. Feeling totally dismayed and disappointed, you go to your colleague and tell them what happened. Here are four hypothetical responses you might receive. Just notice how you feel as you hear your colleague says each of the following:

- "Why didn't you lock your door? Or lock the bag in your closet?"
- "Oh, man. That stinks. I guess you didn't hear about the latest email from the principal? About grades being due next week? I can't believe we have another thing to do!"
- "Ugggh. That sucks. Guess what happened to me last week? My purse was stolen, right out of my desk!"
- "Oh no! What a shame to lose your new things! I know you were so excited to bring those materials into the classroom and share them with the kids. I am so sorry to hear that happened to you!"

Which do you prefer? Is the last one your favorite? I would venture to guess that is because you have the sense that this colleague has deeply listened to you—unlike the previous three! This colleague was sensitive to how you were feeling; they really "got it"! What a relief to be gotten! In fact, this imaginary colleague provided an essential element for building relationships—what is known as an **attuned response**. They showed they were listening to how you were feeling and experienced the situation from *your point of view.*

It reminds me of one family I worked with as a family counselor. My client was a teenage boy who had a difficult relationship with his father but a close, loving relationship with his mom. One day, his mother told me that her son had confided in her that he had tried vaping, something she and his father were firmly against. When he told her, it occurred to her that if she merely repeated to him how much she didn't want him to vape, they wouldn't get anywhere because that would step all over what he thought and felt about it. She knew that a punitive response would only make him want to hide behaviors from her (as he did with his dad). Instead, she knew she needed to see it from his point of view, at least in that moment. "Yeah?" she said in a curious tone of voice. "How did it taste?"

"It was kind of gross, Mom!" he said, laughing.

What my client's mother did there was quite wise! Even though it must have been tempting to muscle him into seeing things her way, in the long run that may have pushed him even farther away, where he would be less open to her influence. Almost like stepping into a little canoe that her son was rowing, she tried to see the view alongside him instead of forcing him to get out of his boat and jump into hers so he could only see her viewpoint.

If you have someone in your life who's a real listener, you know what a relief it is to be in their presence! Instead of listening, most people do a variety of things that frustrate and confuse the speaker. They criticize, make the topic about them, or minimize or distract from what is being said. They only pretend to listen while they get their own response ready. But if it seems so simple, why on earth is listening so hard to do?

Listening can sometimes be difficult because it can be anxiety-producing to listen to other people in pain, especially when we care about them. We want to swoop in with a solution, judgment, or some kind of lesson that we think they need to learn so we can relieve their anxiety (and ours!). We believe our advice will help. But in truth, the thing that most helps others when they're struggling is to kindly acknowledge their feelings and experiences from *their* point of view.

Seeing things from the other's point of view is what your imaginary colleague from the previous example did when they said, "What a shame to lose your things! I know that you were so excited to bring those materials into the classroom and share them with the kids." In psychology, statements that reflect things from the other's point of view in a non-judgmental way are known as **reflective listening statements**, and they are a key component of every counselor's training. Effectively, these statements tell the other person, "I can see/hear/feel/perceive what's going on with you and how it must feel." Reflective listening statements are an *essential* relationship-building tool. They can help you turn many, many moments of crisis into moments of connection and healing, and this is especially true for children and individuals who come from homes where they did not feel seen or heard by those around them.

I'm waiting for your attention

One year, in an effort to help my students develop their relationship skills and self-esteem, I explained to them that when people talk, others should make every effort to pay full attention. I had them repeat the phrase "I deserve to be listened to. I have a right to be heard." We practiced turning to look at our peers when it was our turn to talk. Finally, I taught them that if others were distracted or having side conversations while they were speaking, they should stop and say in a kind but firm voice, "I'm waiting for your attention," and then wait a moment before continuing. This response, like the *Little Teacher* activity I've mentioned, shares "Power With" students. I have seen them grow in confidence each time they say it, and even their body language changes! In my opinion, teaching my students to stop and command the respect and attention of the room is one of the most powerful pieces of learning they can take from my classroom into their futures.

How do reflective listening statements work? They have the therapeutic effect of calming down the other's nervous system. They demonstrate that you've understood the other's core message and the emotional meaning and distilled it into the most essential parts from *their* point of view. So how can you start being a real listener and providing reflective listening statements?

First, set yourself up to be able to listen fully. Turn your body towards the person you are listening to. Maybe take a deep breath. As you listen, try to keep your full attention on the speaker. Maintain a soft but focused gaze, and avoid over-reacting to what they say with your face or body. You can show you are tracking what they say by nodding and saying "hmmm" or "I see" when appropriate. If you are confused, gently interrupt and try to restate the confusing part ("So I heard you say that you had the bags on the floor? And then, when you got a chance to look, they were gone! Did I get that right?") In general, try to stay quiet and just let the other talk until there is a natural silence. Wait a little longer so that you can really sit with what they are trying to convey, as well as the feelings behind what they are saying. Then you can provide a reflective listening statement like:

- "It's so ________________ when ____________."
- "It sounds like you feel ________ when/because of/about __________."
- "If I am hearing you correctly, you feel ___________ when/because of/about _________."
- "It sounds like you must be feeling _____________ when/because of/about ___________."
- "I get a sense that ________."
- "It seems as if ________."
- "How ________!"
- "It feels as though ________."
- "When I listen to you talk, I get that sense that you are feeling _______."

Then, see how the other person responds. If your reflective response hit home with them, they are likely to respond enthusiastically and say things like "Exactly!" "You got it!" "That's just what I'm feeling!" or something like that. They may even seem relieved.

If your guess about what they are feeling is off a bit, don't worry, they will let you know! You may notice this happening because they may become more guarded, defensive, or say something like "No, that's not what I mean. It's more like___." If the other person does seem defensive, it's important to recognize that they may not be ready to hear your thoughts yet. They still need you to hear them out. Defensiveness can indicate that you need to back off and be present to their needs as *they* are expressing them.

It takes work to provide reflective listening statements, so be patient with yourself as you learn this whole new way of listening. Even if you are not perfect, the other person will almost certainly appreciate your effort because being heard and understood is such a rare and special gift. As the saying goes, "It's good to be loved, but it's profound to be understood."

But what if I don't agree???

Providing reflective listening can be tricky for some of us to swallow because, at first, it may feel like you are letting yourself be manipulated or reinforcing bad behavior. It might feel like you're not getting things to turn out the way you'd like (think of my client's mother, who wanted to express her opposition to vaping, for example). But it's just the opposite because when others feel understood, we can gain their cooperation much more quickly and with less drama. It can help to remember that *validating doesn't always mean agreeing.* It means that, for that moment in time, we see the situation fully from their vantage point regardless of whether we ourselves would act, think, or feel the same way they do. It's simply about hopping into their canoe, so to speak, and seeing the world from their vantage point for a while. Then, when they truly feel heard, they will be better able to listen to you!

LISTEN UP: YOUR TURN TO PRACTICE!

In these practices, two participants take turns deeply listening to one another and sharing reflective listening statements. Partners should be assigned randomly.

Deep listening practice

Partner A chooses a topic that they would like to discuss for three minutes. This topic should not focus on venting or criticizing Partner B or mutual colleagues/acquaintances. Meanwhile, Partner B listens without interrupting or asking questions. If Partner A finishes speaking before the three minutes is up, the partners can wait together until the clock runs out. Then the partners switch. At no point does the listening partner speak or weigh in on what the other is saying; they simply listen and "hold the space" for what their partner wants to express.

After both partners have used up their three minutes, they can spend a few additional minutes providing honest and supportive feedback to one another about how it went and how well they feel they heard what was shared and were listened to.

Reflective statement practice

In this practice, two participants take turns listening and providing reflective statements.

Start in the same way as above, but this time Partner A talks about a problem that they feel comfortable sharing. It is best if it is a problem that is neither too serious nor too unimportant. (For example, you could talk about difficulties: finding the right medication for your allergies, deciding where to celebrate the holidays, troubles getting your daughter to take her driver's license test, etc.) Partner A speaks for three to five minutes while Partner B listens attentively. Partner B can give non-verbal cues that they are listening by nodding, maintaining a supportive, warm facial expression, and using eye contact and other gestures if needed. (Note that different cultures feel differently about eye contact.) Partner A should allow Partner B time (gaps in the conversation) and opportunities to provide reflective listening statements to match what Partner A says (the sentence starters above can help). Partner B should be sure to describe the emotion behind the words. When Partner B speaks, they need to reflect the situation from the other's point of view and be on guard to avoid problem-solving for the other, giving them advice, focusing on irrelevant issues, turning the topic to themselves, etc. Then the partners switch.

At the end, both partners can spend a few minutes providing honest and supportive feedback to their partner about how well they feel their partner listened and responded to what they shared.

Questions for reflection

- Think of a challenge that you or someone you know is facing. Craft a reflective listening statement to show how well you really understand what they are going through. Consider starting with a sentence stem such as, "It feels so ________ to ________," or one of the other examples provided in this chapter.
- Do you have any students who are excellent listeners? Where do you think their ability to listen comes from?
- Are you a good listener? Why, or why not? What do you think you might like to do to improve?
- When you listen to others, what do you find to be the most challenging part? For example, do you find it hard to not interrupt, give advice or change the subject? Something else?
- After reading this chapter, do you think you would like to incorporate deep listening and reflective listening statements into your interactions with students? Can you imagine an occasion when this might be useful?
- How might you share information about deep listening and reflective listening statements with your students in a developmentally appropriate and engaging way? For example: "It can feel scary to do something new." Or, "It's so validating to be picked for the play, especially since you spent so many hours practicing!" Or, "It sounds like you feel left out when Leila doesn't ask you to play with her." Or, "When I listen to you talk, I get the sense that you already know what you'd like to do next."

13

Schmooze Sessions and *Just Because*

How to Quickly Build Connections and Use Non-Contingent Positive Reinforcement

Building trusting, securely attached relationships with students takes time and a certain amount of consistency. In fact, many of our insecurely attached students may need to re-establish the safety of that relationship on a daily basis. For many of these children, a teacher's slightest action—a furrowing of their brow as they think over something the child has said, for example—could be misread as a sign that their teacher no longer cares about them. And for so many—especially those with an insecure attachment—the mere fact that they haven't seen you in ten hours may prompt them to imagine that you've changed overnight into a stranger who no longer cares for them. This makes sense considering that so many children have care-takers whose attention and love can seem to vary radically from day to day and moment to moment. As we have discussed, instead of being a source of comfort for them, many children have parents whose affection is unreliable, inconsistent, or contingent on them acting a certain way. That's why it's so important to continually establish ourselves as safe attachment figures whose caring is reliable, safe, and consistent.

It's easy to re-establish this bond when the group comes together each day by making these reunions joyful and light, instead of producing anxiety and dread of a new school day. Think of the festive atmosphere in the Seattle Fish Market, where vendors shout greetings out to one another and passersby as they pitch fish through the air to one another. While they're working, they create a sense of playfulness and welcome for everyone entering their space. We can cultivate this sort of joyful atmosphere and re-establish our relationships with students with what I like to call "Schmooze Sessions."

These sessions offer a chance to smile, laugh, banter, and schmooze to let them know that their return to our classroom culture is something joyful! At my school, I have the opportunity for schmooze sessions each morning as we walk from the basement to the 2nd floor. This quick walk gives me a four- to five-minute block of time to reconnect with the students. These short schmooze sessions let students know that they will continue to receive the same care and attentiveness no matter what.

On any given day, I might know that one of my students finally saw their stepbrother last night, for example, and the schmooze session is a great time to ask about and celebrate the visit. "You have been waiting so long for this visit! Can you believe that it finally happened? How did it feel to be together?" (These kinds of questions, similar to Shelly Gable's "Active Constructive Responding," have been shown to calm our nervous systems down because they make us feel witnessed.) I can compliment hair that looks like someone has put a lot of time (and gel!) into. I have the chance to point out cool light-up shoes and a new hoodie. If someone was absent the day before, I can tell them that we missed them and we're glad they're back. I can comment on a quiet student's facial expression or tell another student that I was thinking about something they said/did the day before. (They are always so blown away to hear that I think about them in my free time!)

Flowers for the teacher

For the last couple of years, I have worked in a community that primarily serves new immigrants to our country. I have found that this community is super appreciative of my work, and my students often bring me little gifts like apples and candies. One day, as I was picking my students up and beginning a schmooze session, I noticed that one of my 2nd graders was crying and covered in tears. I immediately thought someone must've died! "What happened, honey?" I asked him. "Teacher," he said to me in Spanish, "I picked you flowers!" "Oh, that's so sweet!" I replied. "Thank you!" "But," he said, and this brought up another round of sobs, "I left them on the dining-room table!" Gotta love those kiddos!

During these five-minute schmooze sessions, there's also a chance to look into as many eyes as possible to feel out which child is coming in with a heavy heart and to remind them in a whisper (or with a covert sticky note later in the day) that we're here to offer a listening ear, whenever they're ready. You don't have to get to every student every day. Just overhearing someone in charge being kind to others is immensely reassuring to everyone in earshot.

Schmooze session prompts

- It's good to see you today!
- It's good to see your face!
- You're wearing a new ____ today!
- Your (birthday/big game/concert) is coming up. How are you feeling about that?
- Oh, I see you (lost a tooth, brought in a new backpack, did something different with your hair, etc.).
- You're smiling today. Something must be making you happy!
- You don't look like your bright and happy self today. I'm here for you if there's anything I can do to help.
- Tell me one thing you did since I saw you yesterday!
- How was ________ (the movie, your soccer game, karate class, baby brother's birthday, evening, etc.)?

Or, for important events:

- Wow! Where were you when you found out that _______?
- Can you believe that this happened?!
- How did that make you feel?
- How did this change things for you?

A practical note about the noise that can accompany these morning schmooze sessions. Many teachers prefer to set the tone for their day by having the students enter the school building or classroom silently, so you might want to monitor the accompanying noise from schmooze sessions. I find that if you have to move your group from one part of the building to another, you may want to be first or last, so the noise from your moving party doesn't bother other classes. So your students know when they are expected to go from socializing mode to getting back down to business, it's helpful to teach this procedure. You may even want to practice repeatedly with your group at the beginning of the school year. You can also schedule schmooze sessions as informal breaks in the middle of the day when you can close your classroom door and just spend time together. Think of it as an opportunity to teach relational norms—a hugely important skill that students will need for their future.

Just because: Non-contingent positive reinforcement

These schmooze sessions are based on a therapeutic strategy called "non-contingent positive reinforcement." Non-contingent positive reinforcement refers to positive interactions with others that are not contingent on what they do or do not do. They relate to the central idea of Rogerian therapy, **unconditional positive regard.** Carl Rogers, the founder of Rogerian therapy and a famous humanistic psychologist, believed that for a person to grow, they need an environment that provides them unconditional positive regard—being known and loved for exactly who they are. In a classroom, that means respecting and esteeming individuals for their essential core self, regardless of how they are doing academically or how their behavior conforms to the classroom per se. It requires stepping outside of our roles as teacher and student and momentarily letting go of what we want and need from the students and instead enjoying them *just because.*

For example, if a child reads something to you, and they do it badly, you might be tempted to give them feedback on their academic progress ("Slow down, and focus on the hard words, you need to remember to break them into syllables" or "That sounded smooth, good job"). But if at times you want to express non-contingent positive reinforcement for that same situation, you might zoom out a bit from the roles you are in as a teacher and a student and just appreciate the situation. You may say something like "I love to hear you read" or "It's fun to listen to you" or "Thank you, I really appreciate you spending some time reading to me." These kinds of phrases go beyond whether the child is correct or behaving in the way we want them to; they are an expression of seeing them and the situation in their entirety. It's being kind and enjoying the moment—*just because!* It's a tremendously powerful tool in building relationships. In my experience, it's also very rewarding to be allowed to just be a human for a while, not always in the role of a teacher!

Practically speaking, using non-contingent positive reinforcement and showing unconditional positive regard for students are also powerful tools for managing behavior. Since students are already receiving attention in more positive ways, it can reduce how frequently students act up to get attention. Using non-contingent positive reinforcement can also help build self-esteem in students who struggle behaviorally or academically, because it shows your approval of who they are, not just of what they can or cannot do.

Here are some ways to provide non-contingent positive reinforcement:

- Express it verbally:
  - I like your laugh!
  - You've got such a great smile!
  - I love that you think of these things!
  - I like the way you said that!
  - I love to listen to you (read, share your ideas, sing)/watch you (play baseball, interact with others, etc.)!
  - I enjoy hearing how you see things!
- Provide random acts of kindness ("Hey, I picked out this book for you from the library, thought you might like it" or "I want to give you a few more minutes to get settled in. Just for today, why don't you hang out on the beanbag chair you like so much and chill out for a few before we get started?").
- For especially difficult or defiant students, you may want to carve out five minutes a day/week of non-contingent reinforcement time to spend with them leading you through an activity of their choice. They could choose to have you listen to a song they like, teach you a dance, lead a play session with stuffed animals, and so on.

If your student asks why you are being so kind to them, surprise them by saying, "Just because." You might be surprised at the results!

Questions for reflection

- What do you do to welcome your students into the classroom each day? What are some of the first words your students usually hear you say each day?
- To what extent do you think your principal or administrators make you feel welcome as you come into work each day? What might they do to improve?
- Have you ever received or given a random act of kindness? What happened? How did it affect you?
- After reading this chapter, do you have any new ideas for making students feel welcome in your classroom tomorrow? What are they?

Classroom Relationship Map

Using Art to Uncover Hidden Dynamics

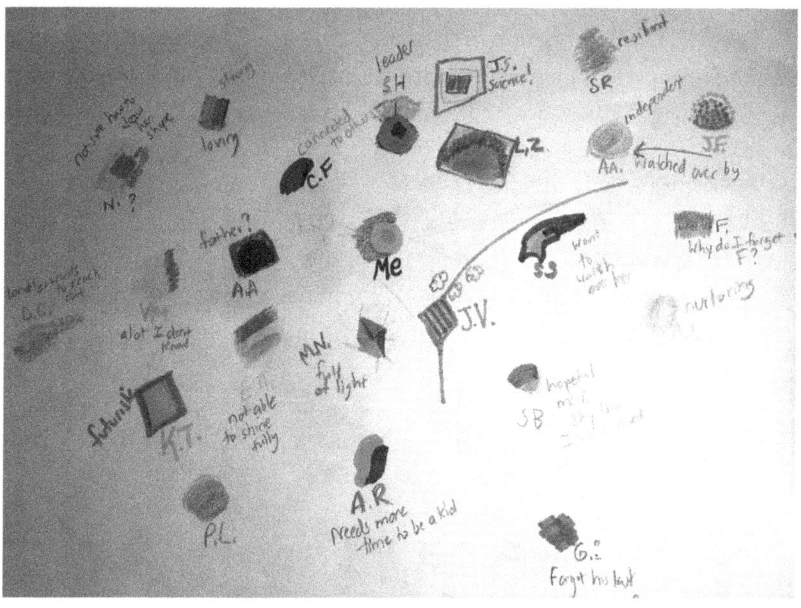

Figure 14.1: A Classroom Relationship Map

When we are in the throes of the hectic school year, we can get lost in the wave of things to do and lose track of our relationships with students. Daily challenges confront us, and soon our awareness of how we interact with students can elude us. At times, we may also sense things about our students' hidden strengths and challenges, but in the hustle and bustle of the day, these crucial feelings and gut instincts about them can get lost. Non-verbal, artistic activities like the following can bring these unconscious patterns and instincts back out into the light.

You will need:

- piece of white paper
- drawing tools such as colored pencils or markers
- pencil or pen.

PART 1: MAKE YOUR CLASSROOM RELATIONSHIP MAP

1. Start by picking a color or colors to represent you and your role in the classroom. Use this color or colors to draw a shape somewhere on your page that represents you. You might want to draw squiggles, or blocks, or a geometric shape like triangles or circles. Or you might want to draw a more abstract shape that you come up with yourself, or one that has personal meaning for you. Just draw a shape that matches you. Color it in with colors that you choose. Then label that shape "Me."
2. Now start to think about the students in your classroom. Who comes to mind first? Just as you did for your own shape, pick a shape and color/colors to represent this student and place this shape somewhere on the page. Don't overthink it and don't rush. Notice what feelings come up as you design each shape.
3. Repeat step number two until you have made a shape for all of your students. To keep track, write their initials or name under their shape and any insights or thoughts that come to mind about them as you draw. This should be very stream of consciousness—don't think about it too much. You are engaging the right hemisphere of your brain, which is mainly insightful, intuitive, and non-verbal.
4. When you've finished, check to see that you've gotten all of your students. You might want to use a roster at this point to make sure you haven't missed any.

PART 2: FIND OUT WHAT IT MEANS

Only read this part after you've finished Part 1: Make your Classroom Relationship Map.

What does my drawing mean?

Specific meanings in artwork and imagery can vary based on many things, including race, culture, gender, socioeconomic background, and other factors. In reading this key, I want you to keep in mind that these are general guidelines; it's most important to pay attention to what resonates for you.

- **Size:** Larger shapes may represent individuals that have more significance. The shape's size might also signify the amount of energy and attention you feel this child requires from you. On that note, smaller images may imply that a child requires less attention from you or is less significant to you.
- **Placement:** Shapes you placed close to you may represent the students you feel closest to or the most protective of. Shapes that are closest to you may signify students who are more prominent in your thoughts or who stand out most to you, while shapes on the outskirts might get less of your focus.
- **Colors:** Bright shapes can signify that you view this individual as strong or see their personality as vibrant or clearly defined. Duller, earthier colors can represent individuals you regard as more shy, stable, or introverted. In comparison, brighter colors may indicate that you see those students as being more dynamic, outspoken, or extroverted.
- **Shapes:** Shapes with straight lines and angles usually symbolize structure and order, precision, and a need for control. This need for control could represent a desire to have more control over that individual, a perception that this child is disciplined, or that they might wish to have more control in some way. Shapes with curves are softer and represent connection and fluidity. They can also indicate that you view those students as more cooperative.
- **Outlining shapes:** If you drew a dark outline around some shapes, this might have to do with boundaries. This could symbolize your sense that this child has strong boundaries or is largely separated from you or others. It may also be interpreted as a desire to protect that student.

Here are some questions to ask

- What color and shape did you choose to represent yourself? Where did you place yourself on the page? How big or small was your shape? What might this tell you about how you see yourself? What might this say about how you view the most important qualities of a classroom leader?
- Looking at where you placed each student on the page, who did you put closer to your symbol? Who did you put farther away? What meaning might that have for you?
- Do you notice any patterns in where you placed students of different ethnicities? Genders? What might that mean to you?
- What students did you think of first? What students did you think of last? Were there any students you forgot or struggled to name?
- Did you group certain students together? What was the meaning of each of those groupings to you?
- Where did you choose to put your more difficult student/s? How did you decide to draw them? What does that mean to you?

PART 3: WRAPPING IT UP

As you were drawing, did anything else become clear to you? Make a list of any new insights that became clear.

"The child who is not embraced by the village will burn it down to feel its warmth."

African proverb

How to Deal with Adverse Childhood Experiences, Trauma, and Chronic Stress in the Classroom

15

What Happened to You?

The Need for Trauma-Informed Education

"Michael" was a sweet boy with bright brown eyes. He was assigned to my counselor caseload at a school in Rhode Island. Before I even met him, though, I became familiar with his sizable reputation. On my first day at Michael's school, the secretary raised one eyebrow when she saw my list of clients. Placing one finger on his name with a knowing look, she warned, "You won't have much trouble finding that one—he's always out wandering the halls." Likewise, Michael's classroom teacher didn't waste any time telling me his many offenses, among which figured the time he kicked the principal in the shins. He seemed to spend just as much time at home on suspension as he did at school.

In our first couple of sessions, Michael seemed cautious, and his hesitant willingness to connect with me was endearing. But on our third session, I noticed that after saying hello and telling me quickly about his day, he gravitated towards drawing a picture. He drew a police car and then several male figures and a house. Without looking at me or speaking, his drawing began to tell a story. He seemed to be telling a story about guns, shooting, hiding, someone dying, and the police. At this point, Michael stopped. He looked deliberately at me and spoke. "Do you know what that was, Miss?" he said grimly. I shook my head, no. "That was what happened to me," he said.

As his family later clarified, Michael had witnessed a shooting that day in which someone had been killed. The entire family feared what might happen to them while awaiting the trial and were especially fearful of the attackers driving by and shooting into the household as retribution for pressing charges. With this vital information, it became clear that this story partially explained Michael's attention-getting behaviors and constant suspensions. Unlike most typically developing children, Michael actually *wanted* to get suspended because whereas he had felt helpless to prevent that initial shooting, he reasoned (in his young mind) that at least if he were sent home, he'd have a chance at saving his mother and other family members from being shot as well. But for the teachers and administrators who weren't privy to the connections between these pieces of information, they looked at his wild behavior and (understandably) thought, "What is the matter with this kid?" The previously mentioned well-known trauma-informed question "What has happened to him?" would have gotten them much closer to the truth. As trauma expert Joe Foderaro observes, the key to trauma-informed care and education is realizing that "It's not what's wrong with others, it's what has happened to them."[1] In this part of the book, we will take a closer look at trauma, how it impacts our students and manifests in our classrooms, and how it can impact us as educators.

trauma n. 1. Any disturbing experience that results in significant fear, helplessness, *dissociation*, confusion, or other disruptive feelings intense enough to have a long-lasting negative effect on a person's attitudes, behavior, and other aspects of functioning.[2]

stress n. 1. Pressure or tension exerted on a material object. 2. a state of mental or emotional strain or tension resulting from adverse or very demanding circumstances.[3]

The need for trauma-sensitive education

Trauma, adverse childhood experiences, and chronic amounts of stress can profoundly shape the extent to which students can engage in learning and exert a powerful effect on how teachers perform in the classroom. Countering this effect requires a profound shift in how we see working with at-risk youth. **Trauma-informed education**, also known as trauma-sensitive education, is that shift. It is not so much a program per se, but rather a shift to using strength-based, less punitive practices that create caring and welcoming environments for communities of learners. The core principles of trauma-informed education are:

- bullying prevention
- staff training

- cultivating safe and supportive environments (the main focus of this book)
- child protection systems
- social emotional learning programs.

It's crucial to note that to have trauma-informed classrooms, we first need to have trauma-informed schools and that starts with administration. Over-burdening teachers with inconsequential paperwork, endless testing, and unreasonable demands on instruction will burn out the very people of whom so much is already asked. As trauma expert Bruce Perry stated, administrators need to know that "the best way to really help kids cognitively and behaviorally in the classroom is to take really good care of teachers."[4]

It's also important to know that trauma-informed education is not just for "those kids." That is because chronic stress, adverse childhood experiences, and trauma are incredibly pervasive, and odds are that you or your students have been or will be impacted by them at some point. Their impact on the way we think, feel, and act affects us all. It might be more helpful for you to think of the strategies in this section of the book as universal precautions for everyone, including you.

My own trauma

As a teenager, I experienced some traumatic events. But at school I continued to attend classes, participate in sports, and keep my grades up. The only noticeable difference was that I seemed spacy. I remember feeling hurt and misunderstood when I was named "Most Out There" by my peers during my senior year and when one of my teachers jokingly called me "Joanna-head-in-the-clouds." Later in life, when I began working as a counselor, I learned that spaciness and dissociation are typical symptoms of trauma. I've since seen and recognized such symptoms in several of my students. But looking back, I don't think that any of my teachers truly saw what was happening. I wasn't naturally a spacy kid; I was a smart kid who was going through a hard time. I wonder what would have happened if someone saw past my behavior and asked me what was happening in my life outside of school. But no one did. Reflecting back, I think it's likely that this experience ultimately drove me to write this book because my hope is that together, we can make sure other children won't suffer in silence or have to act out their pain. My hope is that they'll know that even when things are hard at home, there is a place in the world called "school" where they are truly safe.

First, let's discuss some key information about trauma. The American Psychological Association defines trauma as "an emotional response to a terrible event," such as car accidents, abuse, witnessing violence, natural disasters, and so on. Complex trauma occurs on a repetitive or continuous basis, such as physical or sexual abuse, poverty, and hunger. An individual's reaction to a traumatic event can be short-term or long-term. Post-traumatic stress disorder (PTSD) denotes a longer-term psychiatric disorder that develops in some people after traumatic events. Not everyone who experiences trauma will develop PTSD, and not all stressful events are experienced as traumatic by everyone, even when two people witness the same traumatic event.

A difficult part of defining trauma is that there is almost a limitless amount of potentially traumatizing experiences, because it's not so much about what happened as it is about how one experiences what happened. However, there are generally considered to be three types of trauma. The first is **simple trauma**—painful and overwhelming events that are life-threatening or have the potential to cause serious injury. Some examples are car accidents, fires, earthquakes, and cyclones. **Complex trauma** involves threats, violence, and violation among people, usually people we trust. Some examples of complex trauma are child abuse, bullying, and domestic abuse. Unlike simple trauma, which can usually be talked about comfortably with others, these kinds of traumatic events can feel isolating and shaming. Last, **developmental trauma** occurs in some children who experience neglect or abuse, witness high levels of conflict between parents' and experience separation and divorce, resulting in an impairment in the child's development.

What has happened to trauma-impacted students, and why does trauma translate into such challenging behaviors and such difficulty learning? The ACE study provides us with some perspective. The ACE study[5] was a 1998 landmark study of over 17,000 patients in Southern California. In this gigantic study, the Centers for Disease Control and Prevention (CDC) and Kaiser Permanente asked participants if they had experienced any of ten types of childhood trauma, called **adverse childhood experiences**, or ACEs. These include emotional, physical, and sexual abuse; domestic violence; a family member with substance dependence or mental illness; parental separation or divorce; a household member who was incarcerated; and emotional and physical neglect. The study and subsequent studies on the topic brought to light several key findings that you should be aware of.

- The pervasiveness of ACEs. Nearly two-thirds of the participants were found to have experienced at least one traumatizing childhood event. Of those, 87 percent were found to have two or more types of ACE.
- A direct link between ACEs and major chronic illnesses like diabetes, cancer, and heart disease.
- A direct link between ACEs and social problems. The study found that the more ACEs one experienced, the more likely one was to have mental and behavioral health problems like incarceration, addiction, and problems at work.
- A clear correlation between the number of ACEs and struggles with school. Children with three or more ACEs, for example, were 2.9 times more likely to have problems with schoolwork than children with no ACEs, 4.9 times more likely to have problems with attendance, and 6.1 times more likely to have problems with behavior, etc.[6]

Take care of you!

Trauma is extremely common, and my guess is that you or someone close to you has been impacted by it in some way. In fact, as I write this book, we are in the midst of a climate crisis, a global pandemic, waves of social unrest, and a suspenseful election in the US, all of which can be traumatic. In addition to the usual amounts of violence, these more recent societal conditions make trauma-informed work more vital now than ever. As you read this section of the book, please take care of yourself. If you find that you feel triggered, anxious, or sad revisiting difficult or traumatic experiences in your own life, consider talking to a therapist or a trusted friend, journaling, and taking time out for self-care. This section of the book will be here for you whenever you're ready.

Questions for reflection

- What has been your experience with working with trauma-impacted students? What unique challenges and strengths have you observed in this population?

- Was it surprising to you to learn how prevalent ACEs are? Why or why not?
- Thinking of the students on your roster this year and of the prevalence of ACEs, how many ACEs do you imagine your typical student has? Which students do you estimate would have the fewest ACEs? The most?
- Thinking about several of your students who have the most ACEs, what similarities and differences do you see between them?

16

This Is Your Brain on Stress

To understand how adverse childhood experiences (ACEs), trauma, and chronic stress affect the brain and how this shows up in your classroom, you need to be familiar with two essential parts of your brain. Although they are not the only players, they are two of the most important protagonists. Let's review what each is and the role it plays:

- **Survival brain (the amygdala):** This is the part of the brain responsible for the fight, flight, or freeze response. It is the first to react when you hear "things that go bump in the night." Like an alarm system alerting your body to potential threats, the amygdala's job is to be on the constant lookout for your safety. If this part of the brain could talk, every sentence would end in three exclamation marks. I have heard my colleague Michael McKnight aptly call the prefrontal cortex the "chihuahua brain" because of how readily and energetically it responds to every little threat. Because it responds to stimulus rapidly and instinctively to keep you alive, you can also think of the amygdala as the "reactive brain" or the "survival brain."
- **Thinking brain (prefrontal cortex):** In addition to the hippocampus, which is concerned with memory, the prefrontal cortex, or thinking brain, is responsible for the vast majority of the skills students need for school: cognition, learning, making responsible decisions, and regulating emotions. In contrast to the survival brain, if the thinking brain could speak, it would punctuate its thoughts with pensive ellipses and provide numbered lists and diagrams. If the survival brain is a chihuahua, you can imagine the thinking brain as a wise, brainy professor. While the survival brain issues rapid-fire responses to things, the thinking brain evaluates and analyzes

situations intellectually. The thinking brain is also slower to respond to stimuli than the survival brain.

If we continue to use the metaphor of the survival brain as a chihuahua and the thinking brain as a professor, you can imagine how the two might interact when they are out on a walk in the park. When the chihuahua barks arduously at an overhead plane, the professor might tell the chihuahua to calm down, because the professor can conceptualize how planes operate and calculate the slim odds of the plane crashing down at their exact spot in the park. This is reassuring for the chihuahua, who needs to learn not to regard everything as a threat. To his credit, though, the chihuahua can also sniff out actual danger when it occurs and alert the absent-minded professor, who is too often in his head (pardon the pun!).

Switching metaphors for a moment, you can also imagine that these two parts of the brain are also like two people riding together in the same car, headed to the same destination—towards the shared goal of ensuring your optimal functioning and survival. When the thinking brain has its hands on the wheel and is in charge, we respond thoughtfully and conscientiously to the world around us. Like the professor, we're then able to process and analyze information rationally, solve problems collaboratively, and regulate and express emotions. It's the thinking part of the brain (specifically the left hemisphere of the prefrontal cortex) that we are asking a child to employ when we ask them to "use their words" (instead of kicking their little brother, for example). If there are not too many stressful events occurring in an individual's life, the thinking brain is the one that is driving the car most of the time.

On the other hand, the survival brain only intervenes when life-threatening emergencies occur, as its name suggests. When it perceives that danger is present, the survival brain forcefully grabs the wheel of the car and slams on the emergency brakes, putting a halt to anything the thinking brain was doing. This quick change of who is in charge can occur much more frequently in individuals who have experienced trauma, ACEs, and chronic stress. For them, the survival brain can be in charge almost all the time, and when the survival brain's driving the car, it's time for fight, flight, or freeze.

Fight, flight, or freeze

What is the importance of fight, flight, or freeze to what happens in the classroom? Its influence is powerful and pervasive, largely because of how well and easily such stress responses can be activated. As you may remember from your high school Biology 101 class, when our brain perceives a threat to our survival (when you swerve out of the way of a car accident, for example, or a ferocious dog chases you down the street, or you hear what you believe is someone breaking into your house), the autonomic nervous system activates, and adrenaline and cortisol kick into motion a series of physiological responses meant to help you survive (fight and flight) or prepare to face death (freeze). Among other symptoms, air passages dilate to provide muscles with needed oxygen, and blood vessels contract to redirect blood toward major muscle groups, including the heart and lungs. The ability to feel pain decreases to allow us to run away from or fight the aggressor without being slowed down by our injuries. This is our body's rapid, involuntary response to dangerous or very stressful situations. You can think of this response as your body hitting the gas pedal and holding it all the way down in an attempt to save your life.

To borrow Dr. Dan Goleman's term, when the stress response turns on, it's as though the amygdala "hijacks" the brain by temporarily shutting down parts of the brain unconcerned with anything but immediate survival.[1] Think of it like a binary on and off switch. If one is on, the other is off and vice versa. This hijacking occurs in actual life-threatening situations, but can also happen when we only *perceive* danger or threats (a doctor's voice on the line with your test results, our crush coming over to talk to us, a disruptive student starting to act up again, etc.). Whether the threat is real or perceived, if the nervous system reads it as a threat, the survival brain will take over and put the thinking brain on hold. If you've ever heard the emergency broadcast systems dominating the air and radio waves, you know that all regularly scheduled programming gets suspended until the emergency broadcast system stops sounding the alarm. A very similar thing happens when our emergency broadcast system—the reactive brain—takes over.

By the way, an offline prefrontal cortex is likely why Christina from Chapter 3 found it so hard to pay attention in school on the day her mother was in the hospital. When you think that your life or a loved one's life is in danger, everything else gets put on hold—this is true even on a neurological level!

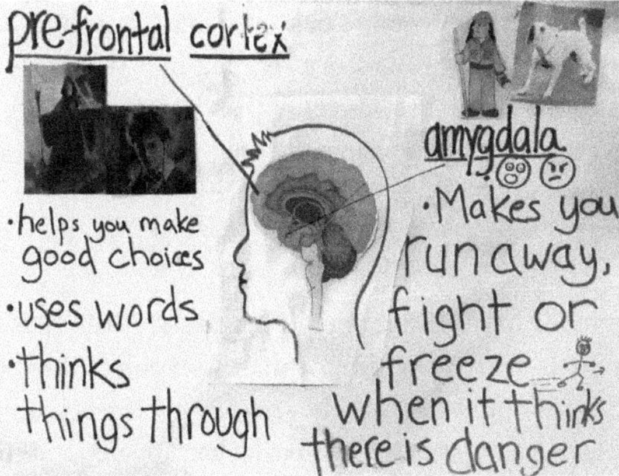

Figure 16.1: Poster from my classroom teaching students about the prefrontal cortex and amygdala

Putting the survival brain in context

If you are thinking in consternation that your survival brain gets in the way of your thinking brain, you're right! But before you start cursing this part of your cerebrum, consider its evolutionary history. Over millennia, the survival brain's response to stress has allowed every one of your ancestors to survive warring tribes, hungry lions, and a million other threats. Its life-saving wisdom about what is and is not safe has been encoded in your DNA and passed down to you for free! While it's true that the survival brain often over-reacts (like a chihuahua), it can also call our attention to important problematic situations (imagine the chihuahua alerting the professor to someone lurking in the bushes, for example). In the classroom, its attention to what is out of place can help us zero in on disruptive behavior before it gets worse. For that reason and many others, the survival brain also deserves our thanks.

If you remember the first wave of the Covid-19 pandemic, you probably have a good idea of how our brain prioritizes survival. When the news started relaying the alarming numbers of rising cases, and cities, states, and countries started to lock down, our usual concerns and routines, which had once seemed so consuming, quickly took a back seat to just staying healthy. Instead of worrying so much about an upcoming dinner party or other day-to-day concerns, many people started thinking instead about where to get masks, hand sanitizer, toilet paper, and non-perishables. People fretted over how often to go to the supermarket and whether our loved ones were following health recommendations. Entire societies shifted into the stress response together and waited for the danger to pass so we could return to our normal level of functioning, and our thinking brains could come back online.

Usually, though, the life-threatening moment passes. The cause of the stress resolves in some measure: the car accident is avoided, the owner reins in her barking dog, you find out that the troubling lump is benign. Soon, the parasympathetic nervous system takes back over, and you start to feel calmer. Your heart rate and breathing settle back into a regular rhythm, and soon you're able to start thinking about more normal concerns again. Your thinking brain comes back online, which means you can return to experiencing the usual ebb and flow of emotions again. Back to your normal baseline, you can think about things not immediately pressing: vacations and quinceanera parties and dinner menus. Your nervous system has returned to homeostasis: a state of calm, restful, alert awareness. This is our regular, natural cycle of dealing with stressful events. Things are okay, then something stressful happens, our nervous system kicks into high gear to respond to it, we deal with it, and then we come back down to our usual baseline stress level. Think of a plane that takes off and flies around for a while, but eventually comes back down to its resting state on the tarmac.

Why am I so tired?

Did you know that your body is still swimming in adrenaline even after the stressful event has passed? By some estimates, adrenaline—one of the key hormones triggered when you feel stressed—lasts up to an hour in your body![2] When we experience multiple stressful events during the day, as happens in our classrooms, we have repeated cycles of adrenaline peaks and valleys. Think of a plane that takes off but never really comes back down to refuel again. This can be physically exhausting, especially if we never really got a chance to completely come down from the last stressful peak. In addition to the physical demands, this adrenaline roller coaster may explain why, compared to many other professions, teachers feel incredibly exhausted at the end of a tough day.

But what happens when the threat is habitual, and the nervous system doesn't get a chance to ever fully come back down to earth? What happens when, day after day, we don't know if there will be enough to eat at home or whether a parent will get drunk and violent? If we will have somewhere safe to sleep at night, or if we'll be evicted from another apartment we just moved into? Whether there will be constant fights in the hallway, or if we will have to work in unsafe conditions? Our nervous systems become like a plane that doesn't have a chance to land; it stays up as long as the threat is present, constantly in motion. Unfortunately, we've entered the airspace of **chronic stress**—a state resulting from repeated exposure to stressful situations and the stress response (fight, flight, or freeze). What happens to the development of young brains in this state of chronic stress?

Use it or lose it: The neuroplastic brain

Before I tell you that, I want you to know what happens is due to the fact that our brains are wonderfully and terribly flexible. They are neuroplastic. Our brains can change and grow the way they do partly because they are *use-dependent.*[3] What does that mean exactly?

Imagine, for example, that you decide to go to the gym for a month to really work out your biceps. You decide that just for this month, you'll give your quadriceps a break and focus on getting your upper arms nice and strong. As you can guess, in a couple of weeks or months, those hard-worked muscles in your arms will grow and expand while your quadricep muscles lose muscle mass. This is because our muscles' growth, like that of our brains, depends on how much they are used. Our bodies pick up on the fact that our bicep muscles are suddenly being used a lot, so the biceps are sent resources that allow them to grow and adapt to the current high demands. The more they're used, the more they grow. For better or worse, our thinking and survival brains function in the same way—their growth depends on how much they are used.

As you can imagine, this can be problematic for children exposed to chaotic, unsafe conditions day after day. Each time a stressful event occurs, the survival brain, also known as the fear brain, will respond by firing, re-wiring, and optimizing its circuits to make up for the giant demand on them. Because past experiences have demonstrated to these children that the world is dangerous and unsafe, the survival brain adapts to fire off easily and readily to each stressful situation. In fact, as it prepares itself to protect against potential danger in the future, it becomes hypersensitive. Like an overly sensitive fire alarm, it may fire off *too* frequently, sending that individual into a persistent state of alarm, even over seemingly trivial things. This can cause individuals to:

- startle easily
- take offense at seemingly trivial things
- have overblown reactions
- misread social cues, often interpreting them as aggressive
- find it hard to relax
- lose sleep
- struggle with interpersonal relationships.

As we've said, because the brain is use-dependent, it will shunt energy and resources away from the thinking brain and divert them instead to the survival brain when stressed. Unfortunately, this means that the survival brain takes center stage in the brain's development and can prevent the thinking brain from fully developing its essential circuitry. Remember, this underdeveloped circuitry is the same circuitry that children need to be responsive, creative, flexible thinkers who can regulate and appropriately manage emotions—in other words, just the circuitry needed to develop most "school skills." In a very real biological sense, it can be more challenging for trauma-impacted children to learn. In many cases, they may have not yet fully developed some of the brain circuitry needed to succeed in school. Put simply, their brain had more important things on its mind!

Window of tolerance

Another way to think about the neurological difference in children impacted by trauma, ACEs, and chronic stress is to think of them as having smaller windows of tolerance. The **window of tolerance**, a term coined by Dr. Dan Siegel, is the normal range, or "bandwidth," of stressful experiences that we can tolerate without becoming very dysregulated. When we are within that window, we feel in control, we can regulate our emotions with relative ease, and life feels manageable. Within our window of tolerance, we can function at our best and handily manage the usual ebb and flow of everyday emotions.

When people frequently face stressful experiences that are too intense or frequent to fit inside their window of tolerance, their window of tolerance can shrink over time, and they can be overwhelmed or triggered by even the tiniest of things. If you ever had a student seem to totally over-react, get angry, or cry at the drop of a hat ("I'm going to get him if he looks at me again!" or "Don't tell me to line up now!" or "You're not the boss of me!"), this could be the reason.

It's also helpful to know that whether individuals have been impacted by trauma, ACEs, and chronic stress or not, the dimensions of someone's window of tolerance can vary greatly. We have a variance in our tolerance for stress, and this variance depends partly on our inherited genetics and partly on our life experiences. So something that might overwhelm one person might be very manageable to another. It's akin to our tolerance for different temperatures. Sixty degrees Fahrenheit (15°C) might be chilly for some, while for others the same 60 degrees might be downright balmy (a helpful thing to remember the next time an argument crops up at home about where to set the thermostat!).

Something else happens when we've experienced too much stress and have been torpedoed outside our window of tolerance. When pushed over the edge, we suddenly feel out of control and unsafe, and we may enter into a state of being that is either over- or under-reactive to things happening around us. In psychological lingo, these are called states of **hyper-** or **hypo-arousal**.

Way up high or way down low: Hyper- and hypo-arousal

When we are overwhelmed with worry and step out of our window of tolerance, our nervous system shifts into one of two gears:

- **Over-reactive (hyper-arousal):** Being over-reactive means being flooded with intense, nerve-wracking emotions like anger, fear, panic, and anxiety. In its attempt to protect us, our nervous system becomes hyper-vigilant, and we can experience hair-trigger reactions to things happening around us that are mistakenly read as threats. From the outside, hyper-aroused people may seem too "hyped up," too aggressive, too "over the top," or too ready to "flip their lid" at any moment.
- **Under-reactive (hypo-arousal):** After people have been through intense periods of over-reactivity (hyper-arousal), they frequently "downshift" into a period of under-reactivity (hypo-arousal). They may start feeling numb, depressed, disengaged, disconnected, and helpless. From the outside, people who are hypo-aroused may just appear "spacey" or disengaged.

Questions for reflection

- Can you think of a time when you or someone else might have been experiencing an amygdala hijack (the survival brain taking over)? What happened?
- Can you think of a time when a student appeared to be lethargic but may have really been in a state of hypo-arousal? Or a student who was bouncing off the walls but may actually have been in a state of hyper-arousal?
- How might the information in this section about how stress affects our brains change how you view hyper- and hypo-arousal?
- How might the information in this section about how stress affects our brains more generally change how you view classroom challenges?
- Do you think it could be helpful to teach your students about the survival brain and the thinking brain and how they function? How might you plan to do this?

17

Trauma, Chronic Stress, ACEs, and Behavior

As we've discussed previously and as you will see again in this chapter, trauma-impacted kids (aka XL kids or "Extra Love" kids, as one of my teacher friends calls them) can have neurobiological reasons that explain their often challenging behavior. In Part 3 of this book, we'll talk all about the most attention-grabbing of those behaviors—meltdowns and tantrums. But for now, you should know that, as we've described above, children impacted by trauma can still be in a perpetual state of alarm and vigilance. This is true even after stressful and traumatic events have long passed; their brains and bodies can continue to react as though the events were still ongoing. This can be incredibly challenging because the traditional behavioral modification strategies—rewards and consequences—used in most schools don't reliably work with students who are habitually dysregulated. These students do much better with lesser-known disciplinary techniques, such as restorative practices that focus on prosocial skills and learning self-regulation. Meanwhile, students like Michael are often labeled as disruptive or defiant. They are also more frequently placed in special education than children not impacted by trauma.[1] Because these children's behavior can be difficult to manage in a classroom, some knowledge of the exact origin of trauma-related behaviors is an essential tool in your toolbox.

Why do children with ACEs, trauma, and chronic stress have such challenging behavior?

As we've said, trauma, ACEs, and chronic stress can change the brain's architecture and impair the brain's capacity to face challenges in the environment effectively. These impairments may make it difficult for individuals to control their emotions and cause them to react instinctively and inappropriately with little understanding of their behavior. This may also explain why psychologist Russell Barkley said, "the children who need love the most will ask for it in the most unloving of ways."[2] However, helping children re-experience relationships differently (called a "corrective experience") is the key to recovering from trauma, and we've discussed many ways to do this in Part 1.

While we will spend considerable time in this part of the book discussing the more noticeable and explosive symptoms of trauma (outbursts, tantrums, aggression, etc.), it's also important to remember that not all trauma-impacted children express the pain of trauma outwardly. There are also many children who have experienced trauma but continue to "behave." Instead of acting in a way that draws attention, they may instead withdraw, focus their pain inwards, or space out. These students may have symptoms, such as depression, and self-harming behaviours, such as cutting and drug use, that are just as serious as those students who act out their pain. But because many of these students who suffer in silence seem to be "okay" to the outside world, they often don't get the referrals for mental services that could help work through their trauma.

When working with trauma-impacted students, it can be hard not to take their behaviors to heart. That's why it's helpful to remember that the child's emotions may actually be intended for another target. **Traumatic re-enactments** occur when people who suffer trauma in their personal relationships attempt to re-enact those dynamics with those close to them in an unconscious attempt to heal. Because teachers are authority figures who are also close to the child, they can easily be mistaken in a child's mind for another authority figure close to them (think of how many times students have accidentally called you Mom or Dad!). They may react (and over-react) to what you say and do as though responding to the person who caused them pain. You are the actor or actress who has been cast unknowingly into this role, assigned to (unconsciously) help the child work out the situation. So even though you had no desire to even audition for this role, you might suddenly find yourself being the stand-in for a loved one who is an Abuser, Tyrant, Victim, Hero, etc. Although the child's behavior in these situations can be frustrating, to say the least, it is reassuring to know that in many cases, it's not that they are doing it *to* you; it's just what they do.

Another symptom to be aware of is the challenge of focusing on the task at hand. Think how hard it was for Christina from Chapter 3 to focus while her mother was in the hospital. In the case of students living with trauma,

ACEs, and chronic stress, they often live in states of high unpredictability, making it exceedingly difficult to focus. Put another way, their nervous system simply has more pressing things to attend to. Questions about safety and survival may be running through their minds during algebra, Spanish class, or circle time. In fact, kids in this sort of perpetual state of alarm can remind you of kids with ADHD, especially if they are in a state of hyper-arousal. They may talk fast, tell stories out of sequence, and be in a perpetual state of motion. In fact, the symptoms of trauma actually can overlap with the symptoms of ADHD. Figure 17.1, from the National Child Traumatic Stress Network, shows the similarities in symptoms between ADHD and trauma. Research shows that this overlap can easily cause doctors to overlook the role of trauma in a child's behavior and focus on ADHD instead.[3]

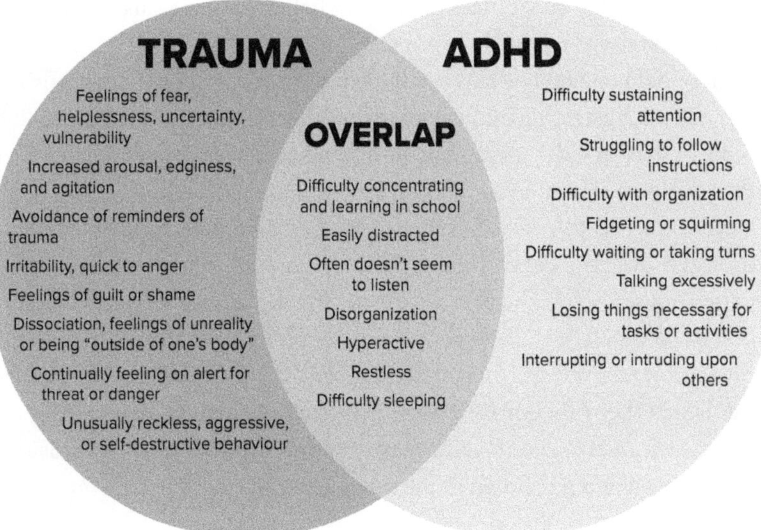

Figure 17.1: The overlap of ADHD and trauma-related symptoms
Source: National Child Traumatic Stress Network

Why is it so hard for trauma-impacted students to manage their emotions?

Traumatized individuals often find it hard to deal with, name, and understand their emotions. There is a biological reason for this. In addition to the brain growing in ways that make it hypersensitive to perceived threats (as we discussed above), trauma can cause an impairment in the bridge between the left and right hemispheres of the brain.[4] Among other things, this causes an impairment in the ability to both experience and name one's emotions—two prerequisites for being able to manage emotions well. It may seem that they can only express their feelings when they are angry, probably because anger is such an intense feeling and is relatively easy to name. It's harder for individuals, especially trauma-impacted individuals, to name the emotions that lie beneath the anger, such as sadness, confusion, loneliness, frustration, etc. For many traumatized children, all of those feelings can just be interpreted as anger.

These children may also shut down or have outbursts because they have a rigid and limited range of coping strategies when they feel distressed. Additionally, these tantrums and patterns of behavior may have been useful in helping them survive in other unsafe situations. Since it's what they know, it's what they continue to do. However, it takes practice and guidance to realize that it's okay to let these patterns of behavior go because they are no longer in situations where there is a real risk to their life.

These old maladaptive coping strategies (and lack of new more positive ones) can be frustrating and tricky for teachers to deal with because they can mean that an older child may act in ways that seem too young, or even infantile, when under stress. That is because, for many trauma-impacted children, the reactive, fear-based area of the brain (the survival brain) is prioritized over the development of other regions that govern executive functioning skills (being able to plan effectively, inhibit impulses, reason, problem solve, etc.).[5, 6] This means there is often a disconnect between a child's chronological age (their actual age) and their developmental age (the age at which they function). So while they may seem much older physically and may act much older in some ways, they can still be missing skills that normally developing children of the same age typically have.

Students do well if they can

As they say, if a child can't do math, we teach them math; if they can't read, we teach them how to read. But what do we do if a child can't behave? Unfortunately, we usually punish them. That doesn't quite make sense, does it? How do we get around this? Dr. Ross Greene's book *Lost at Schoo*l posits that "students do well if they can" and that poor student behavior (attention-seeking, limit testing, etc.) occurs because students have lagging or missing behavioral or coping skills and that these skills can be explicitly taught and targeted.[7] Instead of seeing misbehavior as intentional or only attention-seeking, it can help us to remember that students will choose to act in more constructive ways when given the necessary tools to get their needs met.

Why do they have over-the-top responses to the littlest things?

As we've discussed, chronic stress heightens an individual's base arousal levels as they prepare for the prospect of danger. Think of a smoke detector that is too sensitive to tiny wafts of smoke and sets off all the time, even when there is no real fire. Likewise, it can seem like stressed students are set off by things you would perceive as no big deal (someone looking at them the wrong way, being told they have to wait their turn, being told they can't work with a particular partner, etc.).

The impact of chronic stress on the brain distorts perceptions of social situations, making it harder for trauma-impacted individuals to read interpersonal cues correctly, meaning that ordinary events can trigger deep, unconscious memories. This can cause surprisingly aggressive behaviors, which push people even farther away. Sights, sounds, and shapes can trigger full-blown responses to previous traumatic events. This is especially true of sensory memories from a child's traumatic past that can easily get mixed up with present-day experiences (the sight of a wristwatch, the smell of smoke, the furrowing of a brow, the sight of a tall person, a certain sugary taste, a certain sound, a smoky smell, etc.). In more severe cases, these unconscious triggers can cause a child with PTSD to have a full-blown dissociative episode in which they feel flooded by fragments from their sensory memory and are totally unaware that these are merely responses to past events. (Think of veterans who go into full-blown panic attacks when they hear fireworks or backfiring cars because their brain unconsciously equates the two with memories of battle.) These triggers can cause them to feel that they are re-experiencing that situation in the present moment and that they are separated ("dissociated") from the current reality of what's happening. This can result in behaviors that seem to come out of nowhere and are way out of proportion to the situation at hand. They're actually not coming from nowhere—they're surfacing up from that individual's past.

Other tips for dealing with trauma-impacted behavior

- Be as predictable and structured as possible about what will happen during each part of the day. Have consistent routines for beginning and ending things. Students can relax when they know exactly what is expected of them and when.
- Be deliberate about transitions. Traumatized individuals who are often on the lookout for danger frequently consider any change, even positive change, as a possible threat. When transitions come up, prepare them for what's coming next, how long it will last, and sometimes how it will feel. "Kids, we are going to transition to an activity called ________ now. We haven't done it before, and so it may feel a little new and different to you." "Okay, guys, in about five minutes, we will be pausing our work to get ready for lunch." "In about two minutes, we will switch."
- The words "Find a good stopping place" can be less triggering for students than "Time's up" or "Stop what you're doing now." No one likes to stop doing something they enjoy, and phrasing it this way reminds them that they will be able to come back to this enjoyable activity again later. Make routine a priority because the more familiar the daily routine is, the more calm and confident the student will feel.

Using music during transitions

Music can be a helpful bridge between different classroom activities and can help to cue students that it is time to transition to the next task. For example, one day, my students were having trouble transitioning from looking at the back easel in my classroom to swiveling around and looking at my front blackboard. To help cue them, I made up a song describing what to do—What's next? What's next? Let's turn and take a look, fold your hands, sit up straight, oh isn't math just great?—sung to the tune of Mozart's *Eine Kleine Nachtmusik*. We would begin singing it as we moved through the transition and stop singing when we had finished turning. It worked like a charm!

- Ensure they have access to a Peace Center (aka Amygdala Reset Center or Cool Down Corner) to help them during challenging moments. Stock the Peace Center with sensory items like sequined pillows, hand warmers, hand lotions, mints, squeezy balls and fidgets, velcro strips, scented chapsticks, soft and rough fabrics to touch, clay or Play-Doh, dry erase markers/boards, cards with yoga and breathing activities, and so on. To personalize it even more, you may want to have students include a personalized, encouraging note from a care-giver or special teacher, a photo of a loved one, and a journal to keep track of their feelings, and art supplies like colored pencils. This is also a great place to tuck a few *Check-In Wheels*, which you can find in the Resource section. You can also help them assemble a Calming Box/Bag with some of the Peace Center items so they can take these tools with them to other locations in the school.

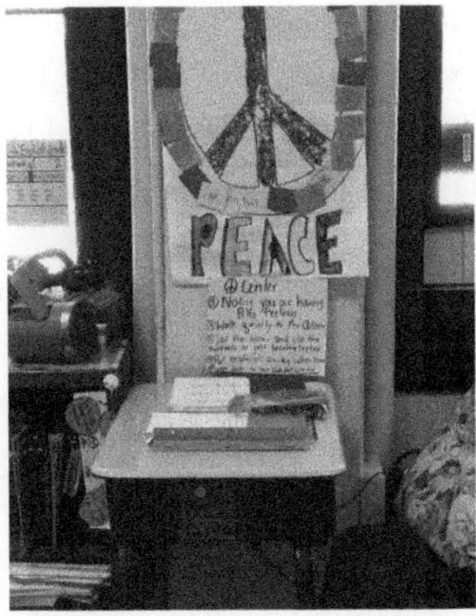

Figure 17.2: Peace Centers can have cozy cushions, coloring sheets, headphones, sand timers, etc., to help students regulate

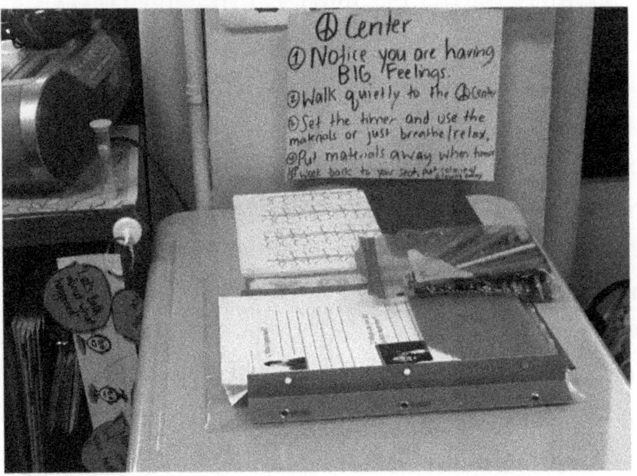

Figure 17.3: A closer look at my Peace Center

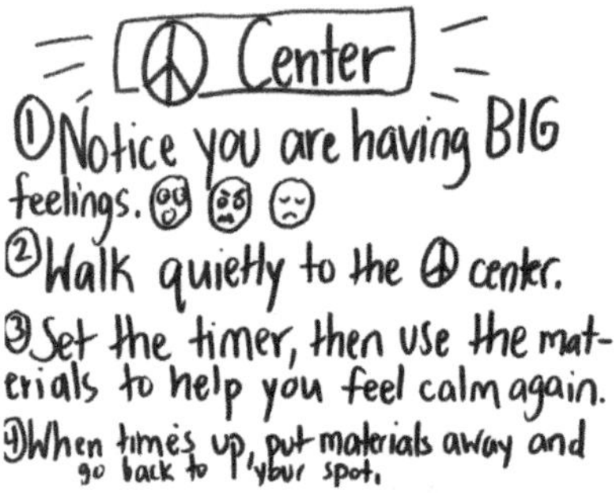

Figure 17.4: Teach and post procedures for how and when to use the Peace Center

- Speaking of helping students feel more calm and confident, you may want to check out many of the strategies listed in Chapter 23, which focuses on anxiety. Many of these strategies (such as instructional best practices like differentiation and a gradual release of responsibility) can help trauma-impacted students to be successful and reduce the number of outbursts and meltdowns.
- Maintain ongoing communication with counselors and social workers at your school. They can help you gain perspective on where troubling behaviors might be coming from and have the potential to be an excellent support for you in dealing with trauma-related behaviors. Although it can be tempting to try to counsel students yourself, remember to stay in your lane when there are big or persistent emotional things happening. Your counselor will be happy to help.
- Establish two or three adults in the school community to be "carers" or "buddies" for trauma-impacted students. These staff or school personnel can provide quick touchpoints (30 seconds or five minutes tops) to just check in with the student each day. This informal but intentionally set aside time can be spent chatting, playing a game, learning about the student's life outside of school, etc. If they have the time, carers can also use this time to quickly process past challenges/successes and prep the student for transitions or changes in the schedule that might provoke anxiety (a test, field trip, fire drill, etc.).
- Give them voice and choice. People who have experienced trauma often feel helpless and victimized by their surroundings and circumstances. We can help convey that they are, in fact, not powerless when we safely and consistently offer choices (seats, partners, books, etc.) and incorporate their ideas into what we do ("I like your idea

for a club! Why don't we start one? What are your ideas about how we can get started?"). It can also help to give them a classroom job, something that powerfully states, "You matter here."

- Seek out their "islands of competence," a term coined by Dr. Robert B. Brooks.[8] Feeling that we are good at something can be transformative, especially for struggling students. Remember, everyone has islands of competence, and finding them is a huge boost to our self-esteem. Part of our job is to help kids spot their hidden superpowers!

Islands of competence

A few years into my work as a counselor, I had a ten-year-old client with perpetually low self-esteem. The fact that he was a 4th grader reading at a kindergarten level only confirmed to him that he couldn't do anything right. He spent most of his time in the classroom crumpling up his work, talking back to the teacher, or walking the hallways when he had had too much. Despite his surly attitude, I had a suspicion that he might perk up if I could find something he felt good at, **an island of competence**. I guessed that he was the kind of kid who liked to tinker around with tools. So one day, I got an idea to help him create a Rube Goldberg machine (one of those kinetic contraptions that cause interesting chain reactions to achieve simple tasks like turning on a light switch). He took to the idea right away, and from then on, when we would meet for therapy at his school, I would spend much of the session letting him work on building this machine and praising his ingenuity at each new development. The most memorable moment happened when one day he proudly invited his teacher to our therapy room to show him his creation. Although he had consistently been angry and aggressive to this teacher, on that day, he changed from being Mr. Angry and Sullen into Mr. Happy and Self-Confident right before our eyes because he was so proud to show his teacher something he was good at! That is the power that an island of competence has to pump up our self-esteem!

- Teach students what to do when they are in the throes of overwhelming emotions (aka *Big Feelings*). You can teach coping skills as part of your morning meeting or as part of a Social Emotional Learning (SEL) program, or in conjunction with other content areas. In addition to communication and intra- and interpersonal skills, don't be afraid to branch out and incorporate out-of-the-box techniques like mindfulness, tapping (Emotional Freedom Technique (EFT)), and sensory calming techniques. Have a Cool Down Corner (aka Amygdala Reset Center/Peace Center) where kids can retreat when they need a break, or a "peace out pass" for kids to communicate to you that they need to take a walk or a moment to cool down.

- Don't get caught up in conflict cycles (easier said than done!). Triggered kids can easily trigger adults (especially when we're scared to lose the appearance of being in charge). Instead, focus on observing, not absorbing what's happening.
- Be sensitive to occasions when the child may be experiencing difficult times, like the anniversary of a death, the birthday of a loved one, the date of a custody hearing, etc. Be willing at those times to modify assignments and expectations while still maintaining a sense of normalcy and predictability.
- Do you. Co-regulation of difficult emotions is key to helping traumatized kids. To do this, though, you will need to be in a good place to manage your own emotions first. Taking care of your own lived trauma through counseling is a smart place to start because this can (1) help you process the challenges of teaching so you don't make your friends and family the sole recipient of your venting, (2) give you insight into some previously unseen ways in which your own past adversity may show up in your relationships with others, and (3) be personally rewarding on many, many levels.
- As we have said, it can be enormously helpful to have a place for kids to escape when they are feeling escalated. But it can be just as helpful for you to have a place to retreat. This could be a cozy corner in your room *just for you*, for example. You could stock it with a tea kettle, scented oils, headphones, quiet music, pictures of friends and family, inspiring notes from your students, and uplifting quotes. If you have the funding, it can also help to have a space outside your classroom just for teachers! Stock this wellness room with at least a few comfortable chairs, Zen music, plants, and other relaxing details (eye pillows, scented oils, foot massager, heating pads, salt lamps, soothing music, even massage chairs, and more). To prevent the wellness room from turning into another place for people to vent (always a temptation), consider making it a whisper-only or silent space.

Questions for reflection

- How do you handle transitions in your classroom? What has helped students transition smoothly?
- Up until now, what resources do you provide to students when they are dealing with big emotions? What has worked best for you?
- How do you feel about the phrase "Children do well if they can"?
- As a child, did you ever have a teacher or another adult highlight one of your islands of competence? What impact did this have on your self-confidence?
- What islands of competence have you discovered in your students? How did this discovery change the way you viewed them? The way they viewed themselves?
- Have you had any students whose chronological (actual age) and developmental age (the age at which they function) seemed quite different? Explain.
- What routines or activities do you already have in place to provide students with a voice and choice in your classroom? What new ideas might you be interested in trying out?

18

Part of the Equation

Teachers and Stress

As you know, stress isn't an experience that only plagues our students. We are often expected to be unflappable and deal with every challenge life throws our way while maintaining perfect teacher composure, but this sets up unrealistic expectations for everyone involved. We are not teacher bots; we have our own challenges to deal with. This situation can put us all in a sticky situation, though, because our emotions are intensely contagious to those around us. Triggered kids can trigger adults and vice versa; if we're not aware of what's happening, one person's state of alarm can easily put others into a state of alarm!

The ordinary demands of teaching and managing behavior alone can cause our amygdala to fire off like a 4th of July firework display. Because our nervous system often perceives students' misbehavior as a threat, responding to misbehavior can send us tumbling out of our window of tolerance and kick off the fight, flight, or freeze response. Unfortunately, this means the thinking part of our brain, the part we most need to help us respond to misbehavior, has been put on pause. Because our brains contain mirror neurons—neurons that mirror the feelings and behaviors of others—our survival brain can come head to head with the child's survival brain. This means that, literally and figuratively, no one is in their right mind!

Here's a question for you. Have you ever found yourself in a stressful situation and suddenly noticed that you are acting just like your parent or childhood teacher? That's because, as the saying goes, *when under stress, we regress*. When we're stressed, our survival brain jumps into action, quickly shutting down our thinking brain! So we revert to using the kind of punitive, "pain-based discipline" that many of us experienced as children: nagging, threatening, shaming, punishing. Unfortunately, children will then only comply out of fear, as you may remember doing as a child. We need our thinking brain to come in with its thoughtful, effective responses, but it has shut off just when we need it most!

To get some perspective on this troubling state of affairs, let's imagine a conversation between the two parts of your brain on a day when a difficult student is acting up. For fun, let's imagine these parts of your brain are managing your reactions just as they would steer a car together, and they must decide what you should say and do.

Survival Brain: Uh-oh! Michael is starting to get irritated again. Watch out, this is going to be bad! (The survival brain switches on the fight, flight, or freeze response and reaches for the wheel.)

Thinking Brain: (Trying to get it together) Wait a moment, I'm not ready yet. I need a moment to think.

Survival Brain: (Momentarily letting go of the wheel to yell) You want to *think*? There's no time for thinking! He just threw his backpack! Someone is going to get hurt!

Teacher says: "Pick that backpack up this second! Who do you think you are to throw things in my classroom? If you don't pick it up right now, I'm going to call your mother and see what she says!" Michael kicks the backpack on the floor, and it bursts open, spilling things all over the floor.

Survival Brain: Oh yeah?!!! Prefrontal cortex, buckle up! Now, we're really going to show him who's in charge!

Choosing a new route

As you can see from the above example, when something triggers, it's incredibly difficult to take a step back and re-route our habitual responses to stress. We instinctively jump into action. If the student is also triggered, we match the student's intensity with our own. Things escalate. How do we get around this age-old cycle? By using new advancements in neuroscience to re-route our responses! Let me explain what I mean.

Did you ever say or do something in the heat of the moment, only to regret it later? Later on, when you felt calmer and had time to think it over and could clearly see what was happening, have you maybe wished you'd responded differently? Insights from neuroscience tell us that our survival brain is much faster to react to stimuli than our thinking brain! So when we pause before we respond to behavior, we are literally giving our thinking brain a chance to catch up! Then it can weigh in with its more thoughtful, clear-headed perspective.

So, with the thinking brain in charge, how might the above scenario play out instead? Let's imagine:

Survival Brain: Uh-oh! Michael is starting to get irritated again. Watch out, this is going to be bad! (Survival Brain switches on the fight, flight, or freeze response and reaches for the wheel.)

Thinking Brain: (In a calm, rational voice, keeping both hands on the wheel) Oh, I see what you're talking about. He does look upset. I'm also noticing that I am starting to sweat, and my heart is beating fast. That means that my body is beginning to panic. But panicking won't help me in this situation. Let me take a moment to think about how I want to respond because I'm not able to manage this well right now.

Survival Brain: Take a moment?!! There's no time for that! He just threw his backpack! Someone is going to get hurt! We need to act *now*! Let's yell at him! Threaten him! Make him stop before all hell breaks loose!

Thinking Brain: (Keeping both hands firmly on the wheel) That's true, I see that. I can feel the impulse to yell at him. But if I do that, things may just blow up more. Survival brain, you don't always make the best decisions, right?

Survival Brain: I guess, but look…

Thinking Brain: (Cutting in) It's important that I handle this calmly, for everyone's sanity. Let me start by taking a few deep breaths. (Breathes slowly and calmly.) Hmmm…now I feel better. (Musing) Let me see. I wonder what this could be about... He must be struggling with something. What seemed to help him the last time this happened? I'll provide reassurance that he can do this and restate my expectations. Thanks for the heads up, amygdala, old friend. I'll handle this one on my own.

See the difference? When the teacher gave themselves a moment to pause, they were able to notice their physical distress signs and ward off the waves of panic. Now aware of what was happening, the teacher re-routed things by choosing to give the thinking brain a chance to speak its mind (pardon the pun!). Then the way forward was clearer. How can one learn to do this?

Four steps to re-routing your response

1. Check in with yourself. What part of your brain seems to be in charge? Notice signs in your body that tell you the survival brain has taken control and that you're on the path to panic. For example, your breathing and heart rate may be rapid, your hands and feet may feel cold and clammy, your muscles may be tense, etc.
2. Ask yourself: is it actually time to panic? Is this a five-alarm fire or just a little smoke and mirrors? Bring yourself back into a calm state. Take several deep breaths, recite a few calming phrases, excuse yourself to get a glass of water. Think about observing, not absorbing, what's happening. Maybe ask a partner teacher to step in for a moment, if you have one.
3. Once you feel calm, ask yourself what the child and situation need. Remember, *you don't have to attend every argument you're invited to*. Not every behavior requires a response, and you may choose to focus on "catching them being good" instead of responding to every infraction.
4. Engage with the student if necessary. Depending on the moment and the child, you may also want to provide calm reassurance, choices, empathetic statements, and/or a calm restatement of your expectations.

Other tips to calm the amygdala

- Take deep, slow breaths. I like to bring the kids into this, and we say we are doing a round of "Take 4 Before." We breathe slowly together for four breaths. For each in-breath, we bring our hands to our heart, and for each slow out-breath, we release our hands back down to our sides. Sometimes we need a couple of cycles of "Take 4 Before!"
- Try doing the opposite of what you feel like doing. If you feel like screaming, try whispering or talking in a soft, soothing voice. If you feel like rushing, try doing things in a slow, methodical way. It sounds weird, but the effect is pretty magical.
- Try the magic of music. Focusing on calming sounds reduces stress. One study done at the University of Pennsylvania even found that letting pre-op patients listen to calming music had the same tranquilizing effect as taking a prescription-strength sedative, without

the side effects.[1] So don't be afraid to pop on some calming tunes to get you grooving to a new track.

- Try self-talk. Say things like: "I am okay." "This, too, shall pass." "I've seen this before, no need to worry." "They are the child. I am the grown-up." "I am at peace." "I am bigger and wiser. I can do this." "I've done hard things before. This is nothing." "All is well. I can handle this." "Exhaling, I exhale my stress like black smoke. Inhaling, I breathe in calm, cool air."
- Cool off with cold water. Marsha Linehan, a psychology professor at the University of Washington, popularized an exercise to help lower the intensity of overwhelming emotions. To do it, you quickly plunge your face into icy cold water for 15–30 seconds and hold your breath, making sure the area underneath your eyes and above your cheekbones feels the icy water. (This might be one that you want to try during your break or a moment alone!) It may sound a bit unusual, and if you have heart issues, you should consult with your doctor before trying it, but apparently it is so helpful because it activates the dive response—a reflex that slows your heart rate and allows blood to more easily flow to your brain.[2] Dive right in the next time you need to cool off!
- While you are trying non-traditional strategies, you might want to try out the Power Pose, also known as Postural Feedback. Harvard researcher Amy Cuddy found that the way we hold our bodies can influence how stressed or powerful we feel in that moment, even on a hormonal level. By maintaining high power poses, Cuddy found that we can increase feelings of being in control while lowering cortisol, a hormone associated with the stress response. To do the Power Pose, stand tall with your chest out and put your hands on your hips like Wonder Woman. Alternately, you can put your hands in the air above your head in a V shape as if you have just won an Olympic medal and are celebrating. Hold for two minutes to set the hormonal changes into motion to help you feel calmer and more in control.[3]
- Try moving to another part of the room and working with another student. Focus your attention totally on them. When you come back into contact with the student who was upsetting you, you may be surprised to find that you have sort of "forgotten" how mad you were, at least partially!
- Display a picture of someone in your life that you admire or who admires you. At difficult moments, look up at the image to recenter

yourself. I have done this with a picture of my grandfather. Even though I never met him, just seeing his face at difficult moments often makes me bite my tongue before I react impulsively to a student's behavior. I want to be the kind of granddaughter he'd be proud of!

- When things get tense or are heading down a bad path, ask for a "re-do." If you don't like the way you acted, stop, pause, and say, "My survival brain seems to be in charge right now, and that's no good. Can I get a re-do?" Then play the situation over again, acting in a way that makes you feel more comfortable.
- If the students are the ones who seem to be struggling, say you'd like to give them a re-do. You can even ask them to go back into the hall, spin around a few times, come back in, and re-do the situation. With younger students, you can show them how to pretend to wind the hands back on an imaginary clock, or hit an imaginary re-wind/back button, and then press *play* on a new scene.

HALT right there!

There is a helpful acronym in the substance abuse recovery world that helps recovering addicts and alcoholics monitor their state of being and HALT before reacting impulsively, It's a great way to check in with ourselves before trying to help children regulate, and it can also be a useful checklist for them to keep in mind. The letters in the acronym HALT stand for:

H—Am I Hungry? Did I eat at the last meal? Or did I skip it?
A—Am I Angry? If so, I may find it hard to think clearly.
L—Am I Lonely? Am I feeling disconnected from other people?
T—Am I Tired? Did I get enough sleep last night and enough moments of rest today?

Questions for reflection

- Think about or draw an imaginary conversation between your survival brain and thinking brain. What do they say to each other when things get tense in your classroom? If you are not happy with how this imaginary conversation usually goes, how might you change it?

- What do you usually do to re-route your responses? After reading this chapter, what new ideas, if any, might you like to try?
- How might you share this information with your students in a developmentally appropriate and engaging way?
- What does the phrase "You don't have to attend every argument you are invited to" mean to you? Can you think of any arguments that you might decide not to attend tomorrow?

19

Social Emotional Learning

A Trauma-Informed Best Practice

The other day I went for a walk with one of my best teacher friends. As is often the case with my teacher friendships (and I'm guessing yours?), our conversations almost inevitably veer towards talking about teaching and our classrooms. "This SEL stuff is the best part of our day!" she exclaims to me, referring to our district's newly implemented **Social Emotional Learning (SEL)** block on our schedule. "It's like, woohoo—finally, we get to talk about the stuff the kids need!"

Indeed! SEL is what kids need, especially those living with trauma, chronic stress, and ACEs. It can be enormously helpful for teachers as well. So, what is it?

SEL, an umbrella term referring to programs and approaches that provide instruction in social emotional intelligence, pro-social or **people skills**, has exploded in popularity in the last several years, and rightly so. These programs posit that social emotional competencies (also referred to as "soft skills" or "21st-century skills") come before academic success (think of Maslow's Hierarchy of Needs before Bloom's Taxonomy of Learning). They are directly in line with the work of researchers like Paul Tough and Angela Duckworth, who argue that kids need more than just book smarts to lead happy, successful lives.

Traditionally, SEL programs and approaches focus on the instruction of five core SEL competencies across different settings, as you can see in Figure 19.1.

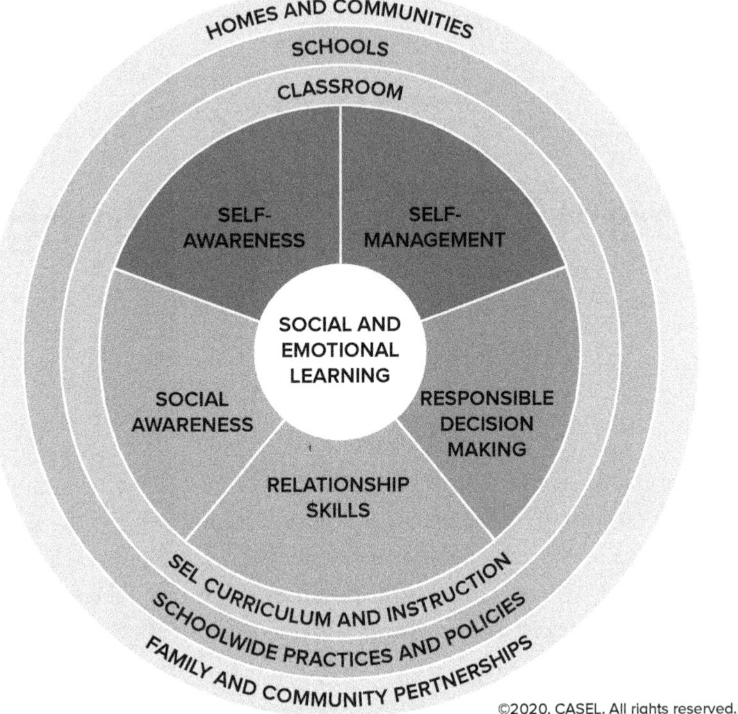

Figure 19.1: The Collaborative for Academic, Social, and Emotional Learning's wheel of SEL competencies

Source: © 2020, CASEL. All rights reserved. http://www.casel.org

Briefly, these competencies are:

- **Self-awareness:** The ability to understand one's feelings, thoughts, and values and how they impact our behavior in different areas of our life. This includes skills like knowing what one is feeling, identifying one's biases, and having a growth mindset.
- **Self-management:** The ability to manage one's feelings, thoughts, and behaviors in different situations and reach one's goals. This includes skills like being able to delay gratification, manage stress, and stay motivated.
- **Responsible decision making:** The ability to make thoughtful, positive, and caring choices about one's behavior and interactions with others. This includes skills like identifying the consequences of one's actions, identifying possible solutions, and evaluating available information.

- **Relationship skills:** The ability to form and maintain healthy, caring relationships and effectively negotiate situations with different kinds of people. This includes skills like communicating well, listening deeply, cooperating to problem solve collaboratively, and managing conflict constructively.
- **Social awareness:** The ability to understand and empathize with the perspectives of other people who may be from different cultures and backgrounds, and to understand the different social norms required for different situations. This includes skills like recognizing others' strengths, showing concern for others' feelings, and knowing where to find support in one's community.

It's not a far leap to see why SEL programs play a crucial role in trauma-informed schools. First, creating safe and supportive communities is a keystone of trauma-informed schools, and SEL programs put a heavy focus on making kids feel they belong and are safe and supported. Second, the brain development of trauma-impacted students deprioritizes the development of healthy coping and self-regulation skills in favor of survival. Since "brains in pain can't learn," as the saying goes, quality SEL programs can provide much-needed coping and self-awareness strategies. These, in turn, help students control and regulate their emotions and behaviors, making for a more positive classroom and school climate. All of this means more instructional time because there are simply fewer interruptions due to behavior!

SEL is not just for trauma-impacted students; it's a tier 1 intervention, something to which most children respond positively. In fact, there is a substantial body of research showing that SEL programs can improve:[1]

- classroom behavior
- ability to manage stress and depression
- attitudes about themselves, others, and school
- academic achievement!

SEL is for teachers too

As it turns out, SEL competencies aren't just good for kids; they're also helpful for teachers. As anyone who attended middle school knows, teachers have to contend with the everyday relational challenges between students in addition to actually teaching them: bullying, peer pressure, social isolation, just to name a few. In addition, to keep a safe and predictable classroom environment, teachers need to appear unflappable as they manage both their own emotions and others' emotions (doing what Dr. Arlie Russell Hochschild called "emotional labor"[2]).

However, like everyone else, teachers enter the workforce with varying degrees of social and emotional competencies. When lacking some of these competencies, teachers, especially new ones, can feel blind sided by teaching's social and emotional nature. As a result, the classroom climate deteriorates, triggering what researchers Patricia Jennings and Marc Greenberg describe as a "burnout cascade." They write:

> When teachers lack the resources to effectively manage the social and emotional challenges...children show lower levels of on-task behavior and performance (Marzano, Marzano, & Pickering, 2003)... The deteriorating climate is marked by increases in troublesome student behaviors, and teachers become emotionally exhausted as they try to manage them. Under these conditions, teachers may resort to reactive and excessively punitive responses that do not teach self-regulation and may contribute to a self-sustaining cycle of classroom disruption (Osher et al., 2007).[3]

When teachers lack SEL skills, student behavior and academic performance suffer, and we descend into the burnout cascade. Before we blame ourselves for not having perfect SEL competencies, let's take a moment to consider two factors that have nothing to do with the failure of individual teachers and everything to do with how educational systems are structured.

First, managing large groups of young human beings in isolation—something teachers do every day—is a new and bizarre development in human history! For the *vast* majority of the roughly 200,000 years of human history, our ancestors lived in tribal communities and shared the work of raising the children together. It takes a village to raise a child, as the saying goes. But modern-day school systems, which are designed using a factory model, aim to move large numbers of students through quickly, meaning teachers are left alone to manage very large groups of students.

Second, our work as teachers requires a similar social emotional skill set to those needed by counselors and psychologists, but for teachers, training in these areas is almost entirely missing! Other fields that require constant social interaction (like clergymen, social workers, and psychologists) prepare their workforce for the social emotional challenges *much* more robustly.[4] Members of those professions receive *thousands* of hours of hands-on practice fine-tuning their social emotional competencies. However, most teachers don't receive any of this hands-on practice or feedback, or access to anyone qualified enough to turn to with their concerns.

So what's a teacher to do if they want to build their SEL competencies? We can start by advocating for quality professional development in our schools. That may take a while, so, meanwhile, we can arm ourselves with knowledge by seeking out information related to each of the SEL competencies (self-awareness, self-management, responsible decision making, relationship skills, and social awareness). In addition to this book, there are many, many books, workshops, and even YouTube videos on the topic of personal growth. If you investigate, you will likely find many public figures who are psychologists, counselors, and self-mastery coaches who appeal to you. You might also want to consider working with a skilled therapist who can help you process the many challenges of the classroom, while at the same time adding to and refining your toolbox of SEL skills!

Every square is someone who cares

Thinking of SEL's emphasis on a caring classroom community, I remember one particularly special student I had. My group of 4th graders that year included a student who really struggled and had a lot going on at home, and my group and I decided to stage a sort of surprise intervention for him. We wanted to remind him that even though he was going through a difficult time, we were there for him. When the day we had planned for came, my students stood up one by one and read aloud to him quick messages of support they had written. He was absolutely blown away and fought back tears. Last, a quiet but brilliant student stood up. He held up a paper where he had carefully drawn a grid of squares and had all his peers sign their names in a square. "Every square is someone who cares," he said and handed the paper over to his astonished peer. Years later, I'm still inspired by this student's creativity, kindness, and generous spirit! Inspired by him, I've put a template for *Each Square Is Someone Who Cares—about YOU!* in the Resources Section at the back of the book.

How to bring SEL into your classroom tomorrow

There are a few ways schools and individual teachers can bring SEL into their classrooms. SEL programs—often referred to as character development programs—can be woven into the curriculum or taught during a separate block in the day, usually led by a counselor, support, or homeroom teacher. SEL mustn't seem like something reserved for only certain blocks of the day, and it can be more easily integrated into daily classroom life when taught by or with the teacher who spends the most time with the group.

If your school doesn't have an SEL program for individual teachers to use, all is not lost. It's relatively easy to thread SEL competencies into the curriculum or make them the focus of morning or classroom meetings. Even if you aren't following a formal SEL curriculum or program, here are a few tips for incorporating SEL into your classroom:

- Provide students with *lots* of opportunities to work in cooperative groups, cooperative learning structures, and pairs. ("Think, Pair, Share," for example, allows students to share with a partner for a certain amount of time while partners listen. Then they switch.) Consider letting students choose their partners sometimes. Consider allowing shyer and more reluctant or introverted students to select their partners first or have the option of working alone.
- For virtual learning, assign each student a virtual study buddy. Over the week, they can partner with their study buddy to complete tasks in small groups on Zoom and/or other video conference platforms. They can also check in with their study buddy to ensure they stay current with assignments and get tech help if needed.
- When students share answers with the group, use helpful facilitation techniques such as wait time. When responding to students' contributions to the group, try responding neutrally instead of praising (which can set up the expectation that students need to please you instead of finding their own solutions to problems). Instead, ask questions to extend thinking and promote discussion: "What do others think of what Ashley said?" "Who would like to add on to what Giovani said?" "Jacob, it looks like you agree with Bella's strategy. Tell us more."
- Use "We Not Me" language to promote a sense of community and inclusion. For example, when a student has turned in excellent work, say, "*We* are so proud of you, Mohammed," not, "I am so proud of you." Or, "Tell *us* the answer to number 5," not, "Tell me the answer to number 5."
- Provide or post talk stems to help kids communicate more easily in group discussions. Some examples are:
  - I agree with ______ because ______.

- I respectfully disagree with what ______ said because I believe ______.
- I'm curious to hear more about what ______ is saying.
- In addition to what ______ shared, I think that ______.
- In my opinion, ______.
- I'm waiting for your attention (said when others are not listening to what the speaker is saying.

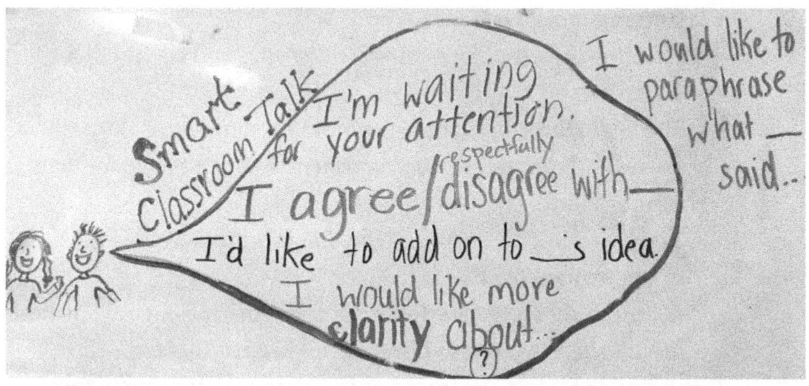

Figure 19.2: It can be helpful to post your talk stems for students' quick reference

- Have a section of your classroom reserved for a social emotional book library. Invite students to contribute to the library with student-authored books about times when they dealt with big or difficult feelings, cared for others, prevented bullying, and so on.
- At the moment when it's happening, try acknowledging the relational, social emotional dynamics of the classroom. For example, if you call a student to speak in front of the classroom, be aware (or even state outright) what they might be feeling ("I know that this can feel scary, but you are doing great").
- Have a shout out at the end of the day for kids to acknowledge others who have been helpful or kind during the day (e.g., "I want to shout out/acknowledge Justina for helping me up when I fell at recess").
- Do role-plays of tricky social situations that can arise in the classroom and discuss tips to navigate them. With permission from kids and parents, you could film a few moments of the students working collaboratively on a project (building a bridge out of tin foil or designing a paper plane, for example) and zero in on social interactions between students. Then play the video for the group

and do a minute-by-minute replay focusing on all the ways students used helpful communication techniques ("Did you notice Sara put her pen down to turn to look at Elena as she spoke? That's some active listening!" "Elena, how did it make you feel to have Sara's full attention?"). Pause frequently and try to pull out the tiniest successes. After a while, your kids will be experts at spotting their successes too!

- Hold regular classroom or morning meetings. Typical parts of morning meetings (especially those that are part of the Responsive Classroom Model[5]) include:
  - Greeting: The members of the classroom and the teacher greet each other.
  - Sharing: Students share an opinion or something about themselves, and the rest of the class listens and can then comment or ask questions.
  - Activity: Students do an activity that promotes teamwork, social, or academic skills.
  - Morning message: Students read a short message from their teacher, usually describing what will happen that day.

  If you decide to do a classroom or morning meeting, make sure you have your group create and agree to classroom or meeting guidelines. Here is a sample set from my classroom:
  - Listen from your heart.
  - No shaming or blaming.
  - One person talks at a time.
  - Use kind words.
  - Say what you mean, but don't say it mean.
  - Take care of feelings.
- In a digital setting, consider having a breakfast club or other club once or twice a week for students to practice their hobbies together or just catch up. You may even want to invite a parent volunteer to host so you can sit back and enjoy!
- With appropriate boundaries, it can help students to hear that you are on a journey to grow SEL skills, too. Sharing your own daily struggles and successes with developing SEL skills shows that you see value in these skills and believe they can improve with practice (growth mindset). It also shows that you see strength in vulnerability—a tremendous social—emotional lesson in itself!
- Provide students with language to express a growth mindset. You might want to provide them with a bulletin board, bookmark, or

other material with helpful growth mindset phrases (see Resources Section for a sample *Mindset Bookmark*).

Questions for reflection

- Can you identify people in your life who excel in any of the SEL skills?
- Think of one student in particular. Which SEL skills do they struggle with the most? How can you tell?
- Which SEL skills are the easiest for them? How can you tell?
- Take a look at the list of SEL competencies in Figure 20.1. How do you feel you do personally with each of them? Are you as self-aware as you'd like to be? How well do you manage your emotions? How empathetic are you? How good are your communication skills, and how responsibly do you make decisions?
- Do you think it would be helpful for your students to know about the SEL competencies? What do you think the best way would be to share this information with them?
- After reading this chapter, are there any strategies for incorporating SEL into your classroom might you like to try out? What are they?

20

A Feather and a Rock

Balancing Kindness and Firmness

Managing trauma-related behaviors can be among the most challenging parts of a teacher's work. These behaviors might even be the reason you are reading this book. Maybe you feel helpless and hopeless. That would make total sense to me, and you would definitely not be alone! I know this both as a teacher and as a therapist who worked with children with very challenging behaviors. I want to stop and just acknowledge how very soul-sucking, demoralizing, and defeating it can be to deal with problematic trauma-related behaviors. It can make you stop wanting to be a teacher; I know that both personally and professionally.

But you *can* do this. While trauma can cause complex, neurobiological changes, and out-of-the-ordinarily challenging behaviors, there is also something simple about managing these behaviors that I bet you may be able to do intuitively. In fact, everyday people who have never read a book about trauma and trauma-impacted behaviors can sometimes be successful with these young people because they know how to do this: balance being a feather and being a rock. Let me explain.

Initially, when you work with challenging kids, you will need to be as soft as a feather. This feather represents your kindness and empathy, your willingness to listen deeply, collaborate, and drop your assumptions and storylines. This warm kindness is a soft place for others to land in what can be a harsh and unforgiving world. This kindness, grace, and warmth is refreshing and transformative for everyone involved.

But there is also a danger in becoming *too soft*. It seems counterintuitive to say, but as a teacher, it can be a mistake to be too kind all the time. If we are only kind and loving in every situation, we may let others off the hook for things they need to take responsibility for. We may forget our own needs because we want to make others feel comfortable. We may be afraid that we will drive others away if we say what we need. Maybe we do this because, deep down, we believe that they are fragile, and we will break and damage them if we are clear and honest about what's okay and what's not. Although potentially hurting others is the *last thing* kind people want to do, being kind all the time can unintentionally cheat others out of the opportunity to grow from honest feedback.

Figure 20.1: A rock and a feather can be the key helping your students

That's why we must also be a rock. The rock represents your firmness, your clear limits, and high expectations. A consistent, firm, clear expression of high expectations is essential to bringing out the best in others. It means putting your foot down and following up with logical consequences and honest truths. But just being the rock doesn't work either. If we are strict and firm all the time, we may alienate and frustrate those around us who feel that we don't get them, don't see their needs or where they are coming from. They may see us as rigid and too demanding. We may fear losing control, so we have a stranglehold on everything others do (think of the *Power Over* style of leadership we discussed earlier). What we need instead is to be both the rock and the feather together, similar to what author Lisa Delpit calls being a "warm demander."[1] Firm and kind in equal doses. While the feather says, "I see your humanity, and I honor it," the rock says, "I also know you can do better, so let's do this!"

As a high school student, I remember when a warm demander's comments pushed me from being an apathetic B and C student to an A student. It happened one day when my high school history teacher pulled me aside after I bombed a test. Even though I didn't come from a background where I had a lot of the financial and social advantages that my peers did, he didn't lower his expectations. "I can see who you are," he said. "And that person should be getting an A in my class." Because of his insistent faith in me, I made that class my priority for the rest of the year and made sure I earned that A!

Still not sure how to balance this? Try thinking about the delicate balance of being simultaneously kind and firm as the same skillset required when teaching someone to swim. We would never throw a novice swimmer off the deep end on the first day. Or the second or third day. There is some teaching to be done first; there is some time we need to spend in the shallow end where things are comfortable and pleasant. But we don't let our budding bather paddle around endlessly in the kiddie pool either. We hold out the expectation that, one day, they will make it to the deep end, even if it makes us both uneasy for a while. We will need to use all the trust we built up with them in the shallow end to ease them into the deep end because we know that's where they can do their best swimming. After all, we don't want them to miss out on the joy of keeping their own body afloat in the water, with all those smooth, cool waves gliding past. We know that just outside of their comfort zone is the magical place where the growth and the healing begin, and it's partially up to us to get them there.

Being the rock and the feather, therefore, means holding two competing truths simultaneously, being both firm and kind. We acknowledge and hold space for difficult events and affirm that, yes, the past can powerfully shape us. But we also refuse to limit ourselves and others to the past, so we insist firmly on our expectations as well. There's no use getting bogged down in the past because, as Henry S. Haskins said, "What lies behind us and what lies before us are small matters compared to what lies within us."[2]

Questions for reflection

- Reflecting on your childhood, can you identify anyone who was only a feather? Only a rock? Anyone who was both? How did these people influence your beliefs about others' abilities? How did they influence the kinds of expectations you have for children in your classroom?
- Do you consider yourself more of a feather or more of a rock? Or both? Explain.
- Are there some children who bring out your kindness more and others who bring out your firmness? Why do you think this is?
- After reading this chapter, what new insights, if any, do you have about your way of interacting with students?

21

It's Not All Bad News

Oprah and the Power of Positive Childhood Experiences

After spending some time reading the previous chapters about ACEs, trauma, and chronic stress, you might be finding yourself feeling down or depressed. You may consider that yes, there are many strategies we can employ, but at the end of the day, can we really help those students who face seemingly insurmountable odds? Well, it's not all bad news; in fact, there's plenty of good news too!

As it turns out, children and young people can and do recover from the devastating effects of ACEs. In fact, Johns Hopkins University has identified seven **Positive Childhood Experiences (PCEs)** that can buffer against the effects of ACEs.[1] They are:

- being able to talk with one's family about their feelings
- feeling that one's family stood by them during difficult times
- having enjoyed participating in community traditions
- feeling a sense of belonging in high school
- feeling supported by friends
- having had at least two non-parent adults who took a genuine interest in one's life
- feeling safe and protected by an adult at home.

Even though we may experience adversity in our lifetimes and childhoods, some factors prevent these events from overwhelming us. Take Oprah Winfrey, for example.

Oprah Winfrey was born into poverty in rural Mississippi to a teenage single mother. She was raised in inner-city Milwaukee, beaten regularly, molested, and raped by a relative at a young age. When she was 14, she was sexually abused and became pregnant with a baby that died in infancy. But today, Oprah is one of the most wealthy, powerful, and successful women in the world. How did she escape the nearly overwhelming odds to go on to lead such an incredibly happy and prosperous life?

When asked if she could pinpoint something or someone who helped turn the tide for her, she responded that it was *school* that made all the difference. According to Oprah, her young life was transformed through a series of caring and supportive relationships with teachers, beginning with one she had in the 4th grade. She has said that her teachers' belief in her helped her build up the self-esteem that would lead her to be so successful. In a CBS 60 Minutes special,[2] she described the transformative power of her teachers in her life, saying that "The moment I felt the most value was in my fourth grade when Mrs. Dunkin said to me I was the one who was chosen to lead the class... Mrs. Dunkin instilled in me this sense of believing that I mattered." Oprah's success, which would never have been predicted by all those things that went wrong for her, was instead predicted by everything that went right for her! In Oprah's case, that was the presence of several loving and supportive teachers. It just goes to show, you never know the depth of your influence and how far and wide into the future your love and caring as a teacher can go. With this love and caring, there is every reason on earth to hope.

Questions for reflection

- When you hear that a student has been through a traumatic event, what is your first thought?
- If others learned that a traumatic event happened to you, what would you like their first thought to be?
- A dear friend once said that people are who they are "because of, and in spite of." As you think about trauma and recovering from difficult life experiences, what does that phrase mean to you?
- As you think about your life and what has influenced you, what factors made you who you are, despite and because of them?
- After reading this section of the book, what other strategies might you now consider developing and implementing to support yourself and your students?

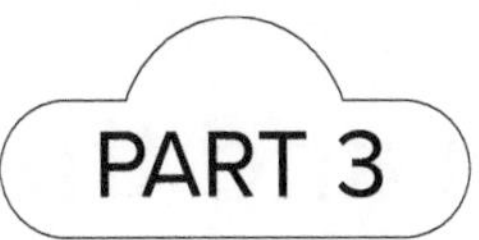

Weathering the Storm

How to Prevent and Process Meltdowns, Burnout, and Other Natural Disasters

"I'm not afraid of storms, for I'm learning how to sail my ship."

Louisa May Alcott

The Storm and the Rainbow

Surviving and Thriving through Hard Times

As you know, sometimes in life, things go very wrong, even in our carefully constructed and well-cared-for classrooms. When this happens, we may find ourselves adrift among the detritus left by the storm and wondering where it all came from. That's why, in this section, we'll pay attention to the sneaky but reliable patterns that can cause things to go very wrong, very quickly. More specifically, we will endeavor to slow down the fast-moving pace of meltdowns and burnouts to see the causes *before* the full-scale storms occur. As we have done throughout this book, we won't make our students the sole focus of our attention; we'll also peer into our own minds to see what's happening when we, too, feel at our wits' end.

Meltdowns

Tempers are flaring, tears streaming down faces, and objects may even be flying through the air. Kicking, punching, throwing, and screaming ensue. If you've ever been around a three-year-old, you are undoubtedly already familiar with what I'm describing! Meltdowns, tantrums, escalations, explosive behavior. Whether it's a teenager, a three-year-old, or a 30-year-old, the bandwidth for constructively managing emotions has been exceeded, and sanity and cool-headedness are now just tiny specks in the rear-view mirror.

Unfortunately, when meltdowns happen in the classroom, the other children—no matter how hard they try to tune them out—are negatively affected and sometimes even traumatized by these escalations. They are also easily among the scariest and most upsetting things that classroom teachers can experience. These extreme behaviors can deprive teachers of sleep and peace of mind and may make us consider quitting, especially if we feel unsupported by administration. Most teachers (myself included!) would love to find a way to make such experiences disappear forever. While it would be an impressive magic trick to get meltdowns to disappear, it might be more helpful to discuss how to prevent them from happening in the first place.

Over the rainbow

Meltdowns often happen so quickly that they can leave you feeling powerless, frustrated, and hopeless, because it's simply not clear where they come from and when they might strike again. That's because it's hard to know precisely when meltdowns begin!

But, for our purposes, I'd like to invite you to think of meltdowns as analogous to thunderstorms or other natural disasters. Although they sometimes seem to sneak up on us, it's also true that forces of nature don't come out of nowhere. In fact, meteorologists who pay close attention can spot them coming from miles away! In the case of a thunderstorm, for example, even if we don't quite pick up on the meteorological conditions changing over time, hot, humid air will have been steadily rising and creating turbulence. We may notice that dark clouds have been gathering, leaves are blowing upwards, birds and animals are looking for cover, etc. Before we know it, the rain, lightning, and thunder are upon us.

To be completely truthful, we might not be able to totally prevent some storms in our classroom from forming. Certain factors are outside of our control, but there are things that we still have the power to change. It's a lot like being out traveling one day when you notice a storm's brewing—what you do next is up to you. You can see the trouble coming and choose to head in another direction entirely. You can safely observe the situation for what it is and wait it out at a cozy rest stop while gaining some perspective on where to go next. If you believe the rainstorm might make you a better driver, you might even turn on your windshield wipers and head straight into the storm. My point is that you have options! You are not stuck, and "troubles don't last always," as the old spiritual says. Besides, who really knows what lies on the other side of that storm? It could be a rainbow or a calmer, more connected classroom—and that's one thing you won't want to miss!

What to do during a meltdown

When a child is deep in the throes of a real meltdown, there is very little that can be done until they are in a more regulated state. We just have to let the waves of strong emotions pass. However, here are some general guidelines for dealing with meltdowns once they have already started:

- Speak very little.
- Give them space.
- Avoid touching them or trying to physically move them from one place to another.
- If you must speak, do so very sparingly, and only provide supportive comments like "This is so hard," "You are feeling so upset," "I am here for you," etc.
- Wait for non-verbal and verbal signs that they are regulated before trying to process what happened with them.

God grant me the serenity...

Inspired by the serenity prayer which asks for serenity during difficult times and the wisdom to know the difference between what we can and cannot control, here's something you can do before or after a rough day. On a piece of paper, make two columns. Label one column "What I can control" and the other "What I can't control." Fill it in with information about the difficult situation. It can be helpful to remember that things that are always under your control include how you think and feel about events, while other people's reactions and actions are largely out of your control. Once you've finished your list, cut your paper in half and throw out (or burn!) the "What I can't control" column. Take a good look at the "What I can control" column, feel the serenity of knowing what you can actually control, and then move on with your day!

Questions for reflection

- Think of a time when a meltdown occurred in your classroom. What did you do that made the situation better? Worse?
- Reflect on your own childhood experiences of having big emotions/ meltdowns. What kinds of messages did your family send you about how to manage your feelings? For example, was it acceptable

for you to explode? Were you expected to bottle your feelings up? Something else?

- How did your care-givers handle strong emotions? How might these early experiences affect the way you expect students to deal when they have strong feelings?
- Fill in the blanks with your first gut-level reaction:
  - When a student melts down, I feel __________.
  - When I melt down, I need __________ to help me recover.

  What insights can you glean from the way you filled in the blanks?

23

Help for Your Nerves

Dealing with Anxiety and Anxiety-Related Behaviors

As we head into Part 3 of this book, let's begin by discussing anxiety. Although certainly not the only reason meltdowns happen in the classroom, anxiety plays a contributing role so frequently that it warrants our attention. Here's a story to get us thinking about anxiety, both ours and our students', and how to best deal with it.

One day in late August, the staff at my school received a professional development session designed to introduce us to the new science program we would be using that year. To demonstrate, our facilitator had brought along an experiment for us to try out. We were told to make a mini cart using popsicle sticks, plastic disks, straws, and tongue depressors. Then the facilitator passed out papers for us to make a sketch. I sat feeling adrift in a sea of other teachers who had already begun to write feverishly. I stared in despair at my blank paper while a dark storm of angry and anxious feelings flooded me. "How can I imagine what to do when I can't touch the materials? How do axles and wheels work again? I need help, but the facilitator said everyone needs to work on their own. Maybe she doesn't care about people like me who don't know how to do the work?!!" I found myself thinking resentfully. Even though I knew I was being silly, I felt more and more nervous and angry with each successive thought. When the facilitator passed by my table, I felt the beginning of frustrated tears springing to my eyes. Gathering myself together, I somehow managed to explain that I couldn't draw a plan to create a mini cart without seeing the materials and that I needed help. She assigned me to a partner and that helped me quell my anxiety and frustration. To this day, I am amazed at the anxiety that welled up inside of me over such a seemingly inconsequential task and the power it had over me!

So what exactly is this powerful thing called anxiety? Why is it so debilitating to those who suffer from it and how can we identify it in our students?

Anxiety can be defined as:

> an abnormal and overwhelming sense of apprehension and fear often marked by physical signs (such as tension, sweating, and increased pulse rate), by doubt concerning the reality and nature of the threat, and by self-doubt about one's capacity to cope with it.[1]

Symptoms of anxiety can include, among other things, sweating, rapid heart rate, hyperventilation, trembling, trouble focusing, stomach aches, and insomnia. Most people experience symptoms of anxiety from time to time, and people with anxiety disorders experience these symptoms for longer and in ways that interfere with their everyday functioning.

Let's stop and think about this on a personal level. What is your experience with anxiety? Can you recall the last time you experienced it? Maybe it's something that you live with continually, or perhaps you can relate to isolated moments of anxiety, such as a challenging high school or college course where you felt you couldn't keep up. Or maybe you can relate to the anxiety you feel in the dentist's chair or in awkward social situations. When trapped in an unpleasant or uncertain situation, your heart may feel like it's in your throat and you may want to escape or do something (anything!) to manage the terrifying emotions you feel!

The same intense emotions grown-ups feel in anxiety-provoking situations, students feel when taking a test, finding a partner, being called on to answer a question, finding someone to sit with at lunch, being told to take out their writing journal and start writing, etc. If we grown-ups feel so desperate and helpless when we experience anxiety, imagine how a child struggling with anxiety might feel!

Not all children who experience anxiety have a diagnosable condition, but the CDC reports that 7.1 percent of children aged three to 17 years (approximately 4.4 million in the US alone) have diagnosed anxiety.[2] Would it surprise you to learn that, in addition to sometimes causing meltdowns, anxiety has also been shown to impair academic performance and verbal working memory?[3] Given how pervasive and damaging anxiety is for children,[4] it's puzzling how little information, guidance, and support teachers are given about how to help students with anxiety! So how do we tell who experiences it, and what should we expect?

Are you up or down? How do you respond to anxiety and stress?

In her book *The Dance of Connection*,[5] Dr. Harriet Lerner explains that people have patterned ways of responding to anxiety and stress called over-functioning and under-functioning (this theory has its roots in Murray Bowen's work on family systems[6]). **Over-functioners** tend to want to jump in and take action at the first sign of a problem; they quickly switch into fixing mode and take responsibility for planning, organizing, and managing (even micro-managing) things. In their eagerness to fix things, they can also take on the responsibility of feeling things for others to prevent others from having to experience the difficult feelings themselves. Over-functioners can also easily burn out and feel resentment because they have taken on so much of the burden for keeping things afloat. On the other hand, **under-functioners** do the opposite; they tend to become less competent under stress, and so others see them as irresponsible, fragile, or vulnerable. Family members may see them as the focus of worry and concern because they may have trouble organizing themselves and taking action to solve problems. They may feel that others only see their weaknesses and that they aren't allowed to do things in their own way.

To continue to act the way they do, both over- and under-functioners depend on the other acting the way *they* do. One person under-functions and, to make up for it, the other over-functions, and vice versa. The cycle repeats each time a challenging situation occurs. Like any time we decide to change our patterned responses to things, the key is realizing what's happening and seeing that the power to change is in our hands.

How to identify anxiety in students

As it turns out, it can be quite challenging to identify students who are experiencing anxiety, whether they have a diagnosable anxiety disorder or not. This is partly because students with anxiety are often capable and creative learners, which can lead teachers to believe they can easily handle more demanding tasks. But this would be a mistake, because when they encounter these harder tasks, their anxiety spikes, and they may shut down.

It may seem that they just don't want to do certain tasks, but strong anxiety has such a stranglehold on our abilities that it may be more accurate to say that they *cannot* do those tasks.

When slow is fast

Sometimes we can be so eager to get our students to learn new material and move on to the next thing that we unintentionally rush them along. This sense of being in a rush can, in turn, make learning new tasks even more stressful for anxious learners who tend to be perfectionists anyway. The next time you find yourself rushing, tune out that little voice in your head that says you have to get things done now; instead, follow the Marines' advice to their recruits that *Slow is smooth and smooth is fast.* Get it?

It can be hard to identify when children are experiencing anxiety because it is largely invisible (although you can be on the lookout for tensed muscles and a flushed face). Anxiety may only show up in its end stages as explosive behavior or having exaggerated responses to things. You ask a child to stop one activity and begin another, and, seemingly out of nowhere, they kick their chair across the room. You tell them the schedule has changed, and they rush out of the room, slamming the door closed. When it's time for writing, they throw their writing journal in the trash. To further confuse matters, these behaviors can look a lot like the behavior of trauma-impacted children, children with attention deficit hyperactivity disorder (ADHD), oppositional defiant disorder (ODD), or other diagnoses in which children get frustrated easily, but the reason behind the behavior is different.

Another reason why it can be hard to figure out who is experiencing anxiety is that there are several types of anxiety disorders, each with different behavior patterns. Here are some of the most common anxiety disorders:

- **Separation anxiety:** This occurs when children worry about being separated from parents and care-givers. These kids can have a hard time coming into the classroom in the morning, may be clingy with care-takers, and may want to contact care-takers throughout the day to calm their anxiety.
- **Social anxiety:** An intense and persistent fear of being watched and

judged by others. While some social anxiety can be developmentally appropriate, students with diagnosable social anxiety can have a tough time socializing with their peers and participating in class, especially when they are called on to "perform" in front of their peers.

- **Selective mutism:** This disorder is characterized by a child's inability to speak and communicate in certain social situations. However, these children can speak and communicate in situations where they feel secure and when they are among people who know them well and with whom they feel comfortable.
- **Generalized anxiety:** The garden variety of anxiety disorder, generalized anxiety disorders are characterized by worrying about a wide variety of everyday things, and for students, particularly about school performance. These students are also likely to struggle with perfectionism.
- **Obsessive-compulsive disorder (OCD):** This disorder occurs when children's minds are filled with unwanted and stressful thoughts, usually about germs, keeping clean, having things in a symmetrical or perfect order, etc. Kids with OCD may alleviate their anxiety by performing compulsive rituals like counting or washing their hands to avoid illness and contamination.
- **Post-traumatic stress disorder (PTSD):** This disorder may occur in some people who have experienced or witnessed a traumatic event such as a natural disaster, a serious accident, rape, the loss of a family member or loved one, serious injury, being threatened with death, and so on. Individuals with PTSD often have intense, disturbing thoughts and feelings about their experience long after the traumatic event has passed. They may be triggered and relive the traumatic event through flashbacks or nightmares; they may feel detached or disconnected from other people. People with PTSD may also expend a lot of energy trying to avoid situations or people that remind them of the traumatic situation, and they may have very negative reactions to ordinary things like loud noises or touch.
- **Specific phobias:** Children may also have an overwhelming fear of particular things, like animals, clowns, storms, heights, enclosed spaces, etc.

It's also worth noting that while traditional behavioral modification models (color-coded behavior charts, earning rewards, or receiving consequences, for example) can be motivating for some children, they don't usually work well with anxious children (or trauma-impacted children for that matter). This is because their fluctuating anxiety levels make it difficult for them to do tasks consistently, even if they'd like to. As is the case with trauma-impacted students, it's better to put into place regulating, relational strategies and restorative justice approaches when disciplining these students. Helping these children learn to regulate symptoms of anxiety in their body and manage their anxiety-provoking thoughts is the name of the game.

How to get "unstuck"

When people (and animals) start to believe that they don't have any control over the bad things that happen to them, their anxiety can lead them to believe, feel, and act as if they are helpless. This is a well-studied phenomenon known as **learned helplessness.**[7] One way around this feeling of being stuck is to question our assumptions. Here are some helpful questions I've found help "unstick" someone who is feeling helpless:

- Can I talk to the part of you that has made it through difficult times?
- What about who you are helped you to make it through? Might that help you now?
- Have you ever failed at anything before this? How did you get over that? Do you think that strategy could work today?
- What do you think is the worst that could happen? How likely is that to actually happen?
- Even if the worst does happen, what can you do to help yourself deal with that situation? What will still be within your control?
- What is one small step you could take right now to deal with this problem/accomplish your goal?

I remember one time when I tried to help "unstick" my friend's daughter who was feeling anxious about taking her driver's license test. Afraid of what could happen, she had been putting it off for months with excuse after excuse. One day on an outing with her, I talked with her about her driver's license test anxiety. "What's the worst thing that would happen if you fail the test?" I asked.

"I don't know...I would feel like a failure!" she said.

"Hmmm...Have you ever failed at anything before?" I asked her. "And did you survive that?"

"Yeah," she said, starting to laugh self-consciously. "I guess I did!"

"So what would prevent you from surviving this time?" She smiled, perhaps realizing she had no rational reason for the fear. "What's one small step you could take tonight towards getting your license," I said.

"Well, I hid the practice booklet in a pile of stuff somewhere under my bed," she said with increasing excitement in her voice. "I could look there tonight and see if I can find it!" I am happy to report that she did indeed find the practice booklet, as well as her way to the driver's license center, where she eventually passed her driver's license test!

Strategies to help anxious students

There is a lot you can do to support students experiencing anxiety. As is the case with most of this book, these strategies can also be adapted to you if you find that you are struggling with anxiety yourself—a very normal reaction to the stresses of teaching!

- Prepare yourself and your anxious students by talking through the events of the day beforehand. For non-readers, this can be a visual schedule, such as those with PECs™ images.[8] Be *very* sure to point out any ways that today's schedule might vary from the norm. Consider providing them with their own printed, laminated schedule of the day. As each subject goes by, they can check off each period of the day with a dry erase marker.
- Transitions can be triggers for kids with anxiety. So help make transitions feel less scary to students by talking through them together. Instead of suddenly telling students to stop doing what they are doing, Minahan and Rappaport suggest **breaking up the transition into different parts**:[9] finding a good stopping place for their work, putting it away, getting their next task ready, and starting their next task. That can mean saying, "Okay, kids, in five minutes, we will find

a good stopping place for our work today… Okay, kids, get ready in two minutes to find a place to pause for today… Okay, kids, now it's time for us to find a good stopping place for our work. You can make sure you will know where to pick up by drawing a star where you left off today (or putting your bookmark/sticky note in that spot, etc.). Great job doing that so smoothly! Now, let's find our math journals. They should be on the right side of your desk; excellent job. Let's put it on our desks and find page 37. When you have your book open to page 37, please give me a big thumbs up. Okay, it looks like we have everyone ready. Now, let's get started. Take a look at the problem on the top of the page…"

- Follow instructional best practices like the **Gradual Release of Responsibility** (I Do, We Do, You Do). For example, during a recent virtual math lesson, I showed students a new skill, solicited their help to complete a new problem, put them in small groups to work on similar problems, and then let them work independently before checking our work together. This scaffolding helped them feel supported for much of the process so they wouldn't feel so terrified when it was time to complete the work independently.
- Another practice that I have found to lower students' anxiety is David Ginsburg's **Hierarchy of Help**.[10] This model reminds students that there are several resources within and around them that they *can* utilize before giving up. In my experience, instead of feeling anxious and asking the teacher for help immediately, this model encourages students to stay in productive struggle longer and use the resources they have at hand first. Also, you can see the "helping house" I created inspired by Mr. Ginsburg's work in Figure 23.1. To use it, at the beginning of our math problem of the day, I put a clothespin on the top tier of the helping house. This means that during this time students are to use their own resources to work independently. After three to four minutes of working independently, I move the clip down to show it's now time to share ideas with peers by asking, for example, "How did you do this one?" or "Can you help me?" After three to four minutes of working with peers, I move the clip to the "bottom floor" of the helping house. This means it's now okay to ask for help from the teacher.

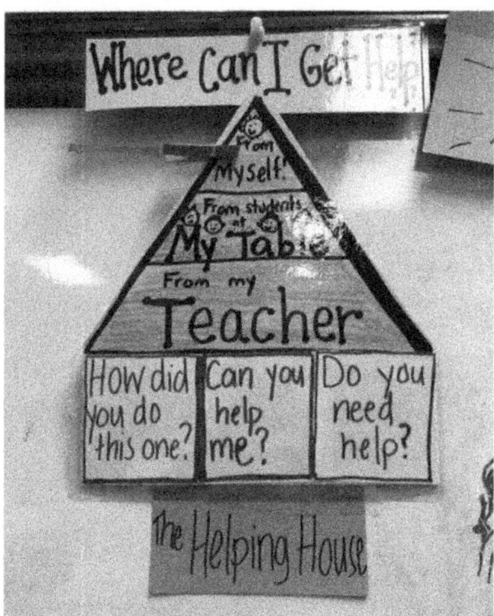

Figure 23.1: My helping house, inspired by David Ginsburg's Hierarchy of Help

- Down-times can be stressful for children with anxiety and they can also wreak havoc with your classroom management. Make a plan for what students can do if they finish early or during slow-moving transitions (sharpening pencils, running a message to the office, organizing the classroom library, etc.). It can help them to have a list on hand of what they can do when they finish early. Items can include word searches, Sudoku, playing with a Rubik's cube, etc.
- Anxious children often have problems waiting for the less fun parts of their day to be over so they can hurry on to more enjoyable moments of the day like lunch, gym class, or whatever they prefer. It can be helpful to aid them with time management. Start by making sure that they have access to a digital clock because many children struggle to read time on analog clocks (saying that we will go to lunch at 11:15 means little to a student who doesn't know what 11:15 looks like on the clock). Encourage them to wear a digital watch to school so you can provide them with feedback about how much time is left before they must stop or start certain activities. Visual timers that show the passage of time (without alarming students) can also be helpful. This is especially true for children with perfectionist tendencies so common with anxiety disorders that make it hard for them to finish their work until it is *perfect.*
- Even though they are often very intelligent, children who experience anxiety may struggle with executive functioning, organizing their material, and keeping their things in order. Have them color-code

their notebooks to match their folders (social studies folder and notebook can marked blue, for example) by marking them with the same colored stickers, or even by coloring the side of the notebook facing out so they can see it at a glance. Help them create a color-coded chart on their desk to identify what color goes with what subject. I have also had success with giving students a bin to put their materials in on the floor next to their desks. I have found it's easier for them to root around in these bins out in the light than inside a dark, messy desk.

- Help them draw a map of where things should go in their desk. In my class, I made a poster of a butterfly with open wings to represent the left and right side of their desk that shows what should go where in which order. When we clean our desks each week or two, they refer to this poster to keep things neat and organized!
- Writing by hand can be a trigger for students with anxiety, perhaps because there are so many ways to mess things up, and students with anxiety are often perfectionists about their work. Offer them the opportunity to use a computer to type their work, and show them how to use voice-to-text technology (Google voice typing, for example) to record their thoughts. This way, they can just get their ideas out there and not agonize so much about spelling!
- Make sure they have access to the Peace Center/Amygdala Reset Center, or help them to assemble a calming box. You can find more information about how to do this in the section *Other Tips for Dealing with Trauma-Impacted Behavior* in Chapter 17.

I Got This! Making a contingency plan

Often when we feel anxious day after day, we can end up feeling as if there is nothing we can do to change a bad situation. We feel powerless in the face of our anxiety or helpless in the face of difficult experiences (dealing with a bully on the playground or facing another day in the classroom with a difficult student, for example). But by focusing on what we *can* do, we take our power back!

One tool I have found helpful is what clinicians call a crisis plan. These lists of coping strategies or possible next steps are traditionally used to help prevent suicides—they are that powerful! The version I am going to share with you here, and which can be found in the Resources Section, is what I call my *I Got This!* Plan.

MY *I GOT THIS* PLAN

Figure 23.2: An I Got This! *Plan, made by an 18-year-old*

MY *I GOT THIS* PLAN

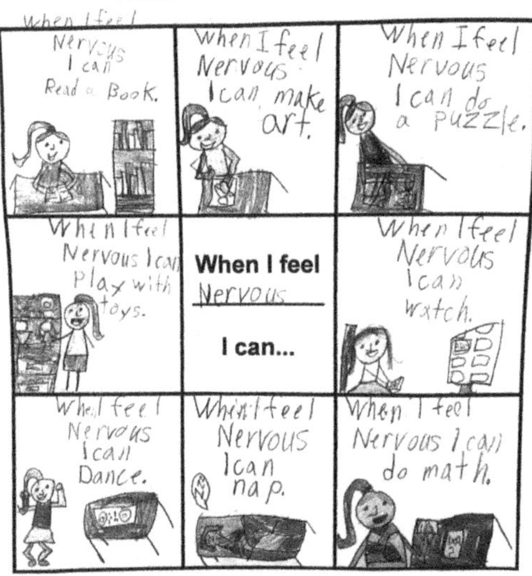

Figure 23.3: An I Got This! *Plan, made by a nine-year-old*

You can use it to brainstorm coping skills or map out alternatives to burning out or melting down. You can fill it out for yourself or help a student to fill it out after brainstorming ideas with them. Simply write ideas for coping in each square of the box. You can find a list of possible coping strategies that you can use to fill in the *I Got This!* Plan in the Resources Section.

This tool can be used to prepare for times when there are strong emotions ("When I feel angry, I can…" "When I feel overwhelmed, I can…" etc.). Students may also want to fill in more specific circumstances ("When I feel scared about taking my final exam, I can…" "When I feel disrespected because people are looking at me the wrong way, I can…" "When I feel impatient because I can't wait for lunch, I can..."). This tool can also be invaluable after a meltdown to help students strategize about what they can do better next time.

It can also help to strategize about little things you can do to help yourself make it through a difficult day or plan for a stressful situation. You can easily fill out the plan yourself, but it can't hurt to ask a close friend, partner, supportive colleague, or therapist to help you brainstorm ideas that best work for you!

Questions for reflection

- As a child, what kind of messages did adults teach you about how to deal with anxiety?
- Can you recall a time when you experienced anxiety in school as a child? What was it about that experience that was so anxiety-producing? How did you cope?
- What experiences have you had with helping students with anxiety in the past? What worked? What didn't?
- As an adult, what do you do to manage anxiety? After reading this chapter, are there any new strategies you'd like to try?
- How might you share the information from this chapter with your students in a developmentally appropriate and engaging way?

24

Like a House on Fire

Feelings First Communication

My friend Maria told me the following story one day during the Covid-19 pandemic of 2020. Her story exemplifies an absolutely crucial component of helping others handle tough situations—dealing with their **feelings first**.

> I was upstairs in my bedroom one day when I heard my eight-year-old daughter trying to make her way upstairs carrying her laptop. I heard noises as she started shuffling across the room, dragging the power cord behind her. I heard more commotion and a bit of yelling from my husband, as she almost dropped the laptop. A few minutes later, I heard a loud thump on the stairs as she apparently tripped over the cord. I came to the stairs and found my daughter, Meadow, in a heap at the bottom of the stairs with her laptop and power cord a tangled mess. "What happened?" I asked. I could sense she was trying to hold back her tears. Seconds later, she burst out crying and shouted, "I fell!" I helped her up and led her to my bedroom. Now she was crying very loudly and intensely. I got the sense she was not just crying about the fall, but about something else. I knew I had to take care of the fall and her state of mind first, though, so I said, "You fell. It can be scary and hurt when you fall. Where does it hurt?" Through the tears, she told me and pointed to where it hurt—her foot, her knee, her elbow. She cried softly for a bit more, then suddenly she started to tell me through tears how upset she was about the coronavirus and our quarantine. She had never said anything before that day, but she told me she was sad to miss things that were planned for the summer, and that she felt angry and afraid. I tried my best to respond with compassion and patience. I told her, "Meadow, it's okay to be upset and to have feelings about this."

> I said, "It makes sense to me that you feel so sad." She cried a little harder, then she looked up and said to me, "Mommy, you make me feel so comfortable." It was one of my proudest moments as a mom!

In addition to being a loving and caring mom, a huge part of my friend's success in helping her daughter has much in common with psychiatrist Dan Siegel's **Connect and Redirect** approach to helping children deal with difficult experiences using their whole brain.[1] In this case, it means that when she addressed the emotional content of the situation first ("It can be scary and hurt when you fall"), it helped her daughter calm down and be more open to logically processing what happened. This feelings first communication, as I call it, is one of the most helpful tools you can have in your toolbox when it comes to tantrums, explosive behavior, and meltdowns. It's also an important framework for your loved ones to be familiar with when you come home from a hard day of teaching and just need someone to listen to how you feel.

Right brain and left brain

To summarize Dan Siegel's explanation of this type of communication, here's how it works. As you may know, our brain is divided into two distinct hemispheres—the right and the left—often referred to as the right and left brain. When the right and left brains work together, they keep us happy, healthy, and functioning well on many levels. They also have unique traits that set them apart.

The left brain, for example, is very logical and linear. It focuses on details and words and is analytical and methodical. When you look at a diagram of how a clock works and understand its functioning using logical, mathematical reasoning, you're using your left brain. When you write an essay detailing the timeline of the Civil War, your left brain is happily humming along, putting things in order, and selecting words to formulate your thoughts.

But there is also the right brain to consider. While the left brain is logical and linear, the right brain is experiential, non-verbal, creative, and looks at the big picture instead of small details. It's emotional, tied to our intuition, and loves to be absorbed in images, sensations, and experiences. While the left brain enjoys the logic of how a clock works, the right brain would prefer to be looking at a painting of Dali's melting clocks in *The Persistence of Memory*. Instead of constructing an exact, linear timeline of the Civil War, the right brain would rather compose an instrumental song or interpretative dance that captures the emotions of the time period.

Together, the two sides of our brain help us live happy, meaningful, successful lives. Using only one side or the other would set us off balance. We wouldn't want to miss out on the logic our left brain provides or be too far from the emotions and intuition that dominate our right brain. But an important thing to know when helping individuals through difficult times like meltdowns is that *when we are upset, our emotional right brain must be dealt with before we introduce left-brain logic.*

Because of the stress response and the brain's architecture, it's almost impossible to get others to hear what we say unless they are calm and regulated enough to listen. When they are upset, it's like trying to reason with someone in the middle of an emergency—a house on fire, for example. When we discover they are in a burning house, we, of course, wouldn't think this is the time to start talking about how long they've been smelling smoke or when they last changed the battery in the smoke detector. This is clearly also not the time to talk about fire safety tips and everything they should do to prevent a fire from happening again. We know that there is an emergency happening, and we need to get them to safety first.

Once we've gotten them a certain distance from the fire and made sure they've recovered and are totally okay again, we can start talking more rationally about what happened. If we try to share advice and reason with them in the midst of the raging fire, they will (understandably) struggle to take in what we're saying. They may even resent us for not noticing that there are more pressing matters to attend to!

In real life, this means that we must deal with the emergency of their feelings before we can reason with them. That's when our logical, rational left brain can finally reach their logical left brain.

This is also consistent with trauma expert Bruce Perry's **Neurosequential Model of Therapeutics,**[2] which describes how children must first be regulated (physically stable and not in a stress response state) before they can relate (connect with others) and then finally be able to reason. Here are a few examples of this feelings first approach:

- J'Lynn was having a fabulous time during kindergarten free choice time. She and her two peers had built a space tower out of blocks. When it came time to clean up and put the bricks away, J'Lynn stormed off and stood in a corner. Her teacher, Mr. Blake, knew he needed to connect with her raging right brain first before he could get her to see that her actions weren't acceptable. Kneeling down, he said kindly, "It can be disappointing to have to take apart something you've worked hard on, huh?" J'Lynn nodded slowly. Mr. Blake continued, "That must have been a hard thing to do."

- Ms. C comes home from a hard day of teaching. Her principal has singled her out for running behind on her schedule and has written up an unfavorable evaluation. She is dismayed, frustrated, and crushed that her administrator has not seen all the hard work she has done and focused instead on one negative aspect. When Ms. C comes home, her spouse listens to her carefully. Even though they are tempted to suggest that she speak up for herself—or even quit her job—they instead say, "Wow, that sounds so frustrating. After all the work you've been putting in, that must have been so demoralizing!"
- High school junior Diego is overwhelmed with finals week. Besides keeping up with his soccer practice, he feels anxious about getting a passing grade in pre-calculus. When he complains angrily to his teacher, she resists the urge to tell him that his focus should be solely on academics right now, not athletics. Instead, she focuses on the feelings behind what he is saying: "You must feel like you have so much to juggle right now. It's stressful to have to manage so many demanding tasks all in one week!"

As you can see, the process of connecting with feelings first takes a little bit more time than a simple redirection. In fact, this process requires you to name the emotional nature of the situation (think of the reflective listening statements we discussed in Part 1) and let your words sit for a while before trying to reason with the other person. You might have to be strategic about how you do this in a classroom because you can't take a half-hour to sensitively attend to very minor meltdowns. For example, after Mr. Blake reassures J'Lynn that it is indeed disappointing to have to take apart something she's created, she might shift into a more regulated state. Then he might say, "Remember that we will get to have free choice time again next week, right? Did you know that's coming right up? If you want, I can show you on our calendar when that will be. Would you like that?" or something similar to get her back on track. If she is still not ready, he can reassure her that he is available to talk when she is prepared to, and then move on with whatever else he needs to do. Once she is totally regulated again and her left brain is engaged (this may be quite a bit later, depending on how upset she was), he might even explore alternatives to her behavior with her (including using the *I Got This!* Plan to map out what she can do next time).

You may be wondering what to do if you disagree with how the other person sees things, though. As we mentioned earlier regarding reflective listening statements, it's helpful to remember that validation does not always mean agreement. When we connect with feelings first (or provide reflective listening statements), it doesn't necessarily mean we are saying the other person is right. But we are recognizing some basic rules about how our brains and emotions work. As brain scientist Jill Bolte Taylor writes, "Most of us think of ourselves as thinking creatures that feel, but we are actually feeling creatures that think."[3] The fact that we are *feeling creatures that think* explains why dealing with feelings first is so effective!

So next time you find yourself dealing with someone (yourself included) who is in the throes of difficult emotions, remember to deal with feelings first like the house is on fire. Then, once the fire's out, you can talk calmly about what comes next...

Questions for reflection

- Have you ever had anyone help you through a problem by addressing your feelings first? What happened?
- Can you think of a time when someone tried to reason with you (use your left brain) while your right brain was still swimming in emotions? How did that go? What would you prefer they did? Can you craft a sentence or two they might have said instead that would have been more helpful?
- Can you think of a time when you helped a child by dealing with their feelings first? What happened? Can you think of a time when this approach might have helped? Explain why.
- What, if any, insights about helping children with difficult emotions will you take away from this chapter?
- How might you share the information from this chapter with your students in a developmentally appropriate and engaging way?

25

Stinking Thinking

How Cognitive Distortions Can Lead You Astray

One day, while the students are working in groups, you notice that Amadi has suddenly flounced away from his group and plopped himself angrily down at his desk. When you go over to find out what's going on, he replies angrily with tears in his eyes, "Marquis wouldn't let me take a turn with the markers! Nobody ever lets me have a turn!"

"That's not true!" you want to tell him. Just yesterday, he was happily taking turns with Mauricio and Kim! You know his outburst is happening because he's not seeing things clearly, but you may not know that it's also because he's suffering from something known as a **cognitive distortion**!

Cognitive distortions are habitual ways of thinking that are inaccurate and reinforce unhelpful patterns of thinking and behaving. These are popularly called "stinking thinking" or "mind traps." (There is a child-friendly template, *Steer Clear of Stinking Thinking!*, in the Resources Section to help you explain them to the kids.) There are many different types of cognitive distortions that people can unknowingly fall into. Here are a few:

- **All or nothing thinking:** Also known as "black-and-white thinking" or "polarized thinking," this kind of thinking happens when people over-generalize and condense events and experiences together to come up with some kind of simplified explanation for them. This kind of thinking can be detected when words like "always," "never," "everything," "nothing," "no one," and "everyone" are present. "No one ever wants to hang out with me!" "I never get recognized for my hard work!" "Things never work out for me," and Amadi's "No one ever lets me have a turn" are all examples of black-and-white thinking.

- **Catastrophizing:** Dreading or assuming the worst when faced with a new or unknown experience. Someone who catastrophizes may be afraid of failing a test, for example, because in their mind failing the test means they will also fail out of school. Then they fear they will never be able to get a college degree and will end up living in their parents' basement. Another example would be equating minor aches and pains with a terrible, terminal illness. Or receiving a slightly unfavorable evaluation and assuming that means you're losing your job tomorrow. The fear is that everything will result in a catastrophe. It's about taking a set of circumstances and jumping lickety-split to the worst possible outcome.
- **Personalization:** As the name implies, this means we take personal responsibility for something that doesn't have to do with us. When people see things this way, they believe that what others do is a direct, individually directed reaction to who they are and not to the many other factors likely involved. After teaching a lesson that bombed, for example, you may think the failure is all about you ("I'm not engaging, interesting, or organized enough"), when, in truth, the failure of the lesson also had a lot to do with the students, the material, the time of day, and many other factors.

Do any of these resonate with you? If they do, you're not alone: we all have these types of thinking from time to time. In my experience, they can be a significant contributor to feeling burned out because they have so many insidious and harmful effects on our ways of thinking, feeling, and behaving!

Reality check! Questioning your thoughts

The good news is that once you're aware of cognitive distortions and their pernicious effects, you can free yourself of them! In fact, the practice of questioning your thoughts is a central tenet of Cognitive Behavioral Therapy (CBT), one of the most evidence-based and popular types of therapy used in the United States. Correcting cognitive distortions by questioning the veracity of your thoughts can be done over time, and there are steps you can take to change unhelpful thought patterns. Martin Seligman's life-changing book, *Learned Optimism*, is a great place to start.[1] Here are some ideas to get you started.

1. First, identify when there is a cognitive distortion (stinking thinking) taking place.

2. Try to figure out which cognitive distortion is taking place. You can use the *Steer Clear of Stinking Thinking!* template in the Resources Section to help or Google the many types of "cognitive distortions" and see if you can find one that matches. In the classroom, you might want to teach students the most common ones, then as problems crop up, ask students to identify what kinds of stinking thinking might be at fault!
3. Question the accuracy of the thought as though you were an investigator trying to determine its truthfulness. You might ask, for example: "How do I know this thought is true?" "Is it always true?" "Can I think of examples of times when it wasn't true?" "Might everyone else see it as true?" "What would I say to a friend who was having this thought about themselves?" "Is there another way to look at this?" "Am I taking this personally when it's not personal?" "Can I check the truthfulness of this belief with a trusted friend?"

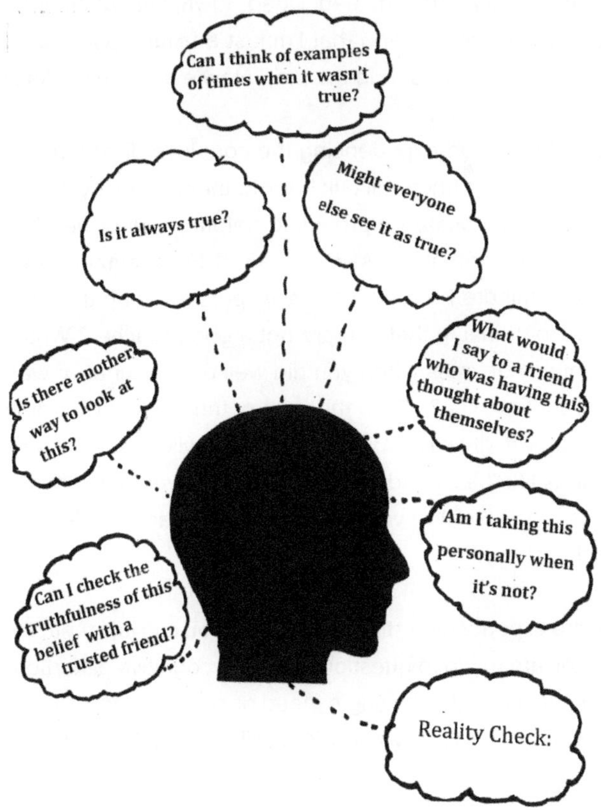

Figure 25.1: Reality check: Are you sure what you are thinking is true?

4. Question the troublesome thought by using the *Prove Me Wrong, Please!* activity described below.

PROVE ME WRONG, PLEASE!

Do you suspect you or someone else has been suffering from a case of stinking thinking? Try this experiment to see if you can get to the truth behind a cognitive distortion.

1. Set out two chairs. Chair #1 will represent the point of view of the cognitive distortion. Chair #2 will be the counter-argument, the (helpful) devil's advocate.
2. The person experiencing the cognitive distortion should sit in Chair #1 and talk aloud about a recent stressful situation in which they may have been having a case of stinking thinking. For example, they might say, "My principal wrote me a negative evaluation. That makes me feel angry and ashamed. Deep down, I am afraid it means I am not a good teacher and that I'm just a failure." Or a student might say, "I didn't get a part in the play! Now everyone thinks I'm a loser. It's a total disaster!"
3. Now the person experiencing the cognitive distortion should sit in Chair #2. Here, they will talk back to themselves by playing the role of devil's advocate by providing helpful, clearer-headed counter-arguments to what was said in Chair #1. For example, they might say, "Wait a minute here. You are over-personalizing this. What is your proof for thinking that you are not a good teacher? What are some examples of times when you did well as a teacher or were praised for your teaching?" Or, in the case of the student who didn't get the part, they might say, "You said everyone will think you're a loser. That sounds like black-and-white thinking. Do you absolutely know that to be true? Would everyone in the world agree? What might they think instead?"

If students are experiencing stinking thinking, you can talk them through this process. If you are trying to question your own cognitive distortions and feel stuck, you might consider inviting a friend or colleague to help you through this and play your devil's advocate. You will be glad they did!

Questions for reflection

- Can you think of a time when you or someone else fell into the trap of "all or nothing" thinking? Catastrophizing? Personalization? What happened?
- What is your reaction to Shakespeare's assertion that "There is nothing either good or bad, but thinking makes it so"?
- Do you think that the material in this chapter might be helpful or interesting to your students? How might you share it with them in a developmentally appropriate and engaging way?

26

Coming to Our Senses about Sensory Differences and Disorders

Just as you need to be aware of the role of anxiety and cognitive distortions in causing meltdowns, another thing to keep your eye out for is students who have sensory differences. So, what exactly are sensory differences?

Have you ever met someone who is always very aware of what music is playing in the background of movies? Or have you ever met anyone who is the first to point out that that color is *just not right on you*, or someone who seems to be especially attuned to the taste, smell, or feel of things? These people may have heightened awareness of sensory input from one or more of our five senses.

Did you also know that input from our five senses, while it can be pleasant and highly calming (relaxing essential oils, classical music, soft fabrics, for example), can also be de-regulating and lead to meltdowns? Why is that?

Let's for a moment reflect on sensory life back when we were babies. Way back then, our little bodies called out for things like movement, rest, water, food, touch, warmth, and coolness. In their effort to take good care of us, our parents tried to meet these needs as best they could. They also probably noticed that when we cried, certain sensory experiences helped calm us down more than others: rocking back and forth, quiet music, soft fabrics, a back rub, a warm bath, etc. (By the way, these preferred sensory experiences might have been different for other babies because they are unique to your particular temperament, genetic make-up, past experiences, etc.) In any case, these sensory-soothing activities were enormously helpful to us as we learned to regulate our emotions and meet our sensory needs. Fast-forward to today. Even though we are no longer babies, we all still seek out behaviors that meet our needs for things that feel good, taste good, sound good, smell good, or are visually pleasing or satisfying. Also, some of us are more tuned in to or repelled by certain sensory stimuli than others.

Many of us are aware that individuals with Autistic Spectrum Disorders have difficulty with sensory input; it's not as apparent that many individuals who *aren't* on the spectrum also have **sensory processing sensitivities and disorders**. In fact, as many as one in six children experience sensory symptoms that interfere with everyday functioning.[1] Many of us experience hyper- and hyposensitivities (over- and under-sensitivities) to different sensory inputs, for example, and these preferences can show up in the classroom.

Suppose an individual is hypersensitive to auditory input, for example. In that case, certain volumes or kinds of noise can be overwhelming to them. They may try to put a buffer between them and the uncomfortable stimulus by putting their fingers in their ears, rocking, humming to themselves in loud places like the recess yard or cafeteria, etc. For individuals with tactile hypersensitivity, they may be bothered by the feel of things (tags on the back of their shirt, chalk, glue on their hands, etc.). They may shrink away from hugs and protest that others are too close to them. On the other hand, hyposensitize individuals crave more stimuli of certain kinds. Depending on which sensory need they are trying to meet, these individuals may fidget, constantly attempt to touch people/textures, stand instead of sit, chew on things, gravitate towards the loudest areas of the playground, accidentally hurt others by unintentionally being too forceful, etc.

Feeling hangry?

Speaking of sensory and physical needs, I confess that I am a mess when I don't get a chance to eat, and this is especially true when I'm teaching. How about you? How well can you focus and stay calm when you're hungry?

Hunger can lead to irritability, and being irritable makes it harder to focus and stay calm. For example, it has been shown that giving children breakfast before school "improves their cognitive or mental abilities, enabling them to be more alert, pay better attention, and to do better in terms of reading, math and other standardized test scores."[2] A study done on judges found that the repeated need to make decisions caused wear and tear on judges' nerves and that they were harsher when they were hungrier.[3] While teachers are not judges, we are certainly called upon to make an incredible number of decisions every day! It makes sense to imagine that we might be likewise impacted and become more punitive when we haven't had a chance to eat.

To keep a lid on hangry behavior in my classroom, I got my principal's permission to give my students a snack mid-morning as they work on their math problem of the day. I have noticed that a couple of little animal cracker cookies make a *huge* difference in both mine and my students' ability to focus and keep it together until lunchtime!

In addition to our five senses, individuals also seek out or avoid stimulus from their proprioceptive and vestibular senses. Our proprioceptive sense has to do with understanding the location and position of our bodies in space. When individuals seek input from their proprioceptive sense, they may do things that help them recover a sense of where they are in space. For example, they may bang books down loudly, bump into objects, lean against people and walls, fall, or stumble frequently. Our vestibular sense refers to our awareness of our body's balance. Sensory-seeking behaviors for this sense include spinning as one walks, twirling around, and rocking in circles.

Because it is likely you will have children with sensory differences in your classroom, it can help to remember that although their behaviors may distract others (or even be socially inappropriate), the child is often completely or partly unaware of it. These sensory differences are very normal for the individual experiencing them. Still, they can become a problem in the classroom, especially when they are disruptive, perceived as weird, or stigmatizing. If you are trying to ascertain whether the behavior is indeed a sensory-seeking behavior, or is motivated by something else, pay attention to how frequently and consistently the behavior occurs. If it happens repeatedly or consistently, even when the child is alone, it's likely a real sensory need and not motivated by something else.

In general, the idea is to recognize that, in many, many cases, sensory-seeking behaviors are not meant to be irritating or bad. Students with sensory differences and disorders are experiencing a normal, natural part of being human—sensory needs—and they are trying to meet them.

How to help with sensory coping strategies in the classroom?

Given how ubiquitous sensory differences are, your classroom likely has children with different sensory needs. So why not meet them where they are? Also, by embedding simple sensory practices, procedures, and routines into your day with all of your students, you can help keep everyone feeling calm and normalize paying attention to sensory sensations. This can help kids start to become aware of times they need to regulate because their bodies are calling out for something and are on the way to a meltdown.

For example, you can:

- Allow students the option to stand at their desks instead of sitting.
- Allow for flexible work stations (e.g., give them a clipboard so they can work somewhere around the room that feels more comfortable).
- Offer noise-cancelling headphones.
- During tests, let students use privacy dividers (or folders propped open on desks) to block out distracting visual stimuli.
- Offer squishy gel seat cushions or other flexible seating options like bean bag chairs or sensory rocking chairs.
- Incorporate bouncy bands (elastic bands placed between the legs of chairs or desks for students to stretch and use their legs and feet).
- Create a sensory path in the hallway where students can crawl, skip, jump, etc. to burn off steam.
- Engage kids in repetitive, rhythmic clapping/drumming activities as brain breaks.
- Incorporate mindfulness/focused awareness/breathing techniques into regular daily routines.
- Make snacks available or find a way to break up long periods before or after lunch with a snack break. This will help reduce "hangry" behaviours.
- Take movement and dance breaks (line dances like the Macarena, Hokey Pokey, Electric Slide, and the Cha-Cha Slide are a big hit in my classroom!).
- Have "fidgets" available like stress balls, flip chains, stretchy strings, spikey balls, magic cubes, etc. Keep them in a basket where students can access as needed, or in a shared basket on tables. You can also use them in Peace Centers (aka Calm Down Corners or Amygdala Reset Centers). You will definitely want to explain that they are "tools not toys," and model and practice your expectations about how and

when to use them. If you wish, you and your students can also make your own stress balls by filling up balloons with four parts baking soda to one part hair conditioner. Decorate with inspiring words like "CALM," "I CAN DO IT!" or a favorite emoji.

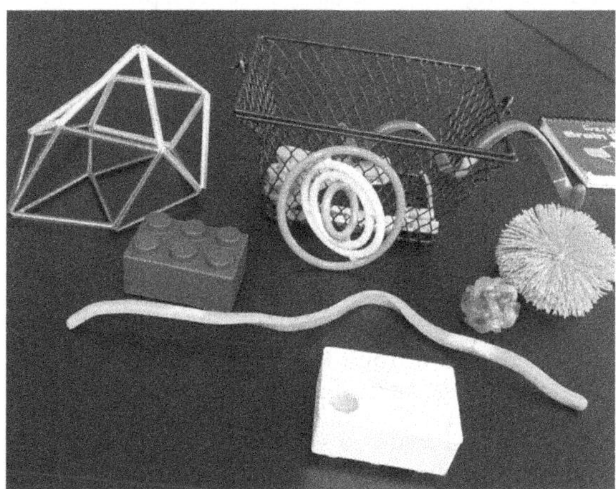

Figure 26.1: Classroom fidgets can help keep fidgeting hands busy

- Have a specially designated place in the room (a quiet spot away from the group) where students can go to hum, rock, pace, or rest quietly when needed without distracting others.
- Have sensory tools in your Cool Down/Calm/Peace Corner (also called an Amygdala Reset Station). They can also have a "sensory to-go bag" or fanny pack to carry around for this purpose. You can find more information about how to create a Peace Center in the section *Other Tips for Dealing with Trauma-Impacted Behavior* in Chapter 17.
- Do left- and right-brain tasks—great to connect both hemispheres of the brain. They are addictive!
  - **Pat your head and rub your stomach** at the same time. Switch sides.
  - **Are you winking at me?** Wink with your left eye, tap with your right foot, switch sides, repeat, and increase your speed!
  - **Eyebrow nose switcharoo:** Put your right hand on your left eyebrow and your left hand on your nose. Now switch by putting your right hand on your nose and your left hand on your right eyebrow. Keep switching, alternating between your two eyebrows and your nose. Go faster and faster!

- **Up and down and left and right:** Students sit at desks. (They may need to lean back in their chair so they can move their legs in the air under their desks) Move the left foot up and down, and the right foot side to side at the same time!

Helpful items for a sensory cool down corner or "sensory to-go bags"

- Sequined pillows
- Hand warmers
- Heating pads
- Mints
- Hand lotion
- Bottles of cold water
- Weighted blanket
- Squeezy balls
- Velcro strips
- Scented chapsticks
- Soft and rough fabrics
- Clay or Play-Doh
- Coloring books
- Dry erase markers/board

Questions for reflection

- Can you identify anyone in your life who might have sensory processing differences or a sensory processing disorder? What special sensitivities do these people have?
- Do you identify with having any special sensory differences yourself? What kind of impact have they had on your daily life? The decisions you make? As a child, to what degree did your teachers accommodate your sensory needs in the classroom and school?
- How might the information in this chapter influence how you view certain members of your class?
- How might you share the information from this chapter with your students in a developmentally appropriate and engaging way?

27

Highly Sensitive People

Even though your colleagues find solace in catching up in the staff lounge, do you often find that you prefer to spend your lunch break alone in your classroom, away from the constant noise and stimulation? Do you feel the need to sit in a dark, quiet room after school to detox from the overwhelming amount of stimuli? Just like students, many teachers are bothered by the fluorescent lighting, loud noises, constant social interactions, and other sensory stimuli so common in schools. But why are only some of us overwhelmed by stimuli? Is there something wrong with us, or could it be that nothing is wrong and we are just what is known as highly sensitive people?

The term **highly sensitive person (HSP)** was coined by psychologists Elaine and Arthur Aron and explained in their ground-breaking book, *The Highly Sensitive Person.*[1] HSPs account for roughly 15–20 percent of the population, whose nervous systems are biologically more sensitive to life's subtleties and who process information more deeply than others. Because of this highly sensitive nature, HSPs commonly have a heightened response to pain, caffeine, hunger, and loud noises and are more susceptible to stress. They can also be more creative, insightful, and empathetic than the average bear because they are so sensitive to what is happening around them. They can struggle with time pressure and absorb other people's emotions. They abhor violence and viscerally react to movies, especially scary ones, as though they were actually happening.

Being a HSP is not a disorder; rather, it's a trait that makes some people more sensitive to different kinds of stimuli. However, because not everyone functions this way, others may tell HSPs that something is wrong with them, that certain things shouldn't bother them, and that they need to toughen up. Actually, all HSPs need to do is realize that they have an increased sensitivity of their nervous system, which is perfectly common and normal.

Because highly sensitive people have such rich inner lives, they often become some of the world's greatest artists, poets, performers, writers, and so on. That's because they have the superpower (and the potential Achilles' heel) of feeling things deeply. It would make sense to assume that individuals like Mahatma Gandhi, Mother Teresa, and Vincent Van Gogh were all HSPs. Because of their increased sensitivity to injustice, the world is a better place!

Do you think that you might be an HSP? Here are some helpful tips:

- Remember, there is *nothing* wrong with you just because you need time and space apart to calm down after a day of teaching. If the data is correct and 15–20 percent of the world's population is highly sensitive, you are not alone in wanting to go home and stare at a blank wall!
- Try to be aware of situations in which your senses are getting overloaded.
- If you are sensitive to them, you probably know that you benefit from avoiding caffeine, violent or scary movies, and loud and stressful people and situations.
- Consider talking to your family and loved ones about this part of you. It might make it easier for them to understand you and others. If you share information about HSPs with students, it might also be a doorway to helping them understand themselves and accepting their unique nature and special gifts.
- Read up about it. Knowledge is power!

Questions for reflection

- Can you identify anyone in your life who might be a HSP?
- What special sensitivities do these people have?
- Have these people ever been told they were too sensitive? How did that make them feel?
- How might the information in this chapter influence how you view certain members of your class? Is there any one student, in particular, that might benefit from this information?
- How might you share the information from this chapter with your students in a developmentally appropriate and engaging way?

28

When You're Always Here

An Overview of Burnout

One holiday season, my former principal did something extraordinary for our staff. As we gathered in the lunchroom for our last meeting before winter break, we noticed that lined up on a cafeteria table were individually wrapped bottles of champagne with pretty little bows tied around each one. Looking out at us, our principal said, "These bottles are for each one of you, to express my appreciation for all you do. I know that you are here working at 2 am, you're here at 5 am, you're here at 9 o'clock at night, and on Sundays." We looked around in confusion, wondering which one of us kept such crazy hours. "I know that you are here, because you're always *here* mentally," she said. "That's why, this winter break, I don't want you to be *here* for one minute. Drink the champagne, enjoy your friends and family, and don't think about this place at all. That way, you will be able to come back refreshed and ready to go!"

What my very wise and caring principal was getting at was the painful reality of how consuming teaching can be and how, without opening the pressure valve from time to time to escape from the relentless demands, even the best of us can burn out. Here are a few important pieces of the burnout puzzle.

First, here's a view of burnout from a relationship-based, trauma-informed perspective. As you may know, human beings are social animals, and that means our moods are contagious. This is especially problematic for educators working with at-risk students, as they are frequently called on to help students self-regulate. To co-regulate (help others with difficult emotions), teachers themselves must be regulated enough to "share our calm, not join their chaos," in the words of L.R. Knost.[1] However, this can be challenging due to the intense social, emotional, and cognitive demands and institutional conditions in schools. An important 2016 study found that teacher burnout and student stress levels may be linked, meaning that students' stress levels were contagious to teachers and vice versa.[2]

You might also find it interesting that in their 2019 book, *Burnout,* Emily and Amelia Nagoski argue that it is not so much the stressors themselves that cause us to suffer and burn out.[3] It's the fact that we never allow ourselves to fully process the emotions we're feeling so we can come out on the other side. They write that this avoidance of our feelings results from societal pressures, especially on women who have been made to feel that it is their moral obligation to take care of everyone else's needs before their own. Sound familiar?

Let it flow!

Since emotions and the stress response are experienced in our bodies, Emily and Amelia Nagoski argue in their 2019 book, *Burnout*, that we need to work through our emotions and let them come to their natural conclusion instead of trying to throw more self-care strategies at them (which also prevents organizational systems from realizing that they can't just keep piling on work while demanding their employees do more self-care to cope!). Instead, according to the authors' theory, we can stay healthy and happy by simply allowing ourselves to complete the stress cycle (think fight, flight, or freeze). They recommend certain activities that help take the focus away from the stressors themselves (since they are largely out of your control) and instead focus on what you can control, letting the physiology of your emotions move through you so you can return to a sense of safety. Some of the techniques they recommend are exercise, breathing, positive social interactions with others, laughter, crying, and creative self-expression (art, music, journaling, etc.). They also recommend connecting with others, especially physical affection and long hugs with loved ones!

What happens to us and our bodies as a result of so much stress? As you may recall from earlier in the book, when we feel stressed, the stress response turns on, and adrenaline and cortisol go up, along with our blood pressure. Our bodies can handle normal cycles of this, but staying in this state of chronically elevated stress negatively affects many systems in our body, including the endocrine, immune, cardiovascular, and digestive systems.

So what can we do? While we wait and fight for institutional and societal conditions to change and learn to take care of teachers, how do we prevent burnout? One crucial strategy is to learn how our students are impacted by trauma and how we, as teachers, are impacted by their trauma and by our own!

Letters from the Principal

I once worked for a principal named Debora Carrera, who did something incredible to keep our staff motivated and positive. Each morning, in the school office, right next to the paper where we signed in each day, she'd lay a handwritten note for all the teachers and staff. It was always directed to us and always had a kind word of encouragement. One day it would say, "Teachers, I am so proud of you. Thank you for your amazing work" Or, "You're the best teachers in the city. You make such a difference each day!" and so on. Even on days when I was tired and discouraged, it always brightened my mood! What a simple gesture it was, yet it meant so much to know all our hard work and sacrifice was seen and appreciated!

Questions for reflection

- In your opinion, what three words or adjectives describe your school's administration's stance on teacher burnout?
- Thinking about emotional contagion, can you recall a time when someone else's emotions rubbed off on you? Or the other way around? What happened?
- What strategies do you use to keep your emotions separate from those of others around you?
- As we've mentioned in this chapter, authors Emily and Amelia Nagoski argue that women have been made to feel that it is their moral obligation to take care of everyone else's needs before their own. Does this statement ring true with your experience? Why or why not?

29

There's a Name for This?

Dealing with Vicarious Trauma

A few years into my teaching career, I stepped into the position of a substitute teacher who had left mid-year. Tellingly, she was the fifth substitute teacher who had left the position that year. There were constant fights in and around my new school; guns and adult gang members often drifted into the school, and mice ran all over. Children often peed in the hall because bathrooms were often kept locked to prevent vandalism. It was a horrible place to be as a teacher and even more so as a student, I imagine. But the stories I heard from the children about their lives outside school were the worst part of all. Despite their undeniable aliveness and charm, my students' neighborhoods also had loads of crime, poverty, and gun violence. I regularly heard about shootings in the neighborhood, robberies at gunpoint, gangs, and drive-by acts of violence. I felt guilty leaving the neighborhood each evening because at least in my neighborhood I didn't have to hear gunshots on my block at night or fear for my life as my students did. I also remember the stress from my job was so bad that I told my boyfriend at the time that I needed a scheduled hour after school every day to just cry before we could meet up and spend time together! He must have thought I was crazy. But I wasn't crazy; I was actually just suffering from **vicarious trauma**, also known as **secondary traumatic stress**, or **compassion/empathy fatigue**.

Vicarious trauma is a well-known and common reaction to working with traumatized individuals. Think about it. Working closely with at-risk children means being in close proximity to traumatic stories and circumstances, including poverty, grief, family problems, racism, drug abuse, and so on. Hearing about these things day after day can take a toll. It may help to know that teachers are not alone in dealing with it. Other people in helping professions like emergency medical technicians (EMTs), social workers, child welfare workers, and other professionals working closely with trauma-impacted individuals also commonly suffer from vicarious trauma. So how do you know if you are suffering from vicarious trauma?

Vicarious trauma symptoms are similar to those of post-traumatic stress disorder, but may not be as severe. When you are suffering from vicarious trauma, you may feel physically, mentally, and/or emotionally worn out. Here is a short list of other symptoms:

- withdrawing from others
- inability to focus
- feeling hopeless
- feeling inexplicably irritable, angry, or numb
- insomnia
- having dreams about students' traumas
- eating too little or too much
- increased irritability with students
- hair-trigger responses to things
- lack of interest or pleasure in things that used to interest you.

Recognizing these symptoms is an excellent first step. It's also important to know that if you are experiencing any of these symptoms, it doesn't mean you are weak or don't have what it takes to be a teacher. We're not teacher-bots who can stand up to anything and everything! We're living, breathing, feeling human beings! As such, we care about others, and this caring can hurt. But while it's sometimes called "the cost of caring," vicarious trauma doesn't have to be the price you pay. Here are some tips to help prevent vicarious trauma from taking a high toll on you, your health, your family, and your quality of life.

- Form or join teacher support groups or make time for discussion during professional learning communities to talk about teaching's mental health challenges. It's crucial to realize that you are not alone; others are also struggling with the same issues. This will help to normalize your challenges and remind you that (a) it's not personal, and (b) you're not alone. A teacher support group such as "The Happy Teacher Revolution" can be, well, revolutionary.

- Self-care. I should confess that I am loath to name self-care on this list for two reasons. One, there are LOADS of books already written about this topic and I can't hope to capture their important content in a quick bullet point. Two, because just telling teachers to "take care of themselves" lets school administrations off the hook too easily for giving teachers excessive amounts of work. At some point, administrations need to stop using self-care as a convenient work-around for giving teachers ridiculous amounts of work. Period.

  Still, I'm including self-care on my list because, in my experience, self-care certainly helps keep teachers sane. Some popular helpful self-care strategies that I have found to be helpful are yoga, exercise, getting together with friends, going to therapy, journaling, drawing, and doing things totally unrelated to the classroom. You can also branch out and try techniques like tapping (aka Emotional Freedom Technique), rolfing, reiki, and acupuncture. Maybe buy yourself flowers—studies show that they can boost mental health.[1] Take your sick days, take your personal days, do what you need to do to take care of the whole you. It's true what they say: *you can't pour from an empty cup*, so make sure you fill your own cup up from time to time!
- Make changes at your school or find a school that is a happier fit for you. Yes, sometimes, that means leaving a job that is making you unhappy. In the above story, I did eventually quit (after trying to organize a group of teachers, providing the superintendent with a list of all my concerns, and writing letters to the paper and the president!). I learned that while it's important to be there for our students, sometimes it can become unhealthy. If your administration is unable to provide strong leadership and you are consistently sad, sick, tired, and overwhelmed, it may be time to get out and find a school that is a better fit for you and your health.
- Have a ritual to separate your workday from your home life. Change your clothes, take a shower, wash your hands, leave your bag in the entranceway, turn off your computer and phone, go for a walk. Anything that signals that the worries and cares of your workplace stay at work where they belong.

How much is it worth to you?

The next time you notice you are worrying too much about managing misbehavior or other stressors in your life, consider:

- If my available energy and happiness today were a $1 bill, how many cents would I want to spend on this situation? How much do I want to save for myself, my friends and family, and activities after school?
- Draw a whole circle to represent your available energy and happiness today. Now, use your pencil to carve out a slice to show how much of the circle you are handing over to a current stressful event. Are you happy with this amount? What are the costs to your family, friends, and your health? Draw a second circle to show how much of the circle you would *like* to hand over to worrying about this situation. Compare the two circles you've drawn. What actions can you take today that will shrink this worry down to the right size?

Questions for reflection

- Have you ever felt "burned out"? What happened?
- Do you know anyone who has burned out? What happened?
- How do you explain why teachers burn out?
- Do you know anyone who has experienced vicarious trauma? Explain.
- What rituals do you use to help separate your work and home life? What about others at your school? Make a list of your favorite strategies.
- How connected and supported do you feel by other teachers? To what extent do you express your support for other teachers? Do you have any ideas of practical ways teachers you work with could uplift and support one another?
- Is there any information from this chapter that you think you'd like to share with teachers who are at risk of burning out/experiencing vicarious trauma?

30

One of These Things Is Not Like the Others

Avoiding the Negativity Bias

As we continue to examine our mental health as teachers, it's worth returning to the topic of cognitive distortions. Let's consider one of the cognitive distortions that come into play every time we look around.

To show you what I mean, take a look at the image below (Figure 30.1). What jumps out at you?

Figure 30.1: What jumps out at you?

I bet it's the light-colored egg. Why did you notice that first? It's likely because of something called the **negativity bias**. The negativity bias is the brain's persistent tendency to see what is different, wrong, or out of place first. Millions of years ago, our brains evolved to notice when things were out of place to cue us to possible danger. A shape that didn't match the other forms in the forest could signal a predator, for example, or food that smelled just a little different could be spoiled and make us sick. Our ancestors' survival depended on paying attention to subtle details like these. Even though we now pay attention to mostly non-life-threatening details, we are still wired to pick up on these inconsistencies first and dwell on them longer.

That means, for example, that while we may have 24 students working diligently, our attention immediately goes to the two who are goofing around in the back of the room. In our evaluation, our principal or supervisor mentions several things that we did well, but we obsess over the one "area of growth" they pointed out. Although 21 of our 24 students remembered to hang up their backpacks, we can't help but zero in on the three who left theirs trailing on the floor. These are examples of the negativity bias at work!

Negativity bias can be particularly nefarious because, as humans, our emotions are highly contagious, and that contagion can leave us feeling stressed.[1] Similarly, in my experience, too much focus on what's going wrong can be transferred by association to your students, who will start to build a similar narrative in their heads. Each time they see something go wrong, they will quickly zero in on it as further evidence of how bad everything is. Things can get very toxic pretty quickly! So how can we fight back against negativity bias?

- For one week, try keeping a jar of pom-poms (those fluffy little balls used for art projects) to keep track of *any* positive moments in the classroom (instead of marbles, which are noisy!). In addition to keeping track of when students follow the rules and answer questions correctly, start keeping track of smiles, laughter, and acts of kindness, too. At the end of the week, count up how many you've got and reward yourself and your students with a feel-good prize like some free time, a dance party, or a fun game you all enjoy.
- Designate each Friday as "Friendly Friday" and put positive, encouraging sticky notes on or in students' desks (especially appreciated by older students who may prefer to be praised privately). Or do this any day of the week!
- Tell students you have selected a "Secret Student of the Day." At the end of the day, share only the positive things that you saw that one student do. Your students will be so excited because the secret student could be anyone and will be on their best behavior. It will also shift your focus to what is going well!
- Assign each student their own "Secret Student of the Day" to keep an eye on. At the beginning of the day, assign them randomly (I use popsicle sticks) and give them each a sticky note to keep track of

positive things that their secret student did during the day. Share the sticky note out loud and exchange them at the end of each day.

"Oh, no! I got that kid in my class?!!" Reframing challenging kids

Another way negativity bias can show up in the classroom has to do with how we see difficult kids, especially the *very* difficult ones. The school community often thinks about these kids in terms of the worst thing they ever did. ("He's the one that did *what*?!!") But remember, as the saying goes, we are not only as bad as the worst thing we've ever done, we're also as good as the best thing we've ever done. So when you find out you have a notoriously difficult kid on your class list this year, try to avoid seeing them only from a deficit model and instead reframe how you view them.

When we reframe something, we **change how we think about what we see, think, and experience**. This is a powerful strategy for good mental health. So in a classroom, while a troublesome behavior or situation may ultimately be in the student's control and not yours, what you can control is your attitude and reaction to them. It has been my experience that reframing how I see difficult students ends up changing the way I see them. Mysteriously, it also seems to positively change the way the student acts (maybe because they are changing to match my new perception of them). As my mentor used to say, "Change the way you see it, and what you see will change."

There are several ways to reframe a difficult student. Here are some helpful reframes inspired by the book *Raising Your Spirited Child* by Mary Sheedy Kurcinka.[2]

- *Stubborn*—Determined
- *Wild*—Free-spirited
- *Fussy*—Discriminating tastes
- *Rigid*—Structured, heightened sense of order
- *Manipulative*—Feels more comfortable when they are in control
- *Nosey*—Curious/social
- *Talkative*—A people person/social
- *Shy*—Has a rich inner world
- *Hyper*—Excited about life, vibrant
- *Spacey or "Out there"*—Visionary
- *Clingy*—Can receive comfort from others
- *Disorganized*—Creative

You can also reframe students by enlisting the help of your colleagues. Seek out colleagues who have had a positive relationship with this student to get a more rounded-out viewpoint. If possible, watch them in action. What tone of voice and attitude do they adopt that make them so successful with this student? Avoid talking about this student with those teachers you know will only get you further down in the dumps about this kid.

Can't find anyone with something good to say? Consider approaching the leading expert on that child—their parent or care-taker! They may have more positive things to share, and this can help you shift your lens towards a sunnier view of the student. Introduce yourself as their child's teacher, tell them you know that this child may have had a difficult time in the past, but you want to make sure this year is different. You may want to ask:

- Can you tell me about _________'s strengths?
- What's your favorite story about _______?
- When you think of __________, what are you most proud of?
- What is something that you wish more people knew about _______?

It can also be helpful to say:

- It's important to me to help students manage their feelings when things get tough. Does _______ ever have trouble staying calm at home? What kinds of things tend to trigger them?
- What strategies have you used to help them calm down? What works?
- When _______ is having a hard day, what's the best way to help?
- To the extent that you feel like sharing, were there any events in _______'s life when they were younger that might be helpful for me to know about?
- Are there any new changes at home that might be helpful for me to know about?
- Is there anything else you want me to know about _______?

If a parent agrees to answer these questions for you, really make them feel appreciated; after all, they are giving you valuable insight into their child that it would be difficult to find elsewhere. It might be exactly what you need to reframe a difficult student, and that can make all the difference to your year!

Questions for reflection

- Do you think you have ever experienced negativity bias? Explain.
- Can you think of a time when a student in your class may have been sucked into the negativity bias?
- Can you think of a time when an administrator experienced negativity bias? How might you explain the information in this chapter to them in a way they would be open to?
- How might you share the information from this chapter with your students in a developmentally appropriate and engaging way?

31

I Thought So!

Watching Out for Confirmation and Implicit Bias

This desire to categorize what we see around us and tell stories about it is part of how our brains are wired. The dangerous tendency to overly categorize things is at the root of two brain biases to be on the lookout for in our classrooms: confirmation bias and implicit bias.

Confirmation bias is our tendency to look for, find, and interpret information in a way that is consistent with what we already believe. In his book, *The Black Swan*, Nassim Nicholas Talib shares the example that swans were once universally thought to only come in one color—white. Every time anyone saw a white swan, that sighting only unconsciously confirmed their belief that all swans were white. Imagine the surprise when black swans were found in Australia!

Another example of confirmation bias is the way we seek out news and social media that only confirm our political preferences. We read social media posts shared by friends who have the same political views, and we seek out media and news outlets that echo our way of seeing the world. Each time we see an event or listen to a political commentary that is interpreted in the same way we already think, it only confirms that what we think must be true. But it also skews how we see the world because it tilts us towards what we already believe and disregards conflicting information about what's really happening.

So, how might this sneaky bias be showing up in your classroom? Consider the following example:

> One day, Ms. G gets a new student in her classroom named Simon. On his first day, while Ms. G is reading to the whole group, she notices that Simon has walked over to the computer and has started to look for *Star*

Wars pictures on Google. "Hmmm..." she thinks. The next day, Simon refuses to begin his work and instead starts ripping papers off the wall.

"Oh no!" thinks Ms. G.

A new neural network is starting to form in Ms. G's brain: "Simon is a kid who causes problems." Every time Simon's behavior catches her eye, this belief is confirmed, thanks to the confirmation bias. Soon, the neurons in Ms. G's brain start to fire off an automatic chain of thoughts every time Simon does anything:

"What's Simon doing out of his seat? I think Simon is a kid who causes problems..."

Quickly becomes:

"What's Simon doing out of his seat? He must be causing problems!"

Because of what she has come to believe about Simon, whenever Ms. G sees Simon doing anything out of the ordinary, she may default to previously confirmed beliefs about him (maybe made worse by negative reports from other teachers).

When we believe that students are difficult, we reinforce this belief by finding examples of it over and over, thereby confirming what we believe to be true. Unfortunately, this means we might assume that misbehavior is happening when it is not. For example, Simon could be out of his seat because he is making his way to the trashcan or going to pick up his glasses off the floor. What's important to know is that incidents of behavior that seem out of place can too quickly confirm our bias. As we've discussed, disruptive behaviors can quickly trigger a stress response in us, and the constant triggering and retriggering of the stress response can lead to exhaustion and frustration!

Implicit bias and race

Another way that confirmation bias shows up in the classroom has to do with who we choose to discipline, how we do it, and why. Negative messages from various media communicate negative stereotypes about people of color, which can result in **implicit bias** (unconscious attitudes and stereotypes that impact behavior) that make their way into our classrooms. As a result of living in an inequitable society, it's safe to assume that all have some degree of implicit bias. This bias is in addition to confirmation bias (which can keep many thinking patterns alive).

Implicit bias around race creates unfair disparities in the classroom. More specifically, research has shown that Black children are disproportionately disciplined and more likely to be suspended for minor discretionary offenses.[1] This is especially unfair given that research has consistently shown that, despite stereotypes to the contrary, Black students do not have higher rates of misconduct than other students.[2,3] As you think about students who may be reluctant to warm up to teachers, it's worth considering that these children may fear that their teachers might single them out unfairly because of their race, as previous teachers have done.

What can you do to both challenge confirmation bias and get at the harmful roots and effects of implicit bias?

- Take a copy of your class list. Without thinking much about each student, write down the first word that comes to your head about them. Then ask yourself, is my perception about this student true all the time? Have there been times when it wasn't? Is this child this way in every classroom and situation?
- Use the Classroom Relationship Map from Chapter 13 to take a look at your implicit bias. What patterns do you see in the race of students closest to you? What role might other implicit biases play? Do you notice a preference or aversion to students of a particular gender, sexual orientation, academic ability, or economic status?
- What are the racial backgrounds of your students? Try substituting the name of a race into the blanks in the following sentences and then complete the sentences with the first thought that comes to mind. What do you notice?
  - "_________ people are..."
  - "The things that are important to _________ people are..."
  - "In school, _________ people are..."
  - "I trust/don't trust _________ people because..."
  - "I am afraid of _________ people because..."
- Look again at how you answered the above questions. Did any patterns stick out? How might unconscious beliefs about these groups influence interactions with them, for better or worse?
- Provide feedback that communicates high expectations. That might mean giving a student feedback on an essay by saying, "Here is my feedback. I am providing it to you because I believe in you, and I know you can make this essay great," instead of, "Here is my feedback. I'm providing it to you so you can fix it and return it."

Questions for reflection

- Think about your favorite students. Can you detect any confirmation bias in the way you think about their behavior, interact with them, or evaluate their work?
- Think about your most challenging students. Can you detect any confirmation bias in the way you think about their behavior, interact with them, or evaluate their work?
- Think back to the school you attended as a child. Can you remember examples of implicit bias?
- How do you see implicit bias currently playing a role at your school?
- Do you feel safe discussing the role of implicit bias at your school with colleagues and administrators? Why or why not?
- What might be a small first step in reversing or at least uncovering implicit bias in your classroom tomorrow? In your school?

32

Room to Breathe

The Practice of Mindfulness

Do you ever lie down and look up at the sky on a beautiful day? Clouds drift by in the silence of the sky, carried along by a soft breeze. Clusters of birds mix and meander or crisscross the vast blue sky while the sun creeps slowly from one horizon to the other. A lot is happening as you watch from your place in the grass. But you are unconcerned, content to let all these events come to pass. The clouds changing shape, the birds choosing their own course, the sun moving determinedly westward; you are aware of it all, but none of it bothers you. Instead, you experience a peaceful awareness of the present moment, a state known as mindfulness.

What does it mean to be mindful? Mindfulness, which has roots in Buddhism, has become a very popular secular practice in recent years. It can be thought of as tuning fully into the present moment with focused awareness and acceptance. No wonder the practice of mindfulness has been known to revolutionize educators' experience of the classroom. In our work, we are constantly called on to *do*, act, and make things happen. We are so accustomed to putting out fire after fire that one of the job's occupational hazards is that we find it hard to sit still, even when we're not working! We feel the need to be in constant motion.

To make matters worse, the compulsion to do things is part of our culture. Think about it: when we meet someone new, to assess who they *are,* we want to know what they *do.* We think that if we are ever caught not doing anything, something must be wrong! But this compulsive doing can drive us crazy, and we need to find time to just stop and rest. Even plants which spend the daylight hours photosynthesizing take time out to simply rest and let the fruits of their labor sink in. Practicing mindfulness is like learning to be a plant, taking time to be in the present moment.

This all may sound a bit new-age, but the mental and physical benefits of mindfulness have been empirically demonstrated by many researchers. For example, mindfulness has been shown to:[1]

- lower high blood pressure
- reduce psychological distress
- decrease symptoms of anxiety and depression
- reduce feelings of anger/hostility
- improve our ability to cope with stressful situations.

In addition, a ground-breaking study led by researcher Patricia Jennings[2] (one of my personal heroines!) provided teachers with a program focusing on mindfulness, stress reduction, and emotional skills. This study found that these interventions reduced teachers' feelings of stress and time urgency (the feeling you have to get things done *now*) and teachers also reported being better able to manage their emotions. Not surprisingly, this mindfulness-based program also was found to improve overall classroom climate and productivity!

What is the science behind mindfulness? Mindfulness works because it activates the parasympathetic nervous system, which puts the body and mind into a state of rest and repair (the opposite of the stress response). On a neurological level, mindfulness builds neurons in the prefrontal cortex (the thinking brain), allowing for more self-awareness, creativity, compassion, and tranquility.

Mindfulness also enables us to become observers of our own thoughts and feelings. Being an observer means not judging or condemning whatever thought pattern, emotional experience, and ups-and-downs run through our minds throughout the day. For example, in the story above, you were likely aware of all that was passing through the sky, the sounds, sights, and sensations; still, you were also bigger and wiser, both in touch with the world and separate from it. You were an observer of your own experience.

Being an observer just means that—we notice our thoughts and emotions as they arise. It's like noticing a butterfly fluttering around in your flower beds outside. You are interested, but not particularly attached to what it's doing (you don't get angry, for example, if it decides to fly up or down or left or right). You're just watching what's happening in each moment with acceptance and interest.

One way of practicing mindfulness is to use this observer to cultivate acceptance and awareness of our everyday experiences in a loving, courageous way. American Tibetan Buddhist nun, Pema Chodron, says that instead of running away from the present moment, we should stay rooted to it and its many emotions and experiences, no matter how painful. This reversing of our age-old instinct to run away from pain leads us to greater peace and a clearer understanding of our humanity and the nature of reality. "This very moment is the perfect teacher," she writes, "and lucky for us, it's with us wherever we are."[3] So, mindfulness is not an exotic activity or about going to sit on a far-off mountain—it's about fully showing up for our lives, day by day, moment by moment.

Mindfulness and me

My own experiences with mindfulness began when a friend challenged me one summer to take part in a month-long, daily yoga practice. Over the course of the month, as each day went by, I noticed that not only was I getting in better shape physically, but my thought processes seem to be shaping up as well. Throughout the day, whether I was washing dishes or walking around town, I began to notice that there was a constant stream of commentary running through my head. I simultaneously realized that another part of me was watching this commentary. Sometimes this observer would have something to say about the arising thought. "Well, that's not a very helpful thought," it would say, or, "Well, that was an interesting reverie." That introduction to mindfulness was the beginning of a life-long practice that I have turned to over and over throughout the years.

One of the first things you will notice when you start to practice mindfulness is that becoming mindful is a really tricky process! It involves reversing many habitual ways of being in the world, especially the habit of continually thinking. It's normal to have other thoughts when we try to practice mindfulness. "Why am I doing this?" "Am I getting this right?" "My feet hurt." "What's for dinner?" This is just what our mind does. Our heart beats, our lungs breathe, our liver filters out toxins. Our brain thinks, processes, wonders, ruminates, imagines, and a million more things. It is rare to ever be fully present in the here and now. Our brain is usually off on errands to the past, where it can re-experience and ruminate on what has already happened, or it may be running ahead to possible storylines concerning the future.

As we've said, mindfulness requires us to stop this pattern of constantly being somewhere else. It requires letting storylines go so that we can clearly see what's happening. It requires softening, slowing down, and relaxing into the present moment.

Given how much urgency we feel to get things done, slowing down can be a very difficult thing for us teachers to do! Who has time to slow down when our demands feel like a never-ending snowstorm that you keep trying to shovel out from under?!! Each time you look up into the sky, hoping that it's finally time to put the shovel down and relax by the fire, you see there is more snow on the way. Thinking we can keep up with shoveling would be madness! Instead, what if you just decided to stop from time to time? What if you instead decided to stop to enjoy the bright white snowflakes whisking around your head, floating down in perfect timing? This is the kind of sanity that mindfulness can offer us.

You've already arrived: Try this!

Next time you feel a sense of needing to get things done (lesson plans turned in, testing done, emails checked, grades submitted, etc.), try this. Find somewhere in your house or the back of your classroom to stand still for a moment. Fix in your eyes on a spot about ten feet away that you would like to reach. Now lift your foot and take a step towards that goal. Now slowly step forward with your other foot. Continue to walk in this manner, but as you do, notice your desire to get from here to there, to get the task done. As you walk, see if you can cultivate the sensation in your body that at every moment you've already arrived. With each step, pause and sit deeply with the experience of being exactly where you already are. Go ahead, try it. What does it feel like to know that there is nowhere else to go, that with each step, you've already arrived?

HOW TO PRACTICE MINDFULNESS MEDITATION

1. Find a chair or cushion to sit on. It should be even, not tilted forwards or backward. Cross your legs comfortably in front of you, or put both feet flat on the floor if you are sitting in a chair.
2. Sit upright with a strong back and an open front. If you are in a chair, try not to lean back in your chair. Sit in a relaxed, upright position with an attitude of openness and dignity.
3. Rest your hands face up or face down on your thighs. You may want to experiment with both to see which feels best to you.
4. Your eyes can be open or closed. If you leave them open, direct your gaze downwards to a spot on the floor a few feet in front of you. If you close your eyes and find you get sleepy or drowsy, you might want to experiment with leaving them halfway open.
5. Once you're comfortably settled into your seat, begin to notice the rise and fall of your breath. You may notice the expansion and contraction of your belly and chest, or the in and out of your breath through your nose.
6. Pay attention to your breath, with no need to control it or breathe in any particular way.
7. Follow your breath with your attention. You will notice that each breath is unique as it comes in and out.
8. When you find your mind wandering, gently and non-judgmentally bring it back, over and over again, to the sensation of your breath moving in and out of your body. As you notice thoughts, feelings, fears, memories, or anything else arising, just label them as "thoughts," and kindly but firmly move your awareness back to experiencing the breath.

A sip of mindfulness

Stopping to pause and be fully present is an entirely different way of being in the world than we're accustomed to. But at the same time, we don't need to go anywhere new or buy any fancy equipment to try it out. We can experience it at any time. Let's try another experiment to see what happens when we practice being fully present. To do it, you'll need a glass of water. Got one? Let's try this together.

Place a glass of water somewhere within arm's reach in front of you with the intention to pick it up and take a sip of water. But before you jump into action, slow down. Pay attention to the feeling of your hand beginning to move up in space to grab the glass. Go nice and slow. Maybe you feel the bending of your elbow joint and the muscles in your bicep starting to engage. Perhaps you feel a soft contact with the air as your arm moves through space towards the glass. Can you notice the temperature of the air on the skin of your hand and arm as they reach through space? As your fingers reach for the glass, can you notice the joints bending and grasping? Can you notice how your hand seems to know what to do already? Do you notice the texture of the glass? Does it feel smooth, or do you sense indentations in it? What is the temperature and texture of the glass in your fingers and on your lips? Cool and polished? Something else? Can you feel the water filling your mouth before you swallow? How does it taste? Is it warm or cool? Can you notice the action of your tongue as the water slides to the back of your throat as you swallow? What was that experience like for you?

Teaching mindfulness to students

Until now, we've mostly talked about how teachers can cultivate mindfulness to avoid the burnout we spoke about in the previous chapter. But it is also worth underscoring that our students benefit greatly when we introduce them to mindfulness practices. There are several ways you can bring mindfulness into the classroom. It's recommended to share the science of why mindfulness works in an age-appropriate way. Then try out some classroom practices (I've included a list for you here).

What's great about mindfulness (aka focused attention practices) in the classroom is that, unlike lesson plans, you don't need a new one every day. Choose a couple of practices to work on for a few weeks, and then choose a few more. Repeat that process, and at the end of the year, you can practice all of the ones incorporated throughout the entire school year.

Figure 32.1: Mindfulness, the practice of being fully in the present moment, can be practiced anywhere!

Quick tips for bringing mindfulness into the classroom

- Try to just dip into the practices at first. Do them for 20–30 seconds and then ask: how did that go? What did you think? Accept all answers with an attitude of curiosity.
- If some students feel shy or awkward about practicing mindfulness, don't worry. Assure them that yes, it is a new and different activity that may feel "weird" at first, and they should feel free to see it as an experiment or new adventure. It may help to remind them that scientists know that mindfulness helps our brains learn and manage our emotions, and that it can also help them through difficult times.
- Be mindful that many students may find it uncomfortable or even triggering to close their eyes. Instead of telling them to close their eyes, you can say something like, "Close your eyes if you feel comfortable, or just find a still spot somewhere on the ground in front of you to let your eyes rest."
- Keep cards describing little mindfulness activities handy at your desk or in your Peace Center (Calm Down/Amygdala Reset Center), where

they are accessible to students. You can find some in the Resource Section. Or better yet, have students create their own to keep on a ring at their desk.

- Although mindfulness has been shown to be more effective for students when the person leading the activity practices mindfulness themselves, if you feel unsure about leading your group, you could try sharing some of the many digital and mindfulness apps online. Many (on Headspace, GoNoodle, and ClassDojo, among others) have free videos and guided meditations for kids and adults.
- Use stuffed animals for the littlest ones. You can have them put a teddy bear or stuffed animal on their belly as they lie on their back and practice belly breathing. They should watch their breathing as the teddy bear goes up and down to match their slow, calm breaths.

Here are some mindfulness activities to get you started:

- **Breathing Exercises:** Using your breathing as a relaxation technique can help clear the mind and unwind the body.
  - **Finger breathing:** Hold one hand up in front of you with your palm facing you. With your other hand, use your index finger to trace the outline of your raised hand. As you trace upwards, breathe in slowly, and as your finger traces downwards, exhale slowly.
  - **Bloom and bud:** Extend your palm out in front of you. As you bend your fingers to contract your hand into a loose first, breathe in slowly. Then open your fist up and extend your fingers as you breathe out. You can imagine that your fist is a flower blooming as it opens and turning back into a bud as it closes.
  - **Box breathing:** Navy SEALs have reportedly used box breathing to help them when their bodies are in fight or flight mode. Close your eyes and inhale through your nose for a count of four. Hold the inhale for four. Exhale fully for a count of four, and try to empty all of the air out of your lungs. Stay empty of breath (don't inhale) for a count of four. Repeat the process for three to five minutes. You can visualize drawing or traveling around the edges of a square: going up one side of the box as you inhale, over to the next side as you hold, down another side as you exhale, and back over to the first side as you hold the exhale. I've noticed this one works particularly well on visual conferencing platforms

where students can trace in the air the invisible edges of their square participant box!

- **Slow mo:** Tell your students to take one entire minute to complete an action in slow motion from beginning to end (e.g., slowly reaching over to pick up a water bottle for an entire minute). The goal is to be mindful and present to each second of the unfolding experience. You can repeat this when picking up a pencil, standing up, sitting down, bringing your hands over your head, tucking your chair in, sipping a cup of water, or even eating a Hershey's chocolate kiss as a special treat.
- **Yoga:** Practice yoga poses with students. A basic sun salutation routine is great, and younger kids often enjoy getting into animal-themed poses like dolphin, crow, and downward-facing dog.
- Try visualizations and affirmations. Famous Buddhist monk, Thich Nhat Hanh, shares one particular visualization that involves seeing yourself first as a flower, then a mountain, then clear water, and finally as space itself.[4] As you breathe in, imagine yourself as a flower and say the word "flower" mentally. Breathing out, say the word "fresh" mentally and imagine the sensation of freshness. Repeat a few times. Then repeat with the words "mountain" and "solid," then "still water" and "reflecting," then finally "space" and "free."
- Try thinking of one word that embodies peace, tolerance, or other mindful qualities you'd like to embody today. Take a minute to write it slowly.
- **Body scan meditation:** This well-known technique requires scanning your body, part by part, for tension or other sensations and non-judgmentally noticing what you encounter. (I find it helpful to do this while lying down in the dark, but in the classroom you may just want to dim the lights.) You can begin by noticing the sensations you feel on the insides of your toes, and then work your way up to your entire foot, focusing on any sensations in the bones, muscles, and skin. Move your attention upwards towards the ankle and lower leg, and repeat this scanning and noticing process. Work your way through every part of your body slowly and lovingly. I also highly recommend listening to mindfulness expert Jon Kabat-Zinn's recordings and writings on body scans (and mindfulness in general!).
- **Loving-kindness meditation:** Inspired by the Buddhist practice of *metta* (loving-kindness), this is the practice of wishing well upon oneself and others. Come to a comfortable seated position or lie

down, and take several calming breaths. When you feel relaxed, begin to visualize positive energy or light shining on you. Gently say or whisper (or say inwardly) some version of the following several times: "May I be happy. May I be well. May I be safe and free from all harm." Soak in the feeling of being deeply cared for by yourself. After repeating these phrases several times and when you feel ready, visualize someone with whom you have a happy, loving, comfortable relationship. Wish those same things on this person by imagining that they are also surrounded by positive energy and light. Repeat the phrase: "May you be happy. May you be well. May you be safe from all harm." Repeat this same process by visualizing sending these well wishes to others you know, and eventually even sending them to those you find difficult to deal with. You can then try extending this loving-kindness to include all living beings en masse. Let the effects of this enormously healing practice sink in, then slowly sit or stand up and go about your day.

Questions for reflection

- How familiar are you with mindfulness? What kinds of experiences have you had?
- If you already have a mindfulness practice, what daily rituals help you keep it alive? After reading this chapter, do you have any new ideas that might keep you motivated to practice? What are they?
- What challenges do you think you might face in finding time to practice mindfulness?
- What challenges do you think you might face in teaching students to practice mindfulness?
- There are loads of virtual mindfulness resources and apps that teach mindfulness. What are the top five that you might like to try out? Make a list.
- How might you share the information from this chapter with your students in a practical and engaging way?

33

Finding the Good

The Practice of Gratefulness

On one particularly tough day, I trudged home feeling exhausted in every way. I called one of my dearest teaching friends, who works in a particularly challenging neighborhood. “How do you survive days like this?” I asked her. Sitting there that night reflecting on it, I was struck by what she said. A true believer in trauma-informed education and mental health, she pointed out that all the self-care and professional development in the world can’t cure what ails us: the broken societal and systemic conditions that can cause kids to act the way they do and the institutional conditions of schools that set us up to burn out. I hear what she’s saying. As much as I know that my challenging students are challenged themselves, that doesn’t mean it’s not exhausting for me, especially with huge class sizes and little support. As much as I know the administration are humans, too, I am still enraged when directives coming from above don’t make sense. That night, and many other nights, I have found myself wrestling with the question: *How can I continue to love teaching every day and not be burned out by the chaos and constant demands, by the emotional labor of teaching?*

The only answer I had that night was sitting on my windowsill. Feeling that I needed something to brighten up my day and my mental health, I had walked to the nearest home improvement store and bought myself two of the prettiest orchids I could find. After the ugliness of the day, I spent some time drinking in their beauty. I made peanut butter cookies, listened to my favorite NPR show, and put my feet in a bubbly foot bath I bought. I decided to feel grateful for it all and for the knowledge that no teacher is ever alone. That night, I felt my heart say a grateful prayer for the invisible community of teachers around the world who sometimes come home feeling demolished.

The practice of **gratefulness**, so helpful on hard days like the one I had, is the practice of shifting our attention away from what we don't have and shining a light on what we do have. Shifting and shining. It not only feels good; it's also a powerful tool that's been shown to have beneficial effects on our mood, wellbeing, and resilience.[1,2] Gratefulness is defined as "being warmly or deeply appreciative of kindness and benefits received; thankful," and the scientifically proven benefits abound. For example, grateful people have been shown to have:

- better physical health[3,4]
- better, longer, sleep[5,6,7]
- fewer symptoms of depression[8]
- more life satisfaction[9]
- less likelihood of burnout[10]
- increased optimism and happiness.[11]

If it's so beneficial, why are we not more grateful more of the time? In my experience, it's because we often spend our moments thinking and focusing on *what goes wrong* in our lives instead of *what goes right.* One way to keep this from happening is to get better at thinking about the things that went well and the things we are grateful for.

Here is a short list of ways you can incorporate gratefulness into your daily life, inside and outside the classroom:

- **Three good things:** Martin Seligman, the founding father of psychology, and his colleagues found that when participants in his study named three good things that happened during the day they significantly increased their feelings of happiness, optimism, and hope over weeks or even months.[12,13,14,15] To do the activity, each day write down three things that went well and why they went well or what you did to make sure they went well. For example: *I had a warm encounter with the secretary today because I remembered to ask her how her son's first day of school went. My small reading group went well because I found a book about space that I knew they would love. During math today, the kids were more focused on their math assignment because I gave them the choice of working with a partner.*
- **Gratitude letter and visit:** Dr. Seligman also suggests calling to mind someone who did something for you for which you feel very grateful, but whom you haven't had a chance to thank properly. Ideally, this could be someone you haven't thought about for a while. It could

be someone from your childhood, a family member, friend, teacher, colleague, or even a student. Try to pick someone who is alive and could meet with you in the next week. Write a letter expressing your gratitude to them. Be specific. Then deliver it to them in person and read it aloud in its entirety. Like Seligman's three good things activity mentioned above, this activity has been found to increase happiness and lower depression, and the effect has been shown to last for months![16]

- **Continuing with the theme of thank you notes:** Encourage your students to write their own thank you notes. Have a thank you card station in your classroom or a table where supplies are available for older students. Supplies might include pre-bought inexpensive thank you cards or blank pre-folded cards made out of cardstock, glue, scissors, markers, old magazines, and prompts like "I appreciate you because..." or "I want to thank you for..." for emerging writers.
- **Find a gratefulness buddy:** Since we are more likely to stick to our commitments when we make them public and have someone we are accountable to, find another teacher or friend who you can text/email or otherwise check in with daily or weekly to exchange the top three things you are grateful for.
- **Start a gratefulness club:** At my school, several teachers and I hold weekly meetings to stay positive. We start each meeting by sharing three things we have felt grateful for this week. It's incredible how good it feels to just listen to positive things that are happening to others you care about!
- Invite students to fill a gratitude jar with notes or use them to make a gratefulness chain or journal about gratefulness. Create a gratefulness bulletin board where class members (or staff members) can share sticky notes about what they are grateful for each day.
- Use the ABCs to brainstorm a list of things students are grateful for. A is for avocados on toast, for example.
- Read books that feature gratefulness and discuss with children what thoughts and observations they have. Examples include *Sylvester and the Magic Pebble* by William Steig, *Giving Thanks: A Native American Good Morning Message* by Chief Jake Swamp, *Thankful* by Eileen Spinelli, *The Magic Fish* by Freya Littledale, *The Giving Tree* by Shel Silverstein, *Thank you, Mr. Falker* by Patricia Polacco, among many others.

- Have students interview their families about what they are grateful for. Invite students to create a newscast reporting on what their family members said were the top one or two things they felt most grateful for.
- **Gratitude shout out:** At the end of the day, ask students to share with the group something or someone they felt grateful for that day. They can start by saying, "Today I feel grateful for/to…because." Have a volunteer record these statements into a gratefulness journal to be placed in the classroom library and read and reread by the class. Invite kids to illustrate their entries. See how many pages you can fill with all the goodness!

Questions for reflection

- What does gratefulness mean to you? What are three things you feel grateful for right now?
- What role does gratefulness play in your life?
- On a practical level, how do you practice gratefulness on a regular basis?
- What messages about gratefulness did you receive from listening to and watching the adults around you as a child?
- In what ways do you incorporate gratefulness in your classroom?
- How might you share the information from this chapter with your students?
- After reading this chapter, are there any new ideas you would like to use to incorporate gratefulness into your classroom?

34

Good Morning, Teacher —What's Ahead?

Finish each day and be done with it. You have done what you could. Some blunders and absurdities no doubt crept in; forget them as soon as you can. Tomorrow is a new day. You shall begin it serenely and with too high a spirit to be encumbered with your old nonsense.

Ralph Waldo Emerson[1]

This morning, as I look through my back window, I can see the sun's rays make their way through the tree in my backyard. My breakfast is on the stove, and my mug is waiting expectantly for its dose of steaming hot tea. It is the morning of a new day.

Yesterday, some mistakes undoubtedly crept in, as Emerson said. Yesterday, we did what humans do; we made mistakes. We bungled things that probably should have been easy for us by now. Perhaps we spoke too much, too little, too early, too late. We fell into traps that we knew were there already. Maybe yesterday, even our best just wasn't good enough. But today, we don't have time to worry about any of that; we've got too much to do. Because our students are out there too this morning, on this dawning of a new day. They're out there waiting for us.

They aren't just waiting for our knowledge—which we will stop at nothing to deliver—they're also waiting for our greatness and our humanity. They are waiting for us to show up exactly as we are and offer ourselves, as imperfect and varied as the offering may be. We know that they will fix us in their minds for later, holding up our myriad facets to the light as they search for their own shape in the world. If we have dared to show them who we are, then they can cling to that example, as a ship seeks out the certainty of a familiar lighthouse, no matter how far removed in time and space. If we point the way to their brilliance and insist upon it, we know we have opened the door to the bright light of their potential. And if we allow them their humanity, exactly as it is, we offer them both healing and freedom.

Because, for all the insanity, we are teachers, after all. Our chosen place on this planet is with the children—there isn't any place we'd prefer. No promise of something better can tear us away because, for us, there *is* nothing better or more soul-satisfying, nothing that defines our course and purpose more than this group of eager young minds.

So, *good morning*, teacher. Today is your day.

Resources Section

RESOURCES TO SHARE WITH STUDENTS

My Mission Statement

This year in school, I would like everyone to remember me as...

CHECK-IN WHEEL

Please follow the instructions below to make a *Check-In Wheel*.

1. In the circle on the next page, make a pie chart that shows how much you are thinking about each of these areas of your life **today**. You can make large pieces for the things that you are thinking about a lot today and smaller pieces for the things you are not thinking about as much.

   School/Work, Friends, Home & Neighborhood, Family, Body

   "Body" means how you're feeling physically—if you are tired, or energetic, sleepy, awake, hungry, full, or if you have body parts that hurt, etc.

2. In each piece of the circle, tell in a few words (or draw) what is happening in each area of your life today.

3. Use the Feelings List (on page 235) to find some words to describe how you are feeling about each of these areas. Write those words in each part of the circle.

4. Color each area with the color or colors that match your feelings.

5. Under the circle, complete the sentence: "Something that I am grateful for is/looking forward to today is ____________________"

CHECK-IN WHEEL (Cont.)

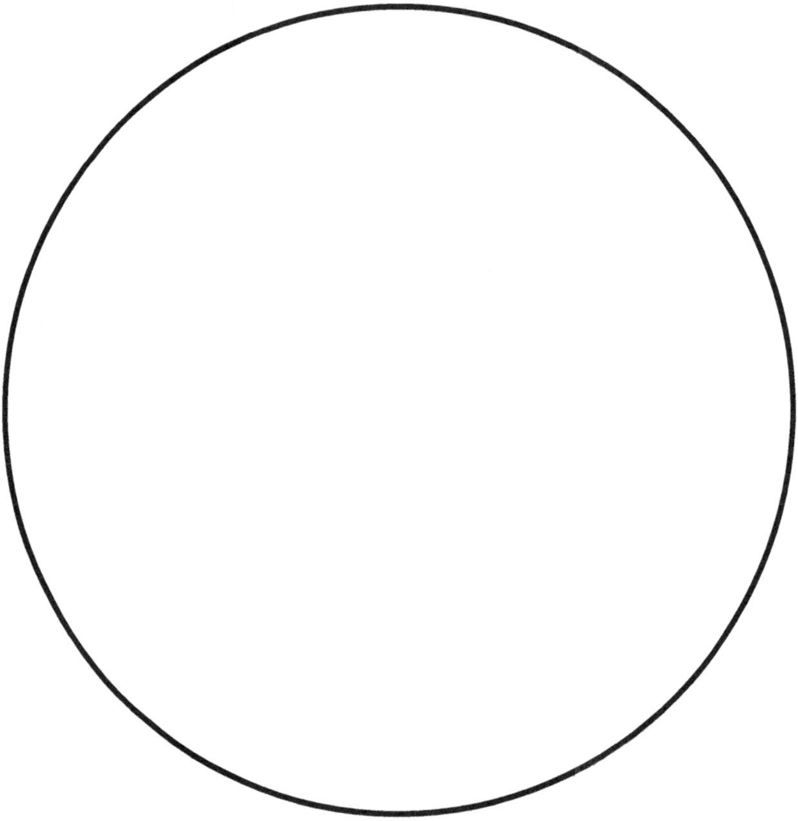

HOW I AM FEELING TODAY

By:______________________________ Date:______________

Something I am grateful for today is

Friends	House/Neighborhood	Family
School	**Today My Body Feels...**	**Other Things I'm Thinking About**

CONNECTING FEELINGS AND SENSATIONS

HAPPY	**SURPRISED**	**AFRAID**
Warm	Sweaty	Heart racing
Light	Jumpy	Cold
Full	Pounding heart	Tense
Tingly	Electrified	Frozen
Awake	Breathless	Chills
Energetic	Jaw drops	Trembly
Bubbly	Eyebrows raise	Shrinking
Smiling		Eyes widen

DISGUSTED	**SAD**	**ANGRY**
Nauseous	Empty	Burning
Queasy	Aching	Hot
Want to get away	Sinking heart	Boiling
Avoiding touch	Heavy	Gut churns
Shuddering	Slow	Tight
Nose wrinkles	Hollow	Seething
Eyes narrow	Eyes look down	Tight jaw
		Clenched fists

FEELINGS LIST

   **PLEASANT**	   **UNPLEASANT**
HAPPY content, peaceful, easy, satisfied, optimistic, delighted, gleeful, joyful, ecstatic	**SAD** upset, disappointed, discouraged, depressed, lonely, apathetic, a sense of loss
ALIVE excited, electrified, interested, thrilled, energetic, animated, inspired, spirited, festive, liberated	**ANGRY** mad, irritated, annoyed, enraged, aggressive, resentful, enraged, provoked, furious
AFFECTIONATE kind, tender, loving, connected to, devoted, close, sensitive	**AFRAID** scared, uncertain, perplexed, shy, unsure, uneasy, hesitant, terrified
OTHER PLEASANT FEELINGS determined, enthusiastic, bold, brave, hopeful, curious, fascinated	**OTHER UNPLEASANT FEELINGS** tense, skeptical, aching, broken-hearted, alone, pessimistic, doubtful, anxious

CLASSROOM COPING STRATEGIES

★ Go to the Peace Center.

★ Ask to take a break.

★ Take five slow belly breaths in and out.

★ Ask to go get water.

★ Do 10 jumping jacks.

★ Stretch!

★ Write down, draw, or say five things you can see right now, four you can hear, three you can touch/feel, two you can smell, and one thing you can taste.

★ Draw your favorite place to be. Imagine you are there.

★ Use dry erase markers/board.

★ Use colored pencils.

★ Fill out a crossword puzzle.

★ Do a Sudoku puzzle.

★ Splash cold water on your face.

★ Find a word to match how you're feeling.

★ Read a book.

★ Do a classroom chore like cleaning your desk, straightening up the classroom library, and so on.

★ Do a *Check-In Wheel.*

★ Write a letter to someone special.

★ When you feel ready to talk about the

★

problem, say how you feel about what is happening. "I feel…when people…"

★ Look at a picture of a loved one. Tell the picture how you're feeling.

★ Ask to talk to a friend or sibling.

★ Ask to talk to a counselor.

★ Read a joke book or think of something that makes you laugh.

★ Listen to calm music.

★ Listen to exciting music and dance out your feelings.

★ Find a word to match how you're feeling.

★ Use a fidget.

★ Ask for a hug.

EACH SQUARE IS SOMEONE WHO CARES—ABOUT YOU!

For: ____

MINDSET BOOKMARK

Instead of "It's too hard!"

I can say...

I will get better with practice.

I can take my time.

I can ask for help when I need it.

I like a challenge.

I've done hard things before.

I know I can do this.

Mistakes mean that I'm trying!

Mistakes are making me smarter.

OR: ______________________________

____

____

____

____

____

MY *I GOT THIS!* PLAN

My *I Got This*! Plan By: ______________

	WHEN I FEEL ______________ **I CAN...**	

★

MINDFULNESS ACTIVITY CARDS

Bloom and Bud

Hold your palm out in front of you. As you bend your fingers to contract your hand into a loose fist, breathe in slowly. Then, as you breathe out, open your fist up and spread your fingers out. Imagine that your fist is a flower blooming as it opens and turning back into a bud as it closes.

Finger Breaths

Hold one hand up in front of you with your palm facing you. With your other hand, use your index finger to trace the outline of your raised hand. As you trace upwards, breathe in slowly, and as your finger traces downwards, exhale slowly.

Box Breathing

Close your eyes and breathe in through your nose for a count of four. Hold your breath for four. Exhale fully for a count of four. Stay empty of breath (don't inhale) for a count of four. Imagine going around the edges of a square as you do each part—start in one corner then go to the next, and the next until you're back where you started!

Share the Love!

Say or whisper to yourself 3 times: "May I be happy. May I be well. May I be safe and free from all harm." Now think of someone you love and imagine saying to them: "May you be happy. May you be well. May you be safe and free from all harm." Next, imagine someone who you don't like a lot. Imagine saying those words to them. Last, imagine saying those words to all the people, animals, and living things on our planet!

SCRIPTS AND TEMPLATES FOR TEACHERS

My Mission Statement

I would like my students to remember me as...

SAMPLE SCRIPT: SHARING CONFIDENTIAL INFORMATION

I've been thinking about how important you are to me, as students, but also as people. We're always so busy learning that I don't always get the chance to remind you that I care about you as people, not just as students. For example, I think that sometimes you come in and you're having a rough time, and you need a little extra TLC. Sometimes you have something really exciting to share. But it's hard for me and others to always know when those days are happening and support you because we're so busy with learning. I want to give you a chance to let me and your peers know how you're doing so we can better support you. Today, I have a new activity that will help you share what's happening with you and how you're doing.

When we do activities like this, your participation is voluntary. That means that it's up to you to decide if you want to do it, and it's up to you to decide if you don't want to do it. You can also decide to share a little bit or a lot, and I will keep it private. The only time I will share what you tell me is if I think you might be in danger, or if I think you might be putting other people or yourself in danger. If this happens, I will need to talk to ____ (guidance counselor) or someone else I think can help keep you safe. But otherwise, I want you to know that whatever you tell me I will keep private and confidential. I am so excited about this because I can't wait to learn more about you and share with you some things about me, too. Does that make sense? So here is how this activity works... (Explain activity).

CARDS ON THE TABLE CONVERSATIONS

1. Hi _______________. How are you? Can we talk?
2. Don't worry—everything is okay. But I want to make sure we can talk when things come up.
3. You're important to me and I'm noticing that ____________ (your work is not getting done, our last conversation made me feel tense, you're coming in late every day, you look frustrated when it's time to work on math, etc.).
4. The story I'm telling myself about this is __________. (Apologize if it's appropriate to do so.)
5. I wonder what's actually happening, though. I'm not sure I have the whole picture. Would you help me to understand?

LIFESAVER

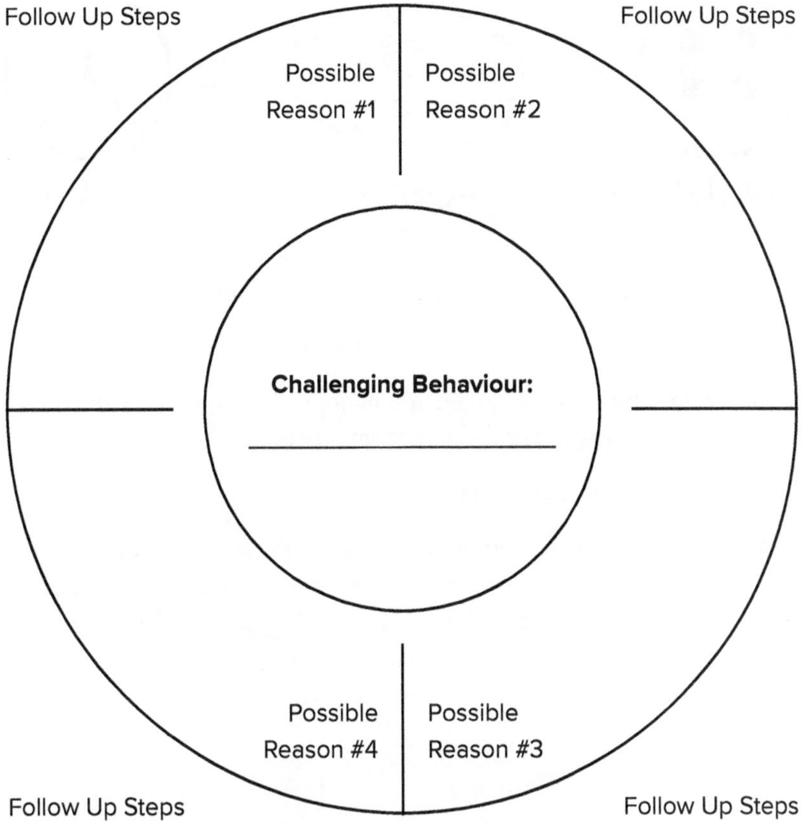

Follow Up Steps

Follow Up Steps

Possible
Reason #1

Possible
Reason #2

Challenging Behaviour:

Possible
Reason #4

Possible
Reason #3

Follow Up Steps

Follow Up Steps

PAUSE AND PONDER EQUALS PEACE

1. Become aware of your response to what's happening.
2. Pause for a few moments to breathe calmly.
3. Ponder the possibility that you might be making up a story about what's happening or be missing information.
4. Decide if you want to act.
5. If you decide to act and inquire about what's happening, use a neutral tone of voice. Say something like "I've noticed ___________. I'm wondering what's actually going on" or "I noticed that ___________. I am wondering what you can tell me about that."

★

PART 1: MAKE YOUR CLASSROOM RELATIONSHIP MAP

1. Start by picking a color or colors to represent you and your role in the classroom. Use this color or colors to draw a shape somewhere on your page that represents you. You might want to draw squiggles, or blocks, or a geometric shape like triangles or circles. Or you might want to draw a more abstract shape that you come up with yourself, or one that has personal meaning for you. Just draw a shape that matches you. Color it in with colors that you choose. Then label that shape "Me."
2. Now start to think about the students in your classroom. Who comes to mind first? Just as you did for your own shape, pick a shape and color/colors to represent this student and place this shape somewhere on the page. Don't overthink it and don't rush. Notice what feelings come up as you design each shape.
3. Repeat step number two until you have made a shape for all of your students. To keep track, write their initials or name under their shape and any insights or thoughts that come to mind about them as you draw. This should be very stream of consciousness—don't think about it too much. You are engaging the right hemisphere of your brain, which is mainly insightful, intuitive, and non-verbal.
4. When you've finished, check to see that you've gotten all of your students. You might want to use a roster at this point to make sure you haven't missed any.

PART 2: FIND OUT WHAT IT MEANS

Only read this part after you've finished Part 1: Make your Classroom Relationship Map.

What does my drawing mean?

Specific meanings in artwork and imagery can vary based on many things, including race, culture, gender, socioeconomic background, and other factors. In reading this key, I want you to keep in mind that these are general guidelines; it's most important to pay attention to what resonates for you.

- **Size:** Larger shapes may represent individuals that have more significance. The shape's size might also signify the amount of energy and attention you feel this child requires from you. On that note, smaller images may imply that a child requires less attention from you or is less significant to you.
- **Placement:** Shapes you placed close to you may represent the students you feel closest to or the most protective of. Shapes that are closest to you may signify students who are more prominent in your thoughts or who stand out most to you, while shapes on the outskirts might get less of your focus.
- **Colors:** Bright shapes can signify that you view this individual as strong or see their personality as vibrant or clearly defined. Duller, earthier colors can represent individuals you regard as more shy, stable, or introverted. In comparison, brighter colors may indicate that you see those students as being more dynamic, outspoken, or extroverted.
- **Shapes:** Shapes with straight lines and angles usually symbolize structure and order, precision, and a need for control. This need for control could represent a desire to have more control over that individual, a perception that this child is disciplined, or that they might wish to have more control in some way. Shapes with curves are softer and represent connection and fluidity. They can also indicate that you view those students as more cooperative.
- **Outlining shapes:** If you drew a dark outline around some shapes, this might have to do with boundaries. This could symbolize your sense that this child has strong boundaries or is largely separated from you or others. It may also be interpreted as a desire to protect that student.

Here are some questions to ask

- What color and shape did you choose to represent yourself? Where did you place yourself on the page? How big or small was your shape? What might this tell you about how you see yourself? What might this say about how you view the most important qualities of a classroom leader?
- Looking at where you placed each student on the page, who did you put closer to your symbol? Who did you put farther away? What meaning might that have for you?

- Do you notice any patterns in where you placed students of different ethnicities? Genders? What might that mean to you?
- What students did you think of first? What students did you think of last? Were there any students you forgot or struggled to name?
- Did you group certain students together? What was the meaning of each of those groupings to you?
- Where did you choose to put your more difficult student/s? How did you decide to draw them? What does that mean to you?

PART 3: WRAPPING IT UP

As you were drawing, did anything else become clear to you? Make a list of any new insights that became clear.

★

STEER CLEAR OF STINKING THINKING!

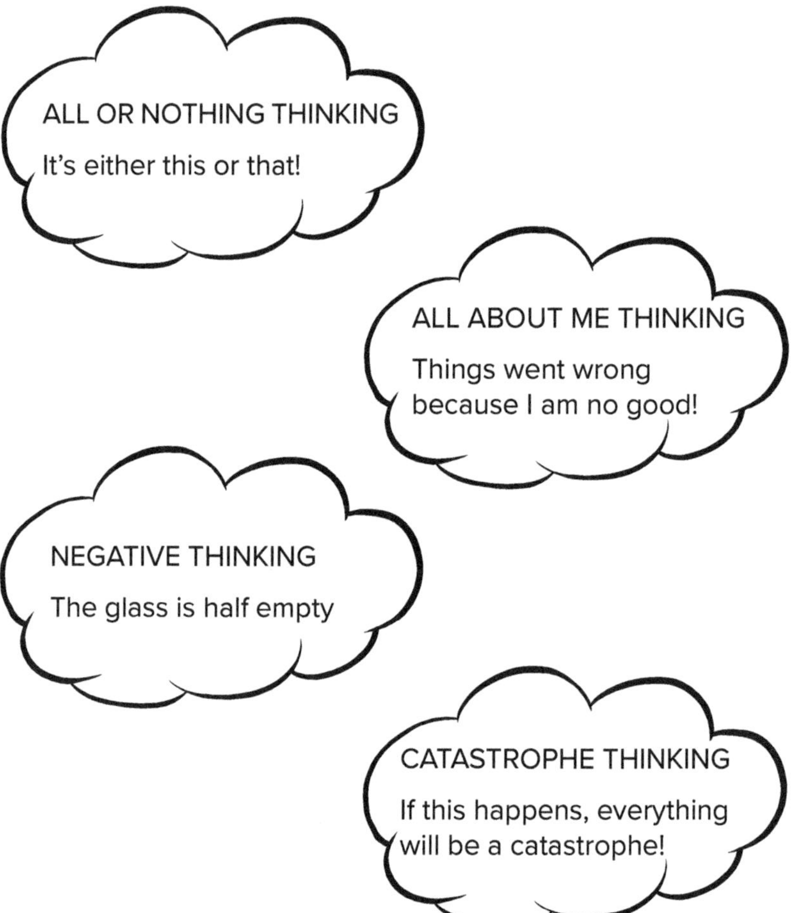

CONNECT CORRECT CONNECT

STEP 1: CONNECT Connect with how the other person is feeling. Authentically try to acknowledge and validate how they feel. Put yourself in their shoes.

I can appreciate that you feel ___________________.

I imagine that it's hard to ___________________.

It makes sense to me that you think/feel ___________________.

I bet you'd prefer it if ___________________.

STEP 2: CORRECT Next, supportively guide the other person to a new, desired behavior.

I also need you to ___________________ so that ___________________.

It's also important that you _________________ so that _________________.

I would appreciate it a lot, though, if you could also _________________.

I think you could be even more ___________________ (productive, confident, efficient, etc.) if you ___________________.

STEP 3: CONNECT Finally, warmly reconnect with the other person.

Does that make sense to you?

What do you think?

I'm here for you/I've got your back. Just let me know if you need help with this.

I'll check back on you later to make sure you're alright. Is that okay?

I really appreciate you trying so hard/doing this/making this effort, etc.

SCHMOOZE SESSION PROMPTS

It's good to see your face today!

You're wearing a new ___________ today!

Your (birthday/big game/concert) is coming up.
How are you feeling about that?

Oh, I see you ___________ (lost a tooth, brought in a new backpack, did something different with your hair, etc.).

You're smiling today. Something must be making you happy!

You don't look like your bright and happy self today.
I'm here for you if you need anything.

Tell me one thing you did since I saw you yesterday.

How was ___________ (the movie, your soccer game, karate class, baby brother's birthday, evening, etc.)?

For important events:

Wow! Where were you when you found out that ___________?

Can you believe that this happened?!

How did that make you feel?

How did this change things for you?

REALITY CHECK

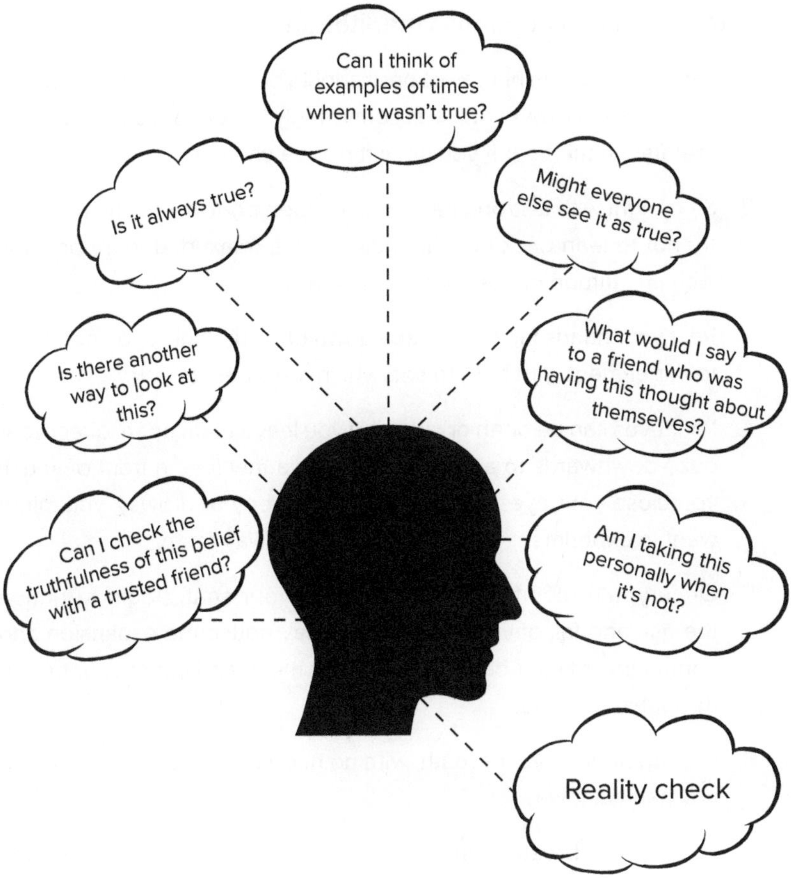

How to practice mindfulness meditation

1. Find a chair or cushion to sit on. It should be even, not tilted forwards or backward. Cross your legs comfortably in front of you, or put both feet flat on the floor if you are sitting in a chair.

2. Sit upright with a strong back and an open front. If you are in a chair, try not to lean back in your chair. Sit in a relaxed, upright position with an attitude of openness and dignity.

3. Rest your hands face up or face down on your thighs. You may want to experiment with both to see which feels best to you.

4. Your eyes can be open or closed. If you leave them open, direct your gaze downwards to a spot on the floor a few feet in front of you. If you close your eyes and find you get sleepy or drowsy, you might want to experiment with leaving them halfway open.

5. Once you're comfortably settled into your seat, begin to notice the rise and fall of your breath. You may notice the expansion and contraction of your belly and chest, or the in and out of your breath through your nose.

6. Pay attention to your breath, with no need to control it or breathe in any particular way.

7. Follow your breath with your attention. You will notice that each breath is unique as it comes in and out.

8. When you find your mind wandering, gently and non-judgmentally bring it back, over and over again, to the sensation of your breath moving in and out of your body. As you notice thoughts, feelings, fears, memories, or anything else arising, just label them as "thoughts," and kindly but firmly move your awareness back to experiencing the breath.

FULL SPECTRUM VIEW OF KIDS

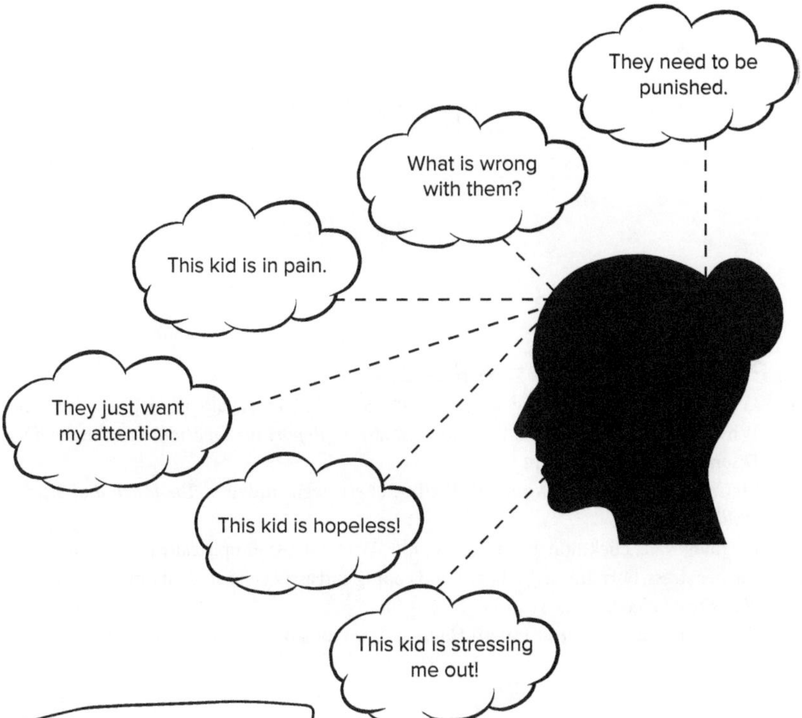

They need to be punished.

What is wrong with them?

This kid is in pain.

They just want my attention.

This kid is hopeless!

This kid is stressing me out!

Full spectrum view

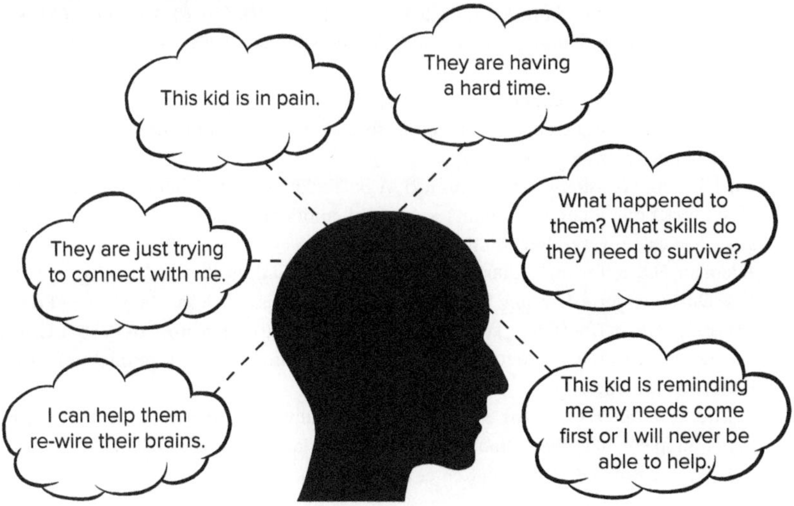

This kid is in pain.

They are having a hard time.

What happened to them? What skills do they need to survive?

They are just trying to connect with me.

I can help them re-wire their brains.

This kid is reminding me my needs come first or I will never be able to help.

Endnotes

A Personal Note to the Reader

1 Lever, N., Mathis, E., & Mayworm, A. (2017) 'School Mental health is not just for students: Why teacher and school staff wellness matters.' *Report on Emotional and Behavioral Disorders in Youth 17*, 6–12.

2 McCallum, F. & Price, D. (2010) 'Well teachers, well students.' *The Journal of Student Wellbeing 4*, 19–34.

3 Herman, K.C., Hickmon-Rosa, J., & Reinke, W.M. (2018) 'Empirically derived profiles of teacher stress, burnout, self-efficacy, and coping and associated student outcomes.' *Journal of Positive Behavior Interventions 20, 90–100.*

4 Oliver, M. & Beacon Press (1990) *House of Light*. Boston, MA: Beacon Press.

Preface: Standard Sizes and the Need for a Full Spectrum View of Schools

1 Sutcher, L., Darling-Hammond, L., & Carver-Thomas, D. (2016) *A Coming Crisis in Teaching? Teacher Supply, Demand, and Shortages in the US*. Palo Alto, CA: Learning Policy Institute.

2 Jennings, P.A. & Greenberg, M.T. (2009) 'The prosocial classroom: Teacher social and emotional competence in relation to student and classroom outcomes.' *Review of Educational Research 79,* 491–525.

3 Durlak, J.A., Weissberg, R.P., Dymnicki, A.B., Taylor, R.D., & Schellinger, K.B. (2011) 'The impact of enhancing students' social and emotional learning: A meta-analysis of school-based universal interventions. *Child Development 82*, 405–432.

4 Adelman, H.S. & Taylor, L. (2006) *The School Leader's Guide to Student Learning Supports: New Directions for Addressing Barriers to Learning*. Thousand Oaks, CA: Corwin Press.

5 Wang, K., Chen, Y., Zhang, J., & Oudekerk, B.A. (2020) 'Indicators of School Crime and Safety: 2019.' NCES 2020-063/NCJ 254485. Washington, DC: National Center for Education Statistics.

6 Lessne, D. & Yanez, C. (2016) 'Student Reports of Bullying: Results from the 2015 School Crime Supplement to the National Crime Victimization Survey. Web Tables. NCES 2017-015.' Washington, DC: National Center for Education Statistics.

7 Herman, K.C., Hickmon-Rosa, J., & Reinke, W.M. (2018) 'Empirically derived profiles of teacher stress, burnout, self-efficacy, and coping and associated student outcomes.' *Journal of Positive Behavior Interventions 20*, 90–100.

8 Haynes, M. (2014) *On the Path to Equity: Improving the Effectiveness of Beginning Teachers.* Washington, DC: Alliance for Excellent Education.

9 Herman, K.C., Hickmon-Rosa, J., & Reinke, W.M. (2018) 'Empirically derived profiles of teacher stress, burnout, self-efficacy, and coping and associated student outcomes.' *Journal of Positive Behavior Interventions 20, 90–100.*

10 Beck, A.T. (1979) *Cognitive Therapy and the Emotional Disorders.* New York: Penguin.

11 Dweck, C.S. (2008) *Mindset: The New Psychology of Success.* New York: Ballantine Books.

12 Dweck, C.S. (2014) *Mindsets and Math/Science Achievement.* New York: Random House.

Chapter 1

1 Segal, J. (1988) 'Teachers have enormous power in affecting a child's self-esteem.' *Brown University Child Behavior and Development Newsletter 10*, 1–3.

2 Rogers, F. (1999) Acceptance Speech: "TV Hall of Fame", New York: March 11. Accessed on 01/27/21 at http://exhibit.fredrogerscenter.org/advocacy-forchildren/videos/view/970.

3 Sparks, S.D. (2019) 'Why teacher-student relationships matter: New findings shed light on best approaches.' *Education Week 38*, 8.

4 Spilt, J.L., Koomen, H.M.Y., & Thijs, J.T. (2011) 'Teacher wellbeing: The importance of teacher–student relationships.' *Educational Psychology Review 23*, 457–477.

Chapter 3

1 Beck, A.T. (1967) *Depression: Clinical, Experimental, and Theoretical Aspects.* New York: Hoeber Medical Division, Harper & Row.

2 Nummenmaa, L., Glerean, E., Hari, R., & Hietanen, J.K. (2014) 'Bodily maps of emotions.' *Proceedings of the National Academy of Sciences of the USA 111*, 646–651.

Chapter 4

1 Katz, M. (1997) *On Playing a Poor Hand Well: Insights from the Lives of Those Who Have Overcome Childhood Risks and Adversities.* New York: W.W. Norton, p.187.

Chapter 5

1 Wlodkowski, R.J. (1983) *Motivational Opportunities for Successful Teaching [Leader's Guide].* Phoenix, AZ: Universal Dimensions.

2 Korbey, H. (2017) 'The power of being seen.' *Edutopia.*

Chapter 6

1 Adichie, C.N. 'The danger of a single story.' TED Talk. Accessed on 01/09/21 at www.ted.com/talks/chimamanda_ngozi_adichie_the_danger_of_a_single_story.

2 Jennings, P.A. *et al.* (2017) 'Impacts of the CARE for Teachers program on teachers' social and emotional competence and classroom interactions.' *Journal of Educational Psychology 109*, 1010.
3 Winfrey, O. (2011) 'The powerful lesson Maya Angelou taught Oprah.' Accessed on 01/27/21 at www.oprah.com/oprahs-lifeclass/the-powerful-lesson-maya-angelou-taught-oprah-video.
4 www.landmarkworldwide.com.
5 Frankl, V. (2006) *Man's Search for Meaning*. Boston, MA: Beacon Press, p.77.

Chapter 7

1 Brown, B. (2019) *The Call to Courage*. www.netflix.com/title/81010166.
2 Farmer Kris, D. (2014) 'The timeless teachings of Mister Rogers.' Accessed on 01/09/21 at www.pbs.org/parents/thrive/the-timeless-teachings-of-mister-rogers.
3 Rogers, C.R. (1957) 'The necessary and sufficient conditions of therapeutic personality change.' *Journal of Consulting Psychology 21*, 95–103.
4 Lerner, H. & Brown, B. (2020) 'I'm sorry: How to apologize and why it matters.' Accessed on 01/09/21 at https://brenebrown.com/podcast/harriet-lerner-and-brene-im-sorry-how-to-apologize-why-it-matters.

Chapter 8

1 Miller, V., Veneklasen, L., Reilly, M., & Clark, C. (2006) *Making Change Happen: Power. Concepts for Revisioning Power for Justice, Equality and Peace*. Washington, DC: Just Associates.
2 For more information on the four types of power, see Miller, V., Veneklasen, L., Reilly, M., & Clark, C. (2006) *Making Change Happen: Power. Concepts for Revisioning Power for Justice, Equality and Peace*. Washington, DC: Just Associates.
3 Pascal, B. (1852) *Pensées*. Paris: Dezobry et E. Magdeleine

Chapter 10

1 Schopenhauer, A. *et al.* (2017) *Parerga and Paralipomena: Short Philosophical Essays*. Cambridge: Cambridge University Press.
2 Winnicott, D.W. (1991) *Playing and Reality*. Hove: Psychology Press.
3 Barkley, R.A. (2020) *Taking Charge of ADHD, Fourth Edition: The Complete, Authoritative Guide for Parents*. New York: Guilford Publications.
4 Cook, C.R. *et al.* (2017) 'Evaluating the impact of increasing general education teachers' ratio of positive-to-negative interactions on students' classroom behavior.' *Journal of Positive Behavioral Intervention 19*, 67–77.
5 Riley, P. (2009) 'An adult attachment perspective on the student–teacher relationship and classroom management difficulties.' *Teaching and Teacher Education 25*, 626–635.
6 Zakrzewski, V. (2014) 'What makes a teacher lose it?' Accessed on 01/09/21 at https://greatergood.berkeley.edu/article/item/what_makes_a_teacher_lose_it.
7 Zakrzewski, V. (2014) 'What makes a teacher lose it?' Accessed on 01/09/21 at https://greatergood.berkeley.edu/article/item/what_makes_a_teacher_lose_it.

Chapter 15

1 Bloom, S. (1995) 'Creating sanctuary in the school.' *Journal for a Just and Caring Education 1*, 403–433.

2 American Psychological Association (2021) 'Trauma.' Accessed on 01/27/21 at https://dictionary.apa.org/trauma.

3 Oxford Online Dictionary (2021) 'Stress.' Accessed on 01/27/21 at https://en.oxforddictionaries.com/definition/stress.

4 PBS Learning Media (2020) 'Regulating Yourself and Your Classroom: Stress, Trauma and the Brain.' Accessed on 01/09/21 at www.pbslearningmedia.org/resource/regulating-yourself-and-your-classroom-video/stress-trauma-and-the-brain-insights-for-educators-thinktv-cet.

5 Felitti, V.J. *et al.* (1998) 'Relationship of childhood abuse and household dysfunction to many of the leading causes of death in adults.' *American Journal of Preventive Medicine 14*, 245–258.

6 Blodgett, C. (2012) 'How adverse childhood experiences and trauma impact school engagement.' Presentation delivered at Becca Conference, Spokane, Washington, 2012.

Chapter 16

1 Goleman, D. (2009) *Emotional Intelligence: Why It Can Matter More Than IQ*. London: A&C Black.

2 Cafasso, J. (2017) 'Adrenaline rush: Symptoms, activities, causes, at night, and anxiety.' Accessed on 01/09/21 at www.healthline.com/health/adrenaline-rush.

3 Perry, B.D., Pollard, R.A., Blakley, T.L., Baker, W.L., & Vigilante, D. (1995) 'Childhood trauma, the neurobiology of adaptation, and "use-dependent" development of the brain: How "states" become "traits."' *Infant Mental Health Journal 16*, 271–291.

Chapter 17

1 National Working Group on Foster Care & Education (2014) 'Fostering success in education: National factsheet on the educational outcomes of children in foster care.' *Research Highlights on Education and Foster Care*, 1–20.

2 Barkley, R.A. (2020) *Taking Charge of ADHD, Fourth Edition: The Complete, Authoritative Guide for Parents*. New York: Guilford Publications.

3 Brown, N.M. *et al.* (2017) 'Associations between Adverse Childhood Experiences and ADHD diagnosis and severity.' *Academic Pediatrics 17*, 349–355.

4 Australian Childhood Foundation (2010) 'Making SPACE for learning: Trauma informed practice in schools.' Accessed on 01/27/21 at www.theactgroup.com.au/documents/makingspaceforlearning-traumainschools.pdf.

5 Perry, B.D., Pollard, R.A., Blakley, T.L., Baker, W.L., & Vigilante, D. (1995) 'Childhood trauma, the neurobiology of adaptation, and "use-dependent" development of the brain: How "states" become "traits."' *Infant Mental Health Journal 16*, 271–291.

6 Kinniburgh, K.J., Blaustein, M., Spinazzola, J., & Van der Kolk, B.A. (2017) 'Attachment, self-regulation, and competency: A comprehensive intervention framework for children with complex trauma.' *Psychiatric Annals 35*, 424–430.

7 Greene, R.W. (2009) *Lost at School: Why Our Kids with Behavioral Challenges Are Falling through the Cracks and How We Can Help Them*. New York: Simon and Schuster.

8 Brooks, R.B. (2001) "Nurturing Islands of Competence: Is There Really Room for a Strength-Based Model in the Treatment of ADHD?" *The ADHD Report* 9, 2, 1–5. doi:10.1521/adhd.9.2.1.19075.

Chapter 18

1 Graff, V., Cai, L., Badiola, I., & Elkassabany, N.M. (2019) 'Music versus midazolam during preoperative nerve block placements: A prospective randomized controlled study.' *Regional Anesthesia and Pain Medicine.* doi:10.1136/rapm-2018-100251.

2 Eist, H.I. (2015) Book review: 'DBT Skills Training Manual, Marsha M. Linehan (2015) New York: The Guilford Press. 504 pp. DBT Skills Training Handouts and Worksheets: Marsha M. Linehan (2015) New York: The Guilford Press. 422 pp.' *The Journal of Nervous and Mental Disease 203*, 11, 887.

3 Cuddy, A.J.C., Jack Schultz, S., & Fosse, N.E.P (2018) 'Curving a more comprehensive body of research on postural feedback reveals clear evidential value for power-posing effects: Reply to Simmons and Simonsohn (2017).' *Psychological Science 29*, 656–666.

Chapter 19

1 Durlak, J.A., Weissberg, R.P., Dymnicki, A.B., Taylor, R.D., & Schellinger, K.B. (2011) 'The impact of enhancing students' social and emotional learning: A meta-analysis of school-based universal interventions.' *Child Development 82*, 405–432.

2 Hochschild, A.R. (2012) *The Managed Heart: Commercialization of Human Feeling.* Berkeley, CA: University of California Press.

3 Jennings, P.A. & Greenberg, M.T. (2009) 'The prosocial classroom: Teacher social and emotional competence in relation to student and classroom outcomes.' *Review of Educational Research 79*, 491–525.

4 Grossman, P. *et al.* (2009) 'Teaching practice: A cross-professional perspective.' *Teachers College Record 111*, 2055–2100.

5 www.responsiveclassroom.org

Chapter 20

1 Lee, R.D. '"Multiplication is for white people": Raising expectations for other people's children by Lisa Delpit.' *Journal of School Choice 8*, 152–155.

2 Haskins, H.S. (1940) *Meditations in Wall Street.* New York: William Morrow & Co.

Chapter 21

1 Bethell, C., Jones, J., Gombojav, N., Linkenbach, J., & Sege, R. (2019) 'Positive childhood experiences and adult mental and relational health in a statewide sample: Associations across adverse childhood experiences levels.' *JAMA Pediatrics 173*, 11, e193007–e193007.

2 CBS News (2018) 'Treating childhood trauma.' Accessed on 01/09/21 at www.cbsnews.com/news/oprah-winfrey-treating-childhood-trauma.

Chapter 23

1 Berg, C. (1952) 'Amended definition of anxiety.' *British Journa of Medical Psychology 25*, 158.

2 Ghandour, R.M. *et al.* (2019) 'Prevalence and treatment of depression, anxiety, and conduct problems in US children.' *The Journal of Pediatrics 206*, 256–267.e3.

3 Hopko, D.R., Crittendon, J.A., Grant, E., & Wilson, S.A. (2005) 'The impact of anxiety on performance IQ.' *Anxiety Stress Coping 18*, 17–35.

4 Costello, E.J. *et al.* (1996) 'The Great Smoky Mountains Study of Youth. Goals, design, methods, and the prevalence of DSM-III-R disorders.' *Archives of General Psychiatry 53*, 1129–1136.

5 Lerner, H.G. & Caruso, B. (2001) *The Dance of Connection: How to Talk to Someone When You're Mad, Hurt, Scared, Frustrated, Insulted, Betrayed, or Desperate*. New York: HarperCollins.

6 Kerr, M.E. & Bowen, M. (1988) *Family Evaluation*. New York: W.W. Norton & Company.

7 Seligman, M.E. (1972) 'Learned helplessness.' *Annual Review of Medicine 23*, 407–412.

8 PECs™ (Picture Exchange Communication System) is a technique which allows individuals to communicate ideas, often by pointing to or using small images and pictures to express needs or desires without having to speak. They can also be helpful visual aids for many other tasks.

9 Minahan, J. & Rappaport, N. (2012) *The Behavior Code: A Practical Guide to Understanding and Teaching the Most Challenging Students*. Cambridge, MA: Harvard Education Press.

10 Ginsburg, D. (2014) 'Ginsburg's Hierarchy of Help.' Accessed on 01/09/21 at https://blogs.edweek.org/teachers/coach_gs_teaching_tips/2014/11/ginsburgs_hierarchy_of_help.html.

Chapter 24

1 Siegel, D.J. & Bryson, T.P. (2012) *The Whole-Brain Child: 12 Revolutionary Strategies to Nurture Your Child's Developing Mind*. New York: Bantam Books.

2 Perry, B.D. *et al.* (2008) 'The neurosequential model of therapeutics.' *Reclaiming Children and Youth 17*, 38–43.

3 Taylor, J.B. (2017) *My Stroke of Insight: A Brain Scientist's Personal Journey*. New York: Viking.

Chapter 25

1 Seligman, M.E.P. (2011) *Learned Optimism: How to Change Your Mind and Your Life*. New York: Knopf Doubleday Publishing Group.

Chapter 26

1 Ben-Sasson, A. *et al.* (2009) 'A meta-analysis of sensory modulation symptoms in individuals with autism spectrum disorders.' *Journal of Autism and Developmental Disorders 39*, 1–11.

2 Brown L.J., Beardslee W.H., & Prothrow, D. (2008) 'Impact of school breakfast on children' s health and learning: An analysis of the scientific research.' Unpublished Manuscript. Harvard School of Public Health. Accessed on 01/24/21 at www.mydigitalchalkboard.org/cognoti/content/file/resources/documents/fa/facfd278/facfd278d9a412ed6d39506bc53e7cdc885f8e0a/Breakfast_Study_sodexofoundation.pdf.

3 Danziger, S., Levav, J., & Avnaim-Pesso, L. (2011) 'Extraneous factors in judicial decisions.' *Proceedings of the National Academy of Sciences of the U SA 108*, 6889–6892.

Chapter 27

1 Aron, E. (2013) *The Highly Sensitive Person*. New York: Kensington Publishing Corp.

Chapter 28

1 Knost, L.R. (2013) *Two Thousand Kisses a Day: Gentle Parenting through the Ages and Stages*. USA: Little Hearts Books, LLC.

2 Oberle, E. & Schonert-Reichl, K.A. (2016) 'Stress contagion in the classroom? The link between classroom teacher burnout and morning cortisol in elementary school students.' *Social Science and Medicine 159*, 30–37.

3 Nagoski, E. & Nagoski, A. (2019) *Burnout: The Secret to Unlocking the Stress Cycle*. New York: Random House Publishing Group.

Chapter 29

1 Ikei, H., Komatsu, M., Song, C., Himoro, E., & Miyazaki, Y. (2014) 'The physiological and psychological relaxing effects of viewing rose flowers in office workers.' *Journal of Physiological Anthropology 33*, 6.

Chapter 30

1 Oberle, E. & Schonert-Reichl, K.A. (2016) 'Stress contagion in the classroom? The link between classroom teacher burnout and morning cortisol in elementary school students.' *Social Science and Medicine 159*, 30–37.

2 Kurcinka, M.S. (2015) *Raising Your Spirited Child, Third Edition: A Guide for Parents Whose Child Is More Intense, Sensitive, Perceptive, Persistent, and Energetic*. New York: HarperCollins.

Chapter 31

1 Gregory, A. & Weinstein, R.S. (2008) 'The discipline gap and African Americans: Defiance or cooperation in the high school classroom.' *Journal of School Psychology 46*, 455–475.

2 Rudd, T. (2014) 'Racial disproportionality in school discipline: Implicit bias is heavily implicated.' Kirwan Institute Issue Brief. Colombus, OH: Kirwan Institute for the Study of Race and Ethnicity.

3 Skiba, R.J., Peterson, R.L., & Williams, T. (1997) 'Office referrals and suspension: Disciplinary intervention in middle schools.' *Education and Treatment of Children 20*, 295–315.

Chapter 32

1 National Center for Complementary and Integrated Health (2016) 'Meditation: In depth.' Accessed on 01/11/21 at www.nccih.nih.gov/health/meditation-in-depth.

2 Jennings, P.A. *et al.* (2017) 'Impacts of the CARE for Teachers program on teachers' social and emotional competence and classroom interactions.' *Journal of Educational Psychology 109*, 1010.

3 Chodron, P. (2000) *When Things Fall Apart: Heart Advice for Difficult Times*. Boulder, CO: Shambhala Publication.

4 Hanh, T.N. (2011) *Planting Seeds: Practicing Mindfulness with Children*. Berkeley, CA: Parallax Press.

Chapter 33

1 Cohn, M.A., Fredrickson, B.L., Brown, S.L., Mikels, J.A., & Conway, A.M. (2009) 'Happiness unpacked: Positive emotions increase life satisfaction by building resilience.' *Emotion 9*, 361.

2 Watkins, P.C., Woodward, K., Stone, T., & Kolts, R.L. (2003) 'Gratitude and happiness: Development of a measure of gratitude, and relationships with subjective well-being.' *Social Behavior and Personality: An International Journal 31*, 431–451.

3 Hayward, R.D. & Krause, N. (2014) 'Religion, Mental Health, and Well-Being: Social Aspects.' In V. Saroglou (ed.) *Religion, Personality, and Social Behavior*. New York: Psychology Press.

4 Hill, P.L., Allemand, M., & Roberts, B.W. (2013) 'Examining the pathways between gratitude and self-rated physical health across adulthood.' *Personality and Individual Differences 54*, 92–96.

5 Mills, P.J. *et al.* (2015) 'The role of gratitude in spiritual well-being in asymptomatic heart failure patients.' *Spirituality in Clinical Practice (Washington DC) 2*, 5–17.

6 Ng, M.-Y. & Wong, W.-S. (2013) 'The differential effects of gratitude and sleep on psychological distress in patients with chronic pain.' *Journal of Health Psychology 18*, 263–271.

7 Wood, A.M., Joseph, S., Lloyd, J., & Atkins, S. (2009) 'Gratitude influences sleep through the mechanism of pre-sleep cognitions.' *Journal of Psychosomatic Research 66*, 43–48.

8 Sirois, F.M. & Wood, A.M. (2017) 'Gratitude uniquely predicts lower depression in chronic illness populations: A longitudinal study of inflammatory bowel disease and arthritis.' *Health Psychology 36*, 122–132.

9 McCullough, M.E., Emmons, R.A., & Tsang, J.-A. (2002) 'The grateful disposition: A conceptual and empirical topography.' *Journal of Personality and Social Psychology 82*, 112–127.

10 Chan, D.W. (2011) 'Burnout and life satisfaction: Does gratitude intervention make a difference among Chinese school teachers in Hong Kong?' *Educational Psychology Review 31*, 809–823.

11 Jackowska, M., Brown, J., Ronaldson, A., & Steptoe, A. (2016) 'The impact of a brief gratitude intervention on subjective well-being, biology and sleep.' *Journal of Health Psychology 21*, 2207–2217.
12 Watkins, P.C., Woodward, K., Stone, T., & Kolts, R.L. (2003) 'Gratitude and happiness: Development of a measure of gratitude, and relationships with subjective well-being.' *Social Behavior and Personality: An International Journal 31*, 431–451.
13 Seligman, M.E.P., Steen, T.A., Park, N., & Peterson, C. (2005) 'Positive psychology progress: Empirical validation of interventions.' *American Psychologist 60*, 410–421.
14 Toepfer, S.M., Cichy, K., & Peters, P. (2012) 'Letters of gratitude: Further evidence for author benefits.' *Journal of Happiness Studies 13*, 187–201.
15 Froh, J.J., Yurkewicz, C., & Kashdan, T.B. (2009) 'Gratitude and subjective well-being in early adolescence: Examining gender differences.' *Journal of Adolescence 32*, 633–650.
16 Seligman, M.E.P., Steen, T.A., Park, N., & Peterson, C. (2005) 'Positive psychology progress: Empirical validation of interventions.' *American Psychologist 60*, 410–421.

Chapter 34

1 Rusk, R.L. (1939) *The Letters of Ralph Waldo Emerson in Six Volumes, Volume 4.* [Letter from Ralph Waldo Emerson to Ellen Emerson, April 8, 1854.] New York: Columbia University Press (Google Books Preview), p.439.

Subject Index

Author Index

The following refer to page numbers and corresponding endnote numbers at back of book.